Food and
Agriculture in
Global Perspective

PERGAMON POLICY STUDIES

ON THE NEW INTERNATIONAL
ECONOMIC ORDER

UNITAR/CEESTEM Library on NIEO

Food and Agriculture in Global Perspective

Discussions in the Committee of the Whole of the United Nations

Edited by
Toivo Miljan
with the cooperation of
Ervin Laszlo
Joel Kurtzman

A volume in the New International
Economic Order (NIEO) Library
Published for UNITAR and the
Center for Economic and Social
Studies of the Third World (CEESTEM)

Pergamon Press
NEW YORK • OXFORD • TORONTO • SYDNEY • FRANKFURT • PARIS

338.19
US8f

Pergamon Press Offices:

U.S.A. — Pergamon Press Inc., Maxwell House, Fairview Park, Elmsford, New York 10523, U.S.A.

U.K. — Pergamon Press Ltd., Headington Hill Hall, Oxford OX3 0BW, England

CANADA — Pergamon of Canada, Ltd., 150 Consumers Road, Willowdale, Ontario M2J, 1P9, Canada

AUSTRALIA — Pergamon Press (Aust) Pty. Ltd., P O Box 544, Potts Point, NSW 2011, Australia

FRANCE — Pergamon Press SARL, 24 rue des Ecoles, 75240 Paris, Cedex 05, France

FEDERAL REPUBLIC OF GERMANY — Pergamon Press GmbH, 6242 Kronberg/Taunus, Pferdstrasse 1, Federal Republic of Germany

Library of Congress Cataloging in Publication Data

United Nations. Committee of the Whole.
  Food and agriculture in global perspective.

  (Pergamon policy studies)
  Bibliography: p.
  Includes index.
  I. Food supply. 2. Agriculture—Economic aspects.
3. Food relief. I. Miljan, Toivo. II. Laszlo,
Ervin, 1932-   III. Kurtzman, Joel. IV. Title.
HD9000.5.U43   1979   338.I'9   79-23I63
ISBN 0-08-025550-7

Contents

Foreword

The unfortunate reality is that as much as 40 percent of
the world's population still must struggle at the edge of poverty. Poor sanitation and health care, lack of suitable housing, unemployment, impoverishment and undernourishment are
realities which face the world's millions, indeed billions,
daily. These perennial problems have so far defied solution in
spite of the fact that the world is rich enough and well en-
dowed enough to feed, clothe, house, and offer employment to
populations even in greater numbers than we currently have.

To solve these problems various United Nations fora have
been created and in 1978 the Committee of the Whole was established by the General Assembly (Res. 22/174) to negotiate
issues crucial to the New International Economic Order and the
future well being of mankind. In March of 1979 the Committee
of the Whole met to discuss the world's situation with respect
to Food and Agriculture. Under the Chairmanship of Mr. Thorvald
Stoltenberg of Norway, the Committee met to look at strategies
for feeding the world's hungry. Various bold and energetic
programmes were presented during the Committee's meetings by
the member States to achieve a more equitable distribution of
the world's Food and Agricultural resources. This volume, one
of sixteen on various aspects of the New International Economic
Order, under the general editorial directorship of Professor
Ervin Laszlo of UNITAR, documents the historic activities of
the Committee of the Whole's Food and Agriculture deliberations,
and it serves to illustrate the world's resolve to eradicate
hunger.

Hunger is a complex and difficult problem and it is highly
unlikely that it can be solved in the discussions and deliberations of only one committee within the United Nations alone.
Yet it is a problem which must be solved and solved quickly.
Each day that passes sees scores of people not only driven to

despair but also to death through starvation. Each day also
sadly sees thousands of children unable to develop and thrive
and live out normal, healthy lifespans for want of food.   To
eradicate these problems, once and for all, is the purpose of
the deliberations presented in this volume, and to that end
the account of those deliberations is presented by UNITAR for
the benefit of all.

                                        Davidson Nicol
                                        Executive Director

Foreword

The Committee of the Whole was established by the 32nd
General Assembly as a high-level political committee with the
purpose of providing necessary impetus to the negotiations for
a New International Economic Order. These negotiations – known
as the North/South dialogue – had for almost two years to a
great extent been conducted outside the United Nations at the
Conference on International Economic Cooperation (CIEC) in Paris.
To many countries, not least developing countries, the outcome
of the Paris negotiations was disappointing. The need was therefore felt to bring the dialogue firmly back to the UN system so
that all Member Countries could participate actively in the
efforts to shape a new and more equitable world order. To emphasize the importance of these efforts the Committee of the
Whole was made responsible directly to the General Assembly.
    The Committee was to deal in a comprehensive manner with
the questions relating to the establishment of the NIEO until
the 1980 Special Session of the General Assembly. It was assumed that from the very outset the Committee would take up
substantive issues, discuss and negotiate in a constructive
manner and produce practical and action-oriented conclusions.
    Unfortunately, differences of view about some aspects of
the Committee's role hampered its work during its first year of
existence. Thanks not least to the resolute efforts and skill
of my predecessor as Chairman, Mr. Idriss Jazairy, to whom I
would here like to pay a special tribute, a clarification of
the mandate of the Committee was reached towards the end of
1978. The Committee thus moved into a new phase of constructive
discussion and negotiation, the first result of which was the
text adopted in January 1979 on the transfer of resources to
developing countries.
    When the Committee at the March session took up the prob-
lems of food production and agriculture it was the first time

that any committee under the General Assembly had devoted a
full session to these questions. Food and agriculture is a
subject matter of major importance, not only on its own merits
but also in the wider perspective of the North/South dialogue.
The political nature of problems like reaching the set targets
for food production and contributing to a more equitable food
distribution and consumption is becoming increasingly clear. I
am convinced that the Committee of the Whole at its March session contributed both to bringing these problems into the centre
of development discussions and to pinpointing some areas of
urgent concern. By doing so, the Committee's competence to
negotiate and adopt decisions on outstanding economic issues of
global dimensions was also demonstrated.

As Chairman of the Committee of the Whole I am deeply concerned about where to go from here in terms of the follow-up of
the conclusions reached at the March session. The World Conference on Agrarian Reform and Rural Development, which was held
in July of this year, represented a new and positive step forward.
However, further efforts on the part of Governments and of United
Nations organs of a more technical nature are clearly called
for. I do hope that the headway we made at the March session
will prove valuable in tackling the many formidable challenges
still ahead.

As Chairman of the Committee of the Whole I have done –
and intend to continue to do my utmost – to see that the Committee functions according to its mandate on North/South relations within the United Nations system. At the same time I
have tried to make it clear beyond any doubt that we are engaged
in a common effort where all parts of the United Nations system
have a role to play and where cooperation and mutual support
are of the utmost importance. The role of the Committee requires that all Governments as well as officials working in the
United Nations system pay very special and urgent attention to
its work. Furthermore, I see a need to establish a much greater
public awareness of the Committee's work and of the issues in
which it is engaged. I am convinced that this study will contribute to this end and would like to express my appreciation to
Mr. Toivo Miljan for his dedicated work and to thank UNITAR for
having undertaken this study.

                                        Thorvald Stoltenberg
                                        Chairman
                                        Committee of the Whole

Introduction—
A World Without
Hunger

The slow progress in agriculture has impeded the narrowing
of the wide gaps between rich and poor countries that is envisaged under the New International Economic Order. The consequent
slow growth of incomes in the developing countries has affected
the developed countries as well. It has limited the markets
for their exports, and has thus restricted incomes and employment in these countries. Shortages and high prices of food and
agricultural products in world markets have also added to inflationary pressures in the developing countries, hampering
their efforts to achieve the economic growth required to overcome their employment problems.
The majority of the people in the developing countries,
indeed the vast majority of the world's poorest people, live in
rural areas and derive their meagre employment and livelihood
from agriculture. The slow progress in agricultural production
in these countries has therefore been a major constraint on the
reduction of poverty, and on the achievement of the basic social
as well as economic goals of development.*

THE ROLE OF THE COMMITTEE OF THE WHOLE
ON FOOD AND AGRICULTURE

Two statements characterize the work of the Committee of
the Whole on food and agriculture. The first Chairman of the
Committee, Mr. Idriss Jazairy once observed, "The New International Economic Order implies a continuous process rather
than an act to be accomplished in a determined period of time."

---

*Nurul Islam, Assistant Director-General, Economic and Social
Policy Department, Food and Agriculture Organization of the
United Nations, speaking to COW on 19 March 1979.

Two hundred years ago the German poet Goethe raised the proposi-
tion, "The question to ask is not whether we are perfectly
agreed, but whether we are proceeding from a common basis of
sentiment." There can be no doubt that the common basis of
sentiment to build a world without hunger was strongly expressed
in the statements by all the participants in the COW deliberations on food and agriculture. But, there is equally no doubt
that there was not perfect agreement on the methods whereby to
wipe out hunger. But, again, there was a common sentiment that
there exists a high degree of inter-relationship between hunger
and the structures of national and international economies and
that concerted international political action is necessary to
eradicate hunger, its causes and effects, from the earth.
Clearly the continuous process that is the NIEO continues, and
COW is an active participant in it.
     The General Assembly of the United Nations by Resolution
32/174 established the Committee of the Whole to assist it in
the establishment of the New International Economic Order (see
appendix). The mandate of the Committee was clarified during
the 33rd Session of the General Assembly by the President of
the Assembly; "Consultations held with the Member States on the
question of the clarification of the mandate of the Committee
Established under General Assembly Resolution 32/174 led me to
the conclusion that in fulfilling its mandate as set out in
resolution 32/174, operative paragraph 4, essentially under
subparagraphs (b) and (c), the Committee will negotiate with a
view to its adopting guidelines on central policy issues as
well as achieving agreement on the resolution of fundamental or
crucial issues underlying problems related to international
economic co-operation. The results of the negotiations will be
expressed in the form of action-oriented agreed conclusions of
the Committee addressed, in accordance with paragraph 5 of resolution 32/174, through the General Assembly, to States and
international organizations concerned."
     At its second session the COW dealt with the problems of
food and agriculture in an integrating manner and arrived at a
set of Agreed Conclusions on these issues. The Committee identified inter alia specific questions to be further considered
at the World Conference on Agrarian Reform and Rural Development
in July 1979, The World Food Council meeting in September 1979
and in the New International Wheat Agreement and the new Food
Aid Convention. Through its discussions and Agreed Conclusions
the Committee also made a valuable contribution to the elaboration of the International Development Strategy.
     From the documentation - the statements of inter-national
agencies and States Members and the reference documentation
provided by the international agencies - presented in edited
form in this collection, as well as from the Agreed Conclusions
it is clear that the Committee of the Whole is fulfilling its
functions in accordance with its mandate to negotiate funda-

mental issues underlying problems related to international economic cooperation. To the question, posed by Chairman Thorvald
Stoltenberg in his introductory address to the Committee, "Can
the Committee of the Whole be of assistance in renewing the
goals and objectives for food and agriculture in the light of
the increasing interdependence in the world today?" the documentation gathered in this collection answers a resounding "Yes".
The Committee did not replicate the work of the specialized
agencies within the United Nations system in the field of food
and agriculture; rather it established a basic framework - a
unifying idea - which brought together the expert work of the
different international agencies and the views of the different
States Members in the Agreed Conclusions of the committee on
Some Aspects Concerning Food and Agriculture.

THE NEGOTIATIONS ON FOOD AND AGRICULTURE

The Mexico Declaration of the World Food Council was used
as a reference text by all sides during the negotiations, and
provided a basis for a common language on controversial issues.
A comparison of the Agreed Conclusions text and the Mexico
Declaration shows progress in several areas:

- The COW test calls for the Governing Council of IFAD
  to decide on replenishment of its resources at the
  end of 1980 and states that the Council should consider the need for an increase in real terms of the
  resources of the Fund.
- The COW text appeals to donors to increase their contributions to the Special Account for the Action Programme for Prevention of Food Losses.
- The COW text asks that donor countries support the
  FAO programme to assist developing coastal states in
  developing their fisheries within their economic zones.
- The COW text urges that special consideration be given
  to the establishment of adequate provisions for special
  international assistance to developing countries in
  establishing food reserves.
- The COW text recommends the developing countries'
  proposal that a reserve stock financing fund be kept
  under consideration.
- The COW text makes a plea for the resumption of negotiations on the New International Wheat Agreement in
  order to stabilize the cereal markets.
- The COW text urges that maximum efforts be made to
  create conditions which would allow for the early
  conclusion of a new Food Aid Convention.

- The COW text welcomes the Five Point Plan of Action
  on World Food Security proposed by the Director-
  General of FAO and passes it on to the Committee on
  World Food Security for action at its next session.

On all the above issues some countries would only accept a
commitment to have the relevant intergovernmental bodies consider the actions outlined, because they did not want to pre-
judge the decisions to be taken by the responsible bodies.
Thus, although there was no major breakthrough on any point of
substance in the Agreed Conclusions, considerable headway was
made in creating openings to be considered fully in the appropriate fora. Some of the issues creating difficulty were those
where certain North-North conflicts exist, primarily between
the United States and some Western European countries, namely
on food security and on agricultural trade. The deadlock between the main parties remained on these issues and the resulting text shows no change over previous well-established positions.
As may be seen in the American negotiation paper the United
States would have supported a strong attack on agricultural
protectionism but this was blocked by a combination of some
Western European countries and Japan. The European Community,
in contrast, would have liked to enlist the support of the Group
of 77 for its scheme of the new International Wheat Agreement
and hence was reluctant to accept any interim proposal on food
security that would lessen pressure to reach agreement on a new
IWA.
A North-South conflict developed over the domestic aspects
of food and agriculture and rural development in developing
countries. This is most clearly seen in the American negotiation paper, which, in comparison to the Group of 77 texts, emphasizes the domestic aspects of food and agriculture in the
developing countries in order to strike a better balance between
the domestic and international aspects. The American amendments
to the Group of 77 negotiation text calling for requisite economic and social reforms in developing countries met resistance
from the Group of 77 and were rejected apart from a few concerning technical cooperation among developing countries (TCDC)
research, the United Nations Conference on Science and Technology for Development (UNCSTD) and conservation. However an
amendment reaffirming that responsibility for the development
of food and agriculture lies primarily in the developing countries themselves, was accepted. But the Group of 77 could not
agree to the attempt to mention any target group, such as small
or landless peasants, for agricultural development. In contrast,
the developed countries made sure that the $ 8.3 billion World
Food Council evaluation for external financing needs of developing countries in agriculture was not considered a target.

Mr. Stoltenberg's role as Chairman cannot be over-empha-
sized in the successful conclusion of the negotiations on the
text of the Agreed Conclusions. In addition to extensive and
thorough preparations for the negotiations, which he organized,
at crucial points during the negotiations he put forward a number of compromise proposals which were incorporated in the final
text.

OBJECTIVE, PURPOSE AND ORGANIZATION OF THIS BOOK

The objective of the book is to present the problem of
food and agriculture in its total global international perspective from the point of view of the specialized agencies of the
United Nations system and the States Members of the United
Nations in the most comprehensive forum in which the question
has so far been discussed - the Committee of the Whole of the
United Nations General Assembly.
More specially, the purpose is to demonstrate that progress
towards the New International Economic Order is a continuous
process. The record provided by international agencies and by
States Members of the UN, shows that although perfect agreement
on the methods and the rate of achievement is not possible among
members of the international community at present, nevertheless,
a sufficiently common basis of sentiment on the question of
eradicating hunger exists for the most comprehensive forum on
the question to date, the Committee of the Whole, to have negotiated a set of comprehensive action-oriented Agreed Conclusions.
Thus the COW is fulfilling its function of negotiating the adoption of guidelines on central policy issues within the process
of achieving the objectives of the New International Economic
Order.
The documents of the COW Second Session dealing with food
and agriculture held at the UN headquarters in New York in March
1979 consist of technical reference papers submitted by the
Specialized Agencies and the Secretariat, and statements by
representatives of Specialized Agencies and Member States, and
proposed negotiation texts. These have been edited and organized into thirteen Chapters in two Parts. The chapters in the
Part One deal with the problem of food and agriculture and its
handling in the global perspective. Hence Chapter Two groups
the statements of the problem around international agency views
and around the views of Member States; Chapter Three presents
the FAO summaries in documents A/AC.191/27 and A/AC.191/37;
Chapter Four the record of action as seen by the different States
Members and the Agencies; Chapter Five the documented record of
progress presented by the FAO in document A/AC.191/34; Chapter
Six the progress report of current efforts by international
agencies and by States; and Chapter Seven the proposals for

action grouped into three parts: the statements of participants
in the COW meeting, the Chairman's non-paper and the negotiation documents, and the Agreed Conclusions of the Committee.
    Part Two of the book presents excerpts from the technical
documents, and statements of Agency representatives and Member
States in the seven specific issue areas found in the Agreed
Conclusions of the Committee.
    The statements by the representatives of Bulgaria and the
USSR were originally made in Russian, the statements of Argentina and Mexico in Spanish, and the statements of the representatives of the European Community, the Group of 77 (Tunisia),
Turkey and Switzerland were originally in French. The transla-
tions into English of these statements in this volume were au-
thorized by UNITAR.

APPENDIX

32/174.   Assessment of progress in the establishment
           of the new international economic order

           Date: 19 December 1977   Meeting: 107
           Adopted without vote   Report: A/32/480

    The General Assembly,
    Recalling its resolutions 3201 (S-VI) and 3202 (S-VI) of 1
May 1974, containing the Declaration and the Programme of Action
on the Establishment of a New International Economic Order,
3281 (XXIX) of 12 December 1974, containing the Charter of Economic Rights and Duties of Status, and 3362 (S-VII) of 16
September 1975 on development and international economic co-
operation, as well as its resolution 2626 (XXV) of 24 October
1970 containing the International Development Strategy for the
Second United Nations Development Decade,
    Recalling the resolutions adopted by the United Nations
Conference on Trade and Development at its fourth session,
    Recalling the results of various United Nations confer-
ences held during recent years on major topics relating to economic and social development, which pertain to the establishment
of the new international economic order,
    Recalling further its resolution 31/178 of 21 December
1976,
    Taking note of Economic and Social Council resolution 2125
(LXIII) of 4 August 1977,
    Noting the report of the Conference on International Eco-
nomic Co-operation, 106/
    Noting the report of the Committee on Review and Appraisal
on its fourth session 107/ and the preliminary proposal of the
developing countries contained in the annex to that report,

Recalling the role of the Economic and Social Council and of other organs, organizations and other bodies and conferences of the United Nations system in the establishment of the new international economic order,

Emphasizing the need to oversee and monitor the implementation of the decisions and agreements reached in the negotiations in various appropriate forums of the United Nations system in their respective fields, and to determine further lines of action and provide impetus for further negotiations for the solution of issues remaining unresolved,

Deeply concerned at the deteriorating economic situation of developing countries and at negative trends in international economic developments,

Deeply concerned also that parts of the developing world are still subjected to colonialism, neo-colonialism, racial discrimination, apartheid, foreign aggression and occupation and alien domination, which constitute major obstacles to the economic emancipation and development of the developing countries and peoples,

Recognizing the concern that the negotiations conducted so far on the establishment of the new international economic order have produced only limited results while the gap between developed and developing countries is growing, and emphasizing that further resolute efforts have to be made, particularly by the developed countries, to reduce the existing imbalance,

1. Affirms that all negotiations of a global nature relating to the establishment of the new international economic order should take place within the framework of the United Nations system;

2. Decides to convene a special session of the General Assembly in 1980 at a high level in order to assess the progress made in the various forums of the United Nations system in the establishment of the new international economic order and, on the basis of that assessment, to take appropriate action for the promotion of the development of developing countries and international economic co-operation, including the adoption of the new international development strategy for the 1980s;

3. Decides to establish a committee of the whole,108/ which shall meet, as and when required, during the intersessional periods until the special session of the General Assembly in 1980;

4. Decides further that this committee shall assist the General Assembly by acting as the focal point in:

(a) Overseeing and monitoring the implementation of decisions and agreements reached in the negotiations on the establishment of the new international economic order in the appropriate bodies of the United Nations system;

(b) Providing impetus for resolving difficulties in negotiations and for encouraging the continuing work in these bodies;

(c) Serving, where appropriate, as a forum for facilitating and expediting agreement on the resolution of outstanding issues;

(d) Exploring and exchanging views on global economic problems and priorities;

5. Requests the committee to submit reports on its work and recommendations to the General Assembly at its thirty-third and thirty-fourth sessions and at the special session to be held in 1980;

6. Recommends that representation on the committee should be at a high level;

7. Decides that the committee may establish appropriate working arrangements to accomplish its task;

8. Decides also that the election of officers of the committee should take place annually;

9. Requests the Secretary-General to ensure that the committee receives the necessary documentation to enable it to accomplish its tasks, as specified in operative paragraph 4 above, and authorizes the committee to request the Secretary-General to provide specific reports in this regard in co-operation with the appropriate organs, organizations, other bodies and conferences of the United Nations system;

10. Requests in this context the Economic and Social Council, in discharging its functions under the Charter of the United Nations, to contribute effectively to the work of the committee, bearing in mind the relationship between the overseeing and monitoring functions of the committee and the role of the Council in the preparations of a new international development strategy;

11. Affirms that in the negotiations undertaken on the various issues in the appropriate bodies of the United Nations system the international community should, with a sense of urgency, make new and resolute efforts to secure positive and concrete results within agreed and specific time-frames.

The food sector and the problem of rural development in general will also require strong, forward-looking policies on the part of both developed and developing countries. New initiatives are called for in order to bring stability to the world market for food grains and to give full and prompt effect to the recommendations of the World Conference on Agrarian Reform and Rural Development. Moreover, the supply of investment funds, both internal and external, and the physical and technical inputs required to increase food production in developing countries and to strengthen their technological capabilities in the agro-industrial sector must be accelerated. Not least, developing countries--and for that matter, developed countries, too--must come to grips with the institutional and social implications of making a rapid transition from a low-level subsistence agriculture, often organized along traditional lines, or as an adjunct to foreign-owned plantations, and of putting to productive use, especially for rural development, the unemployed and underemployed human resources that abound in much of the developing world.

The early conclusion of international agreements on food commodities and the establishment of adequate reserves would also be of great assistance to the attainment of the food security objectives endorsed by the Food and Agriculture Organization of the United Nations.

--Statement by K.K.S. Dadzi,
Director General for Development and International Economic Cooperation,

to the Second Committee, on the first of October, 1979.

I
The Problem

1 The Problem Stated

The problem of food and agriculture is expressed dramatically in the simple word HUNGER, but it is multi-faceted and complex.

THE VIEWS OF THE SPECIALIZED AGENCIES

Each of the Specialized Agency representatives focusses on specific problem areas.

The Problem is the Slow Progress in Agricultural Development

Statement by Mr. Nurul Islam of FAO:
Instead of accelerating to the average rate of 4% a year called for in the International Development Strategy for DD2, the increase in the agricultural production of the developing countries during the 1970s so far has barely matched the rate of about 3% achieved in the 1960s. What is even worse, the increase has been slowest in the poorest developing countries, especially in Africa, where it has not only fallen considerably below the performance of the 1960s but also below population growth. Similarly, instead of decreasing, the number of severely undernourished people in the developing marked economies is estimated to have risen from about 400 million in 1969-71 to about 450 million in 1972-74, or about a quarter of their total population. As with production, the deterioration in the nutritional situation has been very largely in the poorest of the developing countries. Partial data for more recent years indicate little, if any improvement since 1972-74.

The slow progress in the agriculture of the developing
countries has made their food security more and more dependent
on increasingly burdensome imports from a few developed countries, thus thwarting an important part of their efforts to
become more self-reliant. It has also prevented them from taking full advantage of such agricultural export opportunities as
have been available. Industrialization in the developing countries depends heavily on the rapid development of agricultural
processing industries and those manufacturing fertilizers and
other agricultural inputs. However, the increase in their food
imports has pre-empted foreign exchange that would otherwise
have been available not only for agricultural development, but
also for the development of industry and other nonagricultural
sectors. Slow agricultural and rural progress has hampered the
growth of the domestic market as well as the raw material
supplies for their nascent industrial sectors. High food prices
have led to wage and cost increases, and thus reduced the incentive for industrial investment.

In these and other ways the slow progress in agriculture
has impeded the narrowing of the wide gaps between rich and
poor countries that is envisaged under the New International
Economic Order. The consequent slow growth of incomes in the
developing countries has affected the developed countries as
well. It has limited the markets for their exports, and has
thus restricted incomes and employment in these countries.
Shortages and high prices of food and agricultural products in
world markets have also added to inflationary pressures in the
developed countries, hampering their efforts to achieve the
economic growth required to overcome their employment problems.

The majority of the people in the developing countries,
indeed the vast majority of the world's poorest people, live in
rural areas and derive their meagre employment and livelihood
from agriculture. The slow progress in agricultural production
in these countries has therefore been a major constraint on the
reduction of poverty, and on the achievement of the basic social
as well as economic goals of development.

This slow agricultural progress is in striking contrast to
the high degree of international consensus that has been reached
on the diagnosis of world food and agricultural problems, and
on the broad spectrum of measures required to overcome them.
Perhaps in no other major sector is there so wide a range of
agreement, much of it as the level of the General Assembly itself. The numerous targets and measures that have been agreed
are summarized in the documents that are before you. In almost
all cases, their implementation has been disappointingly slow.
I would urge this Committee to look very closely at these
agreed targets and measures, and to use its powerful influence
to promote the practical steps that are still necessary for
their implementation.

Although the action that is required lies to a great extent

in the hands of the developing countries, they also face serious
external constraints on their food and agricultural development.
In particular these concern the inadequacy of external assistance to augment their investment resources, and the instability and inadequacy of their export earnings, partly because
of barriers in the developed countries to the expansion of their
exports. Such obstacles detract from any favourable effects
gained from the success of their domestic policies. The developed countries also have a particular responsibility in the
assurance of world food security. It is in these and related
areas that international action is urgently needed if external
factors are fully to support the internal development efforts
of the developing countries.

The Problem Is International Trade

Statement by Mr. Nurul Islam of the FAO:
International trade in agricultural products has important
implications for the growth and stability of the agricultural
sector. Many developing countries still derive a large proportion of their export earnings from such products. It is therefore a serious matter that, in spite of some apparently temporary improvement in 1976 and 1977, their share in world agricultural export earnings has declined steadily over the longer
term. Their agricultural export earnings, especially from processed products, continue to be limited by tariff and non-tariff
barriers in developed countries, and to suffer from a damaging
degree of instability. Increased export opportunities for processed agricultural products are particularly important for
their industrialization.
Although some progress has been made in the UNCTAD negotiations on a common fund to finance an integrated programme
for commodities, their final outcome is still uncertain. The
same is true of the current round of the Gatt multilateral
trade negotiations. Among the individual agricultural commodities covered by the integrated programme, there has recently
been little significant progress towards new international
agreements except in the case of rubber. Although the international grains negotiation lies outside the integrated programme, it is essential, not only that they should be resumed
as soon as possible, but also that their failure to agree
should not be allowed to prejudice the many other important
negotiations that are under way.
Further extension of the generalized system of preferences
is required, in order to mitigate the resurgence of protectionism, particularly for processed products, in some developed
countries. It is also necessary to expedite   the conclusion
of liberalized general compensatory financing schemes, and of
stabilization arrangements for those individual commodities on
which early agreement appears likely, as well as to stimulate

research and development measures to enhance the competitiveness
of the agricultural exports of the developing countries.

At the present time many developed countries are inhibited
by their problems of unemployment and inflation, in making
trade concessions, expanding development assistance, and facing
up to adjustments in their domestic agricultural economies and
policies. They could, however, give more recognition to the
fact that in the long run such measures, by contributing to the
prosperity of the developing countries and thus their potential
as export markets, would bring benefits to developed as well as
developing countries in an increasingly interdependent world
economy.

The Problem is Lack of Structural Change at Both the International and Domestic Levels

Statement by Mr. S. Aziz of the IFAD:
As already emphasized in the statements from FAO and the World
Food Council, today in 1979, almost half a decade after the
World Food Conference, we are nowhere near the goal of eradicating hunger from this world by 1985. With these successive good
harvests in major food producing regions, the world food prices
have been relatively stable and world grain stocks considerably
higher but there is no indication that the number of people
threatened with the risk of undernutrition has gone down. In
fact in many countries, particularly in Africa, where per capita
food output has declined by 10 percent, the situation may have
worsened. There is thus an urgent need to carry out a critical
evaluation of the progress achieved in implementing the recommendations of the 1974 World Food Conference and to find more
effective solutions for the future.

The World Food Conference had clearly recognized that what
was called the world food problem were really two different but
interrelated problems. One was the recurrent threat of famine
and food shortage that arose from year to year to fluctuations
in production, leading to sudden changes in food prices and
supplies. The second was the chronic hunger and malnutrition
of a large segment of the world population living in Africa,
Asia and Latin America. Even when the world as a whole had
plenty of food and grain prices were relatively stable millions
of people were too poor to buy enough food to meet their minimum requirements.

Recognizing these two dimensions of the world food problem,
the first set of the resolutions adopted by the World Food Conference was aimed at the gradual evolution of a world food security system, through a more dependable food aid policy, an
internationally coordinated system of food reserves and a better
deal for developing countries in international trade in agricultural products. The second set of recommendations was aimed at

the longer term objective of eliminating chronic hunger and
malnutrition, through increased food production and improved
distribution within the developing countries. These recommendations called for stepping up the annual growth of food production from an average of 2.6 percent in the 1960s to a 4.0 percent
in the period 75-85; increasing the flow of external assistance
from $2.0 billion a year to $5 billion a year (in 1972 prices -
which will mean about $10 billion a year in 1978 prices), setting
up a new International Fund for Agricultural Development and
new initiatives in all related fields such as fertilizers and
pesticides, land and water and livestock and fisheries.

The progress so far made in implementing the recommendations of the World Food Conference has already been presented
to this Committee in the documents prepared by FAO and the World
Food Council and in the statements made on their behalf yesterday. The results are obviously disappointing. The world still
does not have a dependable system of food security and the rate
of growth of food production, despite a significant increase in
the flow of external assistance for agriculture is still around
2.6 - 2.8 percent and far below the target of 4 percent per
annum. As a result the cereal imports of developing countries
have gone up from 30 million tons in 69-71 to 70 million tons
in 1978-79 and the number of people suffering from undernutrition has probably gone up rather than diminished.

Mr. Chairman, as you pointed out in your opening statement,
the real task before the Committee is to find ways and means of
transforming the general consensus on agreed measures into concrete action. This in turn will require a careful assessment
of the difficulties and constraints which have so far prevented
more effective results.

Mr. Chairman, the resolutions adopted by the World Food
Conference, provided for the first time, the main elements of a
world food policy. Taken together and implemented effectively,
these elements would have brought about major structural changes
in the world economic system in relation to food, by increasing
food production at a rate faster than demand and by reducing
their dependence on imported food and by evolving more dependable international institutions and mechanisms for channelling
food aid, coordinating stock or regulating trade. This plea
for structural reforms at the international level was matched
with a call for structural changes within countries through
agrarian reforms and higher priority to rural development for
the benefit of small farmers and landless workers.

The Problem is Increasing Dependency on North America
Statement of Mr. Montague Yudelman of the World Bank:

The international community can derive some comfort from
the fact that the world food situation is less ominous than it

was some five years ago. At present global supplies of staple
foods are adequate to meet any sudden shortfall - some 20% of
consumption is presently held in reserve which compares
favorably with the critically low 10% level held only five
years ago. This improved situation has arisen from a combination of factors. Perhaps the two most important of these
has been reasonably good weather in rich and poor countries
alike and a sustained effort in many parts of the globe to
increase food production.

In our view this improvement should not lull the international community into losing its high level of concern about
the prevalence of hunger in the world at large. The recent
improvement in food supplies masks some important problems both
for the present and for the future. These include:

First: The structural changes that have taken place in
world grain trade are leading to an extreme reliance on a single
major source of supply. Today almost every region in the world
is a net importer of grains; the major exception is North
America which has recently become the granary of the world --
providing fully 80% of all grain exports. Most of this grain
is grown under rainfed conditions. A series of poor harvests
in North America could place much of the world in jeopardy,
making the diversification of supply an important consideration.

Second: While there has been a fairly low rate of increase
in food production in most countries in the world this is far
less significant for the richer countries than poorer ones.
The developed world started at a much higher level of output
per capita and with a low rate of population growth. The con-
verse is true for the poorer countries. Consequently even
though some developing countries have the same rate of growth
as the industrialized countries, there remains little slack
between supply and demand in poorer areas, many of which lie in
climatic zones of extreme variability.

Third: The progress which has been made on increasing
food production has not been matched by improvement in food
consumption. Even as bumper crops are harvested on farms in
areas as diverse as the Middle West of the US, the Ukraine of
USSR and the Punjab of India, the number of people who are critically malnourished increases. Some studies have indicated
that in the low income countries as a group, the proportion of
the total population with an inadequate diet has actually increased over the last decade. As stock-piles of food grow,
effective demand is pitifully low and in many parts of the world
we have actually been losing ground.

Fourth: Looking ahead over the next 25 years, we expect
that the more affluent developing countries will shift food
consumption to wheaten and meat diets. Provided growth rates
are not affected by protectionist trade restrictions, these
countries should face little problem in meeting their food requirements either through domestic production or imports. The

poorer developing countries which include the most populous
regions of South Asia and much of Africa face a much different
situation. Even the most optimistic analyses indicate the like-
lihood of only a marginal increase in per capita food output.
Further, future production increases will prove much more expensive than those registered in the last five years because incremental output will have to come primarily through a shift to
higher cost, more intensive farming methods. Even if the poorer
countries are successful in increasing food output, they will
have little margin for error. Food imports could well cost
$10-15 billion annually by 1985, to provide 11% of total con-
sumption (double the proportion in the middle 70s) merely to
maintain existing levels of consumption. Recent World Bank
studies also indicate that even with substantial production
gains and national per capita income growth there will only be
a marginal decline in the number of people who are malnourished.
Thus a realistic analysis indicates that the world hunger problem could well worsen over the next twenty-five years unless
there are greater efforts by all concerned with this issue.

    In summary the world food situation is one in which the
world at large is becoming more and more dependent on North
America for a growing volume of marginal supplies - either to
meet higher consumption levels in richer societies or to sustain
subsistence in poorer countries. However, the poor countries
cannot afford to use their scarce resources to purchase food
which they could grow themselves. Thus it is essential that
these countries with more than half the population in the developing world, make every effort to increase their output. At
the same time there are a very large number of people in the
world - mostly in the rural areas of poor countries - who are
malnourished because they cannot afford to purchase basic
staples.

The Problem is Neglect of Technical Cooperation
Statement by Mr. Bradford Morse of the United Nations Development Programme:

    If I may, Mr. Chairman, I shall draw for my remarks upon
your own opening statement to this Committee, in which you so
astutely observed that, and I quote, "The problem is, as always,
to transform this general consensus of opinion into concrete
action." As the Administrator of the central funding organization for technical co-operation within the United Nations development system, I can attest to the need for operational emphasis, at the developing country level, on increased food production and improved nutritional levels for the hundreds of
millions of impoverished people who you and many other speakers
here have described as chronically hungry and undernourished.
And I can fully agree with your further point that, as FAO has

forthrightly put it: "In most cases the action required is mainly the implementation of measures or targets that have already been agreed upon in various intergovernmental conferences."

As the Administrator of a technical co-operation programme charged precisely with assisting in the implementation of such targets, I wish to call to this Committee's attention the needs and problems of technical co-operation in this area. I recognize that every organization comes here with its own special plea, and because UNDP has experienced a wide range of development needs at the project level, I can fully sympathize with all these pleas. This is because UNDP has a unique cross-sectoral, multi-disciplinary view of what practical development requirements are in almost every sector. But when we struggle to bring all these multiple, integrated requirements together for food production, we find that -- despite the international consensus on what needs to be done -- the operational means to accomplish this intent are too often lacking. Developing countries cannot be expected to meet their targets in increased food production if the technical resources required to obtain that increase are either absent or spread so thinly as to be ineffective. One of the main conclusions reached at the recent Inter-Agency Seminar on Food Production and Distribution held in Washington, D.C. was that most developing countries are unable to maintain a pipeline of projects to speed the flow of capital resources into food production and improved nutrition due to the kind of institutional and organizational bottlenecks which technical co-operation is in part designed to overcome. Lack of adequate technical backstopping has resulted in slow disbursements of loans and credits as well as delays in the delivery of equipment.

I have said before that the international community is neglecting the importance of technical co-operation in the development process despite mounting evidence of both its need and its critical role as a key source of economic growth. UNDP's studies of national development plans show that well below 20 percent of projected technical requirements for development are currently being met through all forms of technical co-operation. At the same time, a growing body of expert economic literature attests to the importance of technical change as the primary source for economic growth -- technical change which leads to an increase in efficiency in the use of productive resources and to economies of scale. Indeed, the studies of one eminent economist show that fully 90 percent of economic growth can be attributed to such factors. So if the international community is to gain full advantage of increased resource transfers through such organizations as the International Fund for Agricultural Development (IFAD), we must keep in mind the corollary need for adequate technical support.

The Health Issue Is Malnutrition

Statement by Mr. S. Malafatopoulos of the World Health
Organization: Malnutrition continues to be a major world problem. It is estimated that according to the criteria used, from
500 to 1000 million people are living with diets inadequate or
insufficient for ensuring health and the full development of
their genetic potential. Nutritional deficiencies of different
types and degrees continue to be one of the major health problems of developing countries and, contrary to earlier expecta-
tions, the problem appears to be increasing both in the number
of individuals affected and in the range of population groups
at risk. In addition, non-dietary factors such as infectious
and parasitic diseases, particularly those associated with diar-
rhoea and adverse environmental factors, contribute to the problem and are aggravated by it. By increasing infant and child
mortality, as well as overall morbidity, and by reducing learn-
ing capacity in children and in work performance in adults,
malnutrition is not only a consequence of unsatisfactory social
and economic development but also one of its major contributing
factors.

Endemic goitre to which I have just referred, is not the
nutritional disease of greatest significance but it is an important one. In many regions of the world, it is responsible for
a significant number of children born with reduced mental capacity, often cretinism and neurological disorders. What is
particular about endemic goitre, caused to a large extent by
iodine deficiency, is that it can be controlled by very simple
inexpensive and effective techniques. In fact, many countries,
including some developing ones, where endemic goitre was highly
prevalent, have been able to control it. WHO and UNICEF have
collaborated in the development and testing of goitre control
techniques and cooperated with interested countries in their
implementation. There are still, however, many countries which
have not given sufficient attention to the problem or have not
been able to solve logistical constraints for the implementation of goitre control measures. For this reason, WHO was particularly gratified by the World Food Council initiative and it
is hoped that the offer of support made jointly by the WFC,
UNICEF and WHO will lead to successful results. In a first
phase of this joint effort, Dr. Mahler, the Director-General of
WHO, wrote around the middle of January this year, to the
Ministers of Health of 19 countries in view of the severity of
the goitre problem they faced and the possibilities of control.
As is indicated in the World Food Council report, the President
of the Council addressed letters to the Ministers of Agriculture or in some cases Heads of States or Governments of the
same countries. The Executive Director of UNICEF wrote to
Ministers of Planning. On the basis of the response to this
first step, a detailed international action programme will be

developed. We feel that this is an important undertaking as coordinated action in the attack of the problem which is relatively easy to solve can create confidence for dealing with more complex ones.

The WFC in Mexico also proposed the eradication of vitamin A deficiency which, in some countries, is the most common cause of blindness in small children. This, however, has already proved a more difficult undertaking than originally envisaged. In this case, further studies are needed to assess the nature of the problem and the effectiveness of the proposed methods of control, before proposing practical programmes at the national and international level.

The Issue Is Hunger

Statement by Mr. Maurice J. Williams of the World Food Council:

There are more hungry people in the world today than ever before. The estimate varies between 450 million and 1.3 billion - depending on the definition of hunger. The 450 million estimate is of those people who get only enough to eat for barest survival - the standard is the absolute minimum food required to support basic metabolism without work or other activity. That we should even collate estimates of need on such a minimal standard itself indicates the enormity of the problem, and the way in which the world has become inured to its human meaning.

Many more than 450 million people - at least 900 million - do not regularly get enough to eat by any reasonable human standard. They know hunger most days of any year. Their energy is sapped by insufficient food; their narrow opportunities are limited by lack of vitality. They are victims of debilitating diseases which they could resist if they were better fed. Their children die from malnutrition and from infant diseases to which lack of food leaves them an easy victim - at a rate as much as nine times the infant mortality rate of the affluent and well fed. Their potential to live fully productive lives, and to contribute to their nation's development remains unrealized. This is what it means to be numbered among the hungry of the world.

Hunger is not new; it has always been part of the human condition for some proportion of the world's people. But two things are new:

-        the number of hungry people is immeasurably greater than ever before, and their numbers are growing rapidly;

- the potential exists to reduce hunger and ultimately to eliminate it; and the world has declared its resolution to do so.

THE VIEWS OF STATES ON THE PROBLEM

The representatives of the States emphasize different aspects of the problem. All express dissatisfaction with common efforts to date and unite around the common objective of eradicating hunger as expressed in the Polish statement.

Poland: Dr. Piotr Feyberg

There is no doubt that the problems of food which we are discussing in this Committee are of primary importance for all countries, and the developing ones in particular. The eradication of hunger and malnutrition in the world should be the leitmotif guiding our activities in the economic field, on both international and national levels. That is why, in our opinion, combating hunger and improving nutrition should stand foremost in the long-term national plans of economic development.

India: Mr. Romesh Bhandari

In our view there can be no more important a subject than that of food. This is very basic to the survival and wellbeing of Man. It is an input which has no substitute. However, what facts we have before us portray a fairly dismal and alarming situation. A large percentage of mankind is impoverished, ill-fed and undernourished. Depending upon the criteria or definitions of hunger, estimates of those who are under-nourished can range from 450 million to anywhere near 1.3 billion. On the basis of 1972-74 figures this would mean that the percentage of undernourished in the developing world would be a minimum of 25% and could go up to 66%.
    While this is the stark reality it highlights both the importance of the subject we are discussing and, the priority and significance which must be placed upon it in the context of our collective efforts to bring about a new International Economic Order. We are all in accord that our global system is both interdependent and interrelated. Peace, Stability and Security can only be ensured through the removal of disparities, by bringing about a more equitable socio-economic order. The main cause of unrest and instability is the economic one. It is only through the removal of want and hunger that mankind can

find permanent insurance against conflicts and wars. If this
indeed is the situation, and, I doubt very much whether any one
in this Chamber would dispute what I have said, then is it not
necessary for us to evaluate as to what the Nations of the world,
individually and collectively, are doing to squarely face the
issues that confront us and to find solutions? In making this
evaluation the picture that emerges is far from reassuring.

The problem of food and agriculture has been discussed for
many years and in many forums. In regard to the substance,
there is nothing new that can be added. We have countless papers,
documents, studies, proposals, recommendations etc. What needs
to be done is known. What is required to achieve what needs to
be done has also been both identified and quantified. Yet,
when we see what has been the implementation of measures to be
adopted, one finds that there is no area in which we have
achieved the targets we have set for ourselves, or, the measures
to which we have agreed.

Against the target of a 4% rate of growth in food and agriculture production our achievement has been 2.5%. Instead of a
growth, this figure is a decline from a level of 2.9% growth of
the previous decade. Flow of external resources for food production are half of the minimum requirement of US$ 8.3 billion
at 1975 prices. We have still not found a solution to food
security. A target of 500,000 tonnes of cereal for International Emergency Food Reserves has not been achieved. A continued availability of at least 10 million tonnes of grains as
food aid has not been realized. Progress in solving long standing problems of international trade in agricultural products of
export interest remains insignificant. Tariff and non-tariff
barriers continue to retard access of such products to the
markets of the developed countries. International Grains negotiations at Geneva have broken down. The pious resolve of the
world food conference to eliminate hunger and malnutrition
within a decade is far from fulfilment. The numbers of undernourished people in the world have grown larger rather than
smaller. In short this is a sad tale of failure of the International community.

The objectives to be achieved in regard to food and agriculture have been identified broadly under four heads:

Firstly, a faster increase in production and a corresponding
need for increased external assistance;

Secondly, finding solutions to the problem of international
trade in agricultural products;

Thirdly, tackling the problem of malnutrition and rural production, and

Fourthly, bringing about international security in the area of
food.

National efforts are thwarted by the lack of adequate response from the international community. It is with a view to
securing such an adequate international response that the Committee of the Whole meets to see how the gap between profession
and performance is bridged. We are not here to identify new
measures or to set down higher targets. This has already been
done. However, various concerned international fora have not
succeeded in bringing about an implementation of what has been
accepted and agreed to. The Committee of the Whole was created
for the purpose of seeing how, through the injection of the
political will, concerned governments can take a fresh and positive look at what has not been achieved in other fora, and, to
see that it is achieved here. In some ways the results of the
outcome of our discussions and deliberations will be a test of
the utility or effectiveness of this Committee. Let us hope
that we will measure up to our responsibilities and see that we
have been able to move forward where others have not.

Sweden: Mr. Per Jödahl

The majority of the population in the developing countries live
in rural areas and outside the urban economy. About 60% of the
population in developing countries derive their livelihood from
agriculture. In most of the developing countries, over 80% of
the gross national product comes from agriculture. It is therefore obvious that agriculture must play a central role in development efforts.

This central role of agriculture is reflected in the many
and sometimes conflicting demands made upon it. Agriculture
should produce food for the people and cash crops for export in
order to finance the import of essential goods; it should provide employment for the majority of the population and generate
an economic surplus for investment in other sectors.

There are many potential conflicts between these demands:
Land reform and labor-intensive farming will improve the living
conditions of the rural masses. It may, however, also lead to
decreases in food deliveries to the urban sector and in the
generation of surpluses for investment in other sectors and
exports.

Rapid increases in agricultural production can be achieved
through mechanization and large-scale farming, but often at the
cost of increased unemployment and malnutrition in rural areas.

Ecological factors may limit the possibilities for increased
production, and a limited availability of land and other production factors can cause difficult choices between the production
of food and cash crops.

These different demands have to be balanced against each other,
and integrated into a national development strategy. There is

no standard solution to this problem, and it is therefore natural
that different countries arrive at different conclusions. Each
country has to take account of its available resources and its
present conditions, and make its own decisions in accordance
with its priorities. Freedom of choice concerning national
development strategies is a very important aspect of national
sovereignty.

Still, certain observations of a general nature can be
made. One is that development should be concerned about people,
and that one of the main tasks of development therefore is the
eradication of hunger and malnutrition. Those who starve are,
invariably, the poor and the unemployed. Development policies
should therefore aim at generating employment and promote an
equitable distribution of incomes and assets.

This is very much a matter of social justice and of the
overall of goals of development efforts. But at the same time,
it is a matter of economic policy and economic efficiency.
Such development policies would create local markets for simple
products that could be produced locally. This production would
not have to be capital-intensive in order to be competitive
even internationally. Instead, it could be small-scale, labour-
intensive and based on local resources. It would also interact
with similar production strategies in agriculture to provide a
self-generating growth process in rural areas.

I should also like to make some comments on appropriate
technology. This has become quite a catch-word over the last
years. The concept has been used in many ways, which has
created some confusion and even suspicion. Hopefully, some of
this confusion will be sorted out at the UN Conference on
Science and Technology. For our part, we attach great importance to the ideas that lie behind this concept, although we are
at the same time aware that it would easily lead to an over-
simplification of the problem.

There is no reason to prescribe a certain type of technology as being particularly suited for developing countries.
The important thing is that all countries should be free to
choose, and be able to adopt or develop technologies that are
suited for their national needs and development strategies.
Such an approach would also permit full use of the considerable
technological know-how which exists in areas where agricultural
production has a tradition of thousands of years. This can be
called a strategy for self-reliance in science and technology,
a strategy which leaves much room for imagination and un-
orthodox thinking. It is important to remember that it does
not necessarily entail focussing on simple technology. It can
equally well imply advanced techniques, e.g. for the utilization of solar energy. Generally speaking, technology should be
prescribed by the choice of production and not the other way
around.

An emphasis on rural development does not mean that it

should be seen as the only goal of development, or as an argument against the promotion of industrialization. Instead, rural development should be seen as a necessary complement to industrialization and as the mobilization of internal resources in support of industrialization.

We had looked forward to the Committee of the Whole having a thorough discussion of the agriculture and industrialization at the same session. That would have made it possible to focus on the interrelation and interaction between these two sectors, and to add an important dimension to these deliberations that is missing at the World Food Council sessions.

Tunisia, Representing the Group of 77:
Mr. Mahmoud Mestiri

The developing countries, taken together, have certainly not achieved the 4 percent goal for food and agricultural production set in the International Development Strategy. In actual fact, the average for this decade has barely reached the level of the preceding decade. The developing countries are very concerned by this situation which affects them all, but has a special impact on those countries which have nutritional priority, as well as other developing countries with substantial nutritional deficits. We are always conscious of the special problems of the African region and, in particular, of the Sudano-Sahelian zone. Without denying that increased efforts are required at the national level to make up for lost time, we cannot avoid the fear that constraints at the international level, which have contributed substantially to the delays which have already been encountered, may continue to make themselves · felt and may even increase in years to come.

In the document which we are submitting to the Committee we have concrete proposals aimed at correcting current trends in both bilateral and multilateral foreign aid intended to increase food and agricultural production in the developing countries. We have also drawn attention, once again, to the fact that agricultural production would be stimulated by the elimination of the obstacles which are being progressively introduced into trade in those agricultural products which are of special interest to the developing countries. We hope that the close linkage which exists between these two aspects will be recognized by the Committee, as it has been by other international agencies, and that our proposals will be given serious consideration.

The increase of agricultural production is equally linked to the accelerated industrialization of the developing countries. Under another item of the Committee's agenda for the present session, we have submitted proposals designed to give appropriate impetus to the Conference which resumes today in

Vienna for the purpose of transforming UNIDO into a specialized
agency which will be in a position to give effective support to
the efforts of our countries to industrialize. Nevertheless,
under the item on food and agriculture, we invite the Plenary
Committee to examine, at this stage, one special aspect of the
problems of industrialization, namely, the development of those
industries which are linked to agriculture.

The European Community: Mr. Jacques Leprette

According to the latest FAO statistics, food production in the
developing countries increased at the average annual rate of 3
percent between 1970 and 1977. While the situation is not
identical in all the developing countries and a number of them
have achieved above-average growth, this rate - which is the
same as that achieved during the 1960s - is below the goal of 4
percent.
    Generally speaking, the analysis establishes that the
poverty zones of the world coincide substantially with the
zones having a nutritional deficiency; this is the most disturbing element.
    While the developing countries substantially met their
nutritional needs during the 1960s, their cereal imports
doubled between 1968 and 1977/1978, rising from 33 to 66 million tons. Forecasts indicate that the situation could de-
teriorate further.

Turkey: Mr. Tahsin Tarlan

Five years have not elapsed since the Conference of Rome at
which public opinion was made aware of the long-term dangers
which would threaten humanity if production did not reach the
stipulated goal. Nevertheless, available statistics show that
the average rate of production of the developing countries
forecast in the international strategy has fallen short of the
goal of 4 percent. It is true that progress has been achieved
in a number of developing countries but the increase in production has nevertheless remained below population growth in
the countries with a nutritional deficit. Consequently their
export receipts are in chronic decline and national income is
threatened.
    Steadily increasing production has been achieved in parti-
cular by those industrialized countries which employ expensive,
high-productivity techniques. The World Bank's report on productivity estimates that, from the present time to 1985, the
total production of the developing countries will be below
their needs and that they will be forced to purchase substantial quantities of cereals from the industrialized coun-

tries and this in turn will create substantial new problems for
them. The same report estimates that the industrialized countries can only continue to increase production at the expense
of increased marginal costs which will, in turn, be reflected
in prices.

The nutritional deficit compensated at the cost of rising
imports will entail severe additional pressures on the balances
of payments of the developing countries. If production in the
developing countries is not intensified very quickly, the capacity of such countries to import capital equipment will be com-
promised. This cumulative development would affect the aggregate demand of the developing countries for the products of the
industrialized countries which, hit by a deep recession, will
make substantial efforts to ensure a rapid recovery.

Nevertheless, the current situation differs from the
periods of recovery of earlier cycles, insofar as it is characterized by the lack of a healthy and non-inflationary demand
from the industrialized countries to compensate for the losses
caused by recession. The reason underlying this negative situation is, in our view, to be found in the feeble growth of investment resulting from the structure of such demand.

New Zealand: Mr. H. H. Francis

As a country whose economic well-being depends on agriculture
and food production, New Zealand welcomes the decision to devote this Committee's second session to consideration of measures regarding world food problems and agricultural development. Our perception of the importance of this subject is not
simply a product of New Zealand's national experience and economic self-interest. Rather, it is a measure of our conviction
that the agricultural sector is of fundamental importance to
economic growth and development. This point was made very suc-
cinctly by the Secretariat of the Committee for Development
Planning in a 1978 study in which it said:

> For much of the developing world, nowhere is the
> need for a dynamic expansion of production greater
> than in agricultural activity. The lagging output
> of agriculture has severely impeded the economic and
> social progress of many developing countries.

The statement on Monday by the distinguished Assistant
Director-General of the Food and Agriculture Organisation may
be read as an elaboration upon that quotation. It makes explicit, in a very telling manner, the linkages between agricultural and other sectors in developing countries and the negative impact of constraints in the agricultural sector on the
achievement of basic social and economic goals. His statement
also demonstrates very clearly the way in which these impedi-

ments to growth and development in developing countries are
felt in the economies of the developed nations. It reminds us
again of the fact, and significance, of the interdependence of
the components of the global economy which was such a major
theme in the debates at this Committee's first session.

Argentina: Mr. Enrique J. Ros

It is the conviction of the Government of the Argentine Republic
that the problem of hunger will be finally solved only once
concrete measures are put into practice to create a world-wide
structure having enough stability to enable the developing countries to adopt a national plan of agricultural development that
will be efficient and lasting. We reiterate that there is need
for concerted action on all fronts of the agricultural
spectrum.

The Union of Soviet Socialist Republics:
Mr. Evgeny Nikolaevich Makayev

The Soviet delegation would like to emphasize some main aspects
of the world food problem and of the means to solve it. The
documents presented to the World Food Council and the FAO in-
contestably testify not to an improvement but to progressive
deterioration in the food situation in many developing countries. In spite of the numerous resolutions of various organizations of the United Nations to solve this problem,
hundreds of millions of people throughout the world continue to
starve, and their number is increasing.
     The main obstacles to solving the world food problem are
the severe consequences of colonialism, profound social inequalities, the neocolonialist policies of the imperialist governments, their stubborn opposition to the restructuring of
international economic relations on the just, equitable, and
mutually advantageous basis, that is the only framework within
which this problem can be solved.
     In the violation of the progressive provisions set forth
in the Declaration of the establishment of a New International
Economic Order of the 6th special session of the General Assembly of the United Nations, in the Charter on Economic Rights
and Duties of Governments, and other resolutions of the United
Nations, the monopolistic circles of the West are still attempting to solve their economic difficulties for the most part
at the cost of the developing countries by utilizing the present
unjust mechanism of commercial-economic and currency-financial
relations.
     The inequitable conditions of trade, the protectionist

policies to which the developed capitalist countries have increasing recourse, inflation, and the export of profits are a
heavy burden above all in the economies of the developing countries, which are especially vulnerable not only to the impact
of the general crisis but also to any instability of the commodity and exchange markets. All this leads directly to the
aggravation of the food situation for the absolute majority of
developing countries.

The Soviet Union has repeatedly called attention to the
necessity of assisting developing countries in their own efforts to solve the food problem. Through international co-
operation based on really democratic principles and aimed
toward the restructuring of international economic relations
and the establishment of a New International Economic Order in
conformity with real United Nations solutions. As a member of
the Politburo of the Central Committee of the Soviet of Ministers of the USSR, A. N. Kosygin emphasized at a meeting with
the electorate,

> International collaboration is a factor of the
> greatest significance both in world politics and in
> the world economy.... For all countries and regions
> of the world as a whole this is the only possible
> way to solve the global problems that confront all
> of humanity and that can be solved only by the col-
> lective efforts of all nations. It is a question of
> preserving peace, of ensuring energy and food, of
> defending the environment, etc.

The solution of the food problem, like the problem of economic development in general, depends above all on ensuring
universal peace and security, on the exclusion of acts of
aggression and the use of force from the everyday relations
between peoples, on the carrying out of active measures for
disarmament and the reduction of military budgets.

The continuing arms race consumes hundreds of billions of
dollars that might be directed toward the solution of the most
severe problems of humanity including that of hunger.

In the connection, I would once more like to attract the
attention of the Committee to the position of the Soviet Union,
advanced before the 5th special session and 33rd regular session of the General Assembly of the United Nations, on the
achievement of an understanding of relative curtailment by governments with great economic and military potential, of their
military budgets to a size on the same order and on the ap-
portionment of the means thus saved to the purposes of development.

As the member nations of the Warsaw Pact stated in a Declaration made at the conference of its Political Consultative Committee in Moscow, November 23, 1978, the implementation of such measures

> will not only set real limits to the arms race, but
> will also release a large amount of money for peaceful
> purposes - for the development of industry and agri-
> culture, science, culture and enlightenment, for
> increased aid to the developing nations to accelerate
> their economic and social development.... This would
> be a tangible gain for disarmament and for the wel-
> fare of nations.

2 The Current Situation: FAO Summaries

The FAO summed up the current global situation in food and agriculture and the measures being undertaken by the Specialized Agencies and States Members of the United Nations in technical papers A/AC.191/27 and A/AC.191/37. The contents of the two documents have been grouped around the seven headings of the Agreed Conclusions of the Committee of the Whole, and are presented in edited form.

INTERNATIONAL STRATEGY FOR FOOD AND AGRICULTURE

The last few years have seen a growing consensus on the principal elements of an international strategy for food and agriculture. The International Development Strategy (IDS) adopted for the Second United Nations Development Decade (DD2) contains the basic target that the expansion of agricultural production in the developing countries should be accelerated to an average rate of 4 percent a year. The review and appraisal of progress in DD2 has highlighted the effects of the lagging performance of agriculture on the achievement of the over-all objectives of the IDS.

The United Nations World Food Conference, which met in November 1974 in the shadow of the food crisis that began in 1972, dramatized the need for greater priority for food and agriculture. It adopted the Universal Declaration on the Eradication of Hunger and Malnutrition, and agreed on a wide range of measures to overcome world food problems, which were endorsed by the twenty-ninth session of the United Nations General Assembly. The measures adopted by other conferences, including the sixth and seventh special sessions of the General Assembly (especially the Declaration and Programme of Action on

a New International Economic Order adopted by the former), the
fourth session of UNCTAD, the Conference on International Economic Co-operation, the biennial sessions of the FAO Conference,
and sectoral conferences, such as those on water and desertification, contain further elements of an international
strategy for food and agriculture.

The eighteenth session of the FAO Conference in 1975
adopted a Strategy of International Agricultural Adjustment,
including 11 Guidelines, and charged FAO to monitor progress.
The World Food Council (WFC) was established by the General
Assembly to monitor and co-ordinate the response of the international community to world food problems. Its third session
in 1977 issued the "Manila Communique" which is a synthesis of
measures to give effect to the resolutions of the World Food
Conference.

Although the global food and agricultural situation has
recovered from the serious short-term crisis, almost all of the
longer-term problems remain basically unchanged, and the estimated number of undernourished people has increased. There
is increasing evidence of a growing commitment by the developing countries to the accelerated development of their food
and agricultural sectors, but the implementation of most of the
recommendations of the World Food Conference is still far from
adequate. Now that the world food situation appears to have
recovered from the immediate crisis, it is imperative that international concern with the problems of food and agriculture
should not once again be allowed to lapse.

In recent years there has been a general widening of international concern, going beyond the food and agricultural
sector to encompass other elements of a broad-based strategy of
rural development designed to reduce poverty and hunger and
meet the basic needs of the poorest people. This was highlighted at the World Employment Conference in 1976. The ACC
Task Force on Rural Development, in which FAO has assumed the
role of lead agency this year, is making efforts to strengthen
the poverty-oriented rural development activities of the international agencies. The World Conference on Agrarian Reform and
Rural Development, which is to be held in July 1979 under the
aegis of FAO in co-operation with other agencies, should further
contribute to the evolution of guidelines for national and international action for the mobilization of investment and for
the institutional and policy changes necessary for the alleviation of rural poverty.

FOOD AND AGRICULTURAL PRODUCTION IN DEVELOPING
COUNTRIES AND THE FLOW OF EXTERNAL RESOURCES

Food and Agricultural Production

World food and agricultural production has resumed its long-
term upward trend, after declining in 1972. This is mainly the
result of generally better weather, but it also reflects increased government attention to agriculture in many developing
countries. There are other signs of improvement, for example
in the supply of fertilizers and pesticides, and the recovery
of world cereal stocks to what may be regarded, at least on a
global basis, as reasonably safe levels. Yet viewed in a
longer-term perspective and in relation to basic development
goals, the situation remains highly unsatisfactory.
      The agricultural production of the developing countries
increased at an average rate of 2.5 percent a year in 1970-77.
This is slower than in the 1960s, and must be compared with the
IDS target of 4 percent. A number of countries have achieved
high rates of growth. But in the developing countries as a
whole agricultural production has increased only slightly
faster than population, and the large gap in levels of production per head between the developed and developing countries
has continued to widen. In Africa, production rose by only 1.2
percent a year in 1970-77, and thus declined substantially in
relation to population. In no less than 62 of the 157 developing countries for which FAO calculates production index numbers (representing 43 percent of their total population), agricultural production failed to match population growth in
1970-77.
      The most disquieting aspect of the production situation is
that the slowest increases have been in the poorest of the developing countries. The 45 most seriously affected (MSA) countries provide a clear indication. Agricultural production in
the MSA countries rose by only 1.9 percent a year in 1970-77,
as compared with 2.8 percent in the other developing countries,
and fell considerably behind population growth. It is thus
clear that the overriding priority for national and international action on food and agriculture remains the acceleration of
the increase in production in the developing countries, and
above all the poorest among them.
      FAO's preliminary estimates indicate that world food and
agricultural production rose by almost 3 percent in 1978. For
the first time since 1973, however, the largest increases were
in the developed countries. Revised data have slightly raised
the annual growth of food production in the developing countries
in 1970-77 to 3 percent, or the same as that in the 1960s.
However, for total agricultural production in these countries
and for both food and agricultural production in the developing

market economies, the rate remains less than in the previous
decade. This is almost entirely due to Africa, where the annual production increase in the 1970s so far is only about half
that of the 1960s, and much less than half that achieved in
each of the other developing regions in the 1970s. In the most
seriously affected (MSA) countries, many of which are in Africa,
the average annual increase in food production fell from 2.6
percent in the 1960s to 2.2 percent in 1970-77, whereas in the
other developing countries it rose slightly from 3.1 to 3.2
percent. The 1978 results, if confirmed by later data, are
unlikely to bring much change in these longer-term rates of
growth.
        The deteriorating situation in Africa led the Ministers of
Agriculture of that region to call for the preparation of a
Regional Food Plan. This was presented to the Tenth FAO Regional Conference for Africa in September 1978 and is likely to
lead to increased requests for assistance in the preparation of
national plans and programmes within this regional framework.

                              Agricultural Inputs

The "horizontal" expansion of production, through the extension
of the cultivable area, must be complemented by "vertical" expansion through raising yields per unit of land. This is
especially necessary in such densely populated areas as the Far
East, but it is also required even where unused land is available. Important requirements are the soil conservation and
water development measures mentioned above, but increased yields
are particularly dependent, with existing technology, on adequate supplies of modern inputs, such as improved seeds, fertilizers, crop protection means, and farm machinery. If the
developing countries are to achieve the necessary acceleration
of the increase in their production, they require much greater
assistance to obtain supplies of such inputs.
        The high-yielding varieties (HYVs) of cereals have played
a major part in the increase in food production, especially in
Asia, since the late 1960s. If 60 percent of the wheat area,
half of the rice area, 40 percent of the maize area and 20 percent of that of millets and sorghums are to be under HYVs by
1985, it would require the annual production of about 70,000
tons of seed for wheat, 230,000 tons for rice, 200,000 tons for
maize, and 40,000 tons for millet and sorghum. This would entail
a very big expansion of the facilities in the developing countries for the production, processing, quality control, storage
and distribution of improved seeds, and a concommitant increase
in the financial and technical assistance available for this
purpose. The Conference on International Economic Co-operation
called for at least $20 million either through bilateral pro-
grammes or through the FAO Seed Improvement and Development Pro-

gramme (SIDP, and the nineteenth session of the FAO Conference
in 1977 appealed for contributions of at least $20 million for
the SIDP alone). However, contributions have so far been made
only on a project basis, amounting to about $3 million for
training and a further $3 million for seed production projects.
A principal requirement for the expansion of agricultural
production is adequate supplies of chemical fertilizers at
reasonable and stable prices. According to the projections
prepared by the FAO/UNIDO/ World Bank Working Group on Fertilizers, supplies are likely to be adequate to meet effective
demand at least up to 1981/82. However, because of inadequate
purchasing power and foreign exchange, the effective demand of
most developing countries falls short of their requirements for
increasing production. In line with a recommendation of the
seventh special session of the General Assembly, the first session of the WFC recommended that donor countries should increase
their fertilizer assistance to MSA countries to 1 million
nutrient tons per year, but such assistance to all developing
countries in fact fell from 570,000 tons in 1974-75 to 540,000
tons in 1975-76 and 430,000 tons in 1976-77. There has been a
sharp decline in the fertilizers made available under FAO's
International Fertilizer Supply Scheme, which fell from 18 percent of the total fertilizer assistance in 1975-76 to only 8
percent of the smaller total in 1976-77. The scheme has been
extended to the end of 1979, and is seeking the replenishment
of its resources. The FAO Fertilizer Programme, which aims to
promote fertilizer use at farm level, is receiving increasing
support from donor Governments, although more resources are
still required to meet requests for assistance.
Many developing countries still have difficulty in obtaining their requirements of pesticides, not only because of the
shortage of foreign exchange but also because certain products
have been banned for environmental reasons in the developed
countries that produce them, and adequate substitutes at com-
parable prices are not yet available. The development of systems of integrated pest control, teaching them to farmers and
providing advisory and monitoring services will require the
building up of technical capability in the developing countries,
including training, the strengthening of extension services,
and adaptive research.

Research and Technology

Agricultural research to devise and adapt appropriate technologies for improved production and processing is still weak
in many developing countries. A major international effort on
the production technology for important food crops and related
farming systems is under way through the centres and programmes
supported by the Consultative Group on International Agricul-

tural Research (CGIAR), which is co-sponsored by FAO, UNDP and
the World Bank. The World Food Conference called for a substantial enlargement of the resources of the CGIAR, and the
resources of the international agricultural research centres
have in fact increased from $34.5 million in 1974 to $80 million in 1977, and $88 million in 1978, and $103 million in 1979.
The CGIAR has endorsed the proposal for the establishment of a
special service to strengthen national agricultural research.

    This international effort has not yet been matched in most
of the developing countries by the development of adequate
national research findings. As was stressed by the eighteenth
session of the FAO Conference in 1975, considerable additional
efforts are required to strengthen national research capabilities, to promote co-operation among developing countries in
this field, and to forge effective links with the international
centres. The CGIAR is considering a proposal for the establishment of a new international mechanism for strengthening
national agricultural research. The nineteenth session of the
FAO Conference in 1977 expressed its concern about this proposal.
It "stressed that FAO was fully experienced and equipped to
provide assistance to national agricultural research" and
"would continue to work to ensure that the essential link between research, extension and production was maintained," and
it "therefore urged the CGIAR to take full account of FAO's
role and capacity in its consideration of the proposal." The
World Employment Conference emphasized that research should
mainly be undertaken within and under the direction of the developing countries themselves. The United Nations Conference
on Technical Co-operation among Developing Countries (TCDC) was
held in August-September 1978. It agreed on the Buenos Aires
Plan of Action, which provides a new stimulus for the continuation and expansion of TCDC activities and calls for the
mobilization of increased resources for this purpose. The whole
complex of policy considerations concerning the accelerated
application of science and technology to development at the
national level and with increased international co-operation
will be discussed at the United Nations Conference on Science
and Technology for Development, to be held in August 1979.

    It is necessary for improved technology to cover a still
wider range of crops, to be applicable in less favorable ecological conditions, and to be consistent with local socio-
economic constraints. More specific areas requiring further
emphasis include economies in energy use, and the development
of appropriate technologies for the reduction of food losses by
preservation and processing. Above all, however, improved
technology must be suitable for use by small farmers, and systems devised and established for its effective transfer to them,
through a co-ordinated effort by the research and extension
services, including the feeding back of the actual needs of
small farmers to the research services. It should also make

fuller use of on-farm resources and traditional skills by means
of appropriate identification of alternative labour-using technologies that may be economically competitive, especially concerning farm tools and equipment.
    The growing awareness in developing countries that the
technologies developed in the industrialized countries are not
necessarily the most appropriate for them has stimulated interest in technical co-operation among developing countries
(TCDC). Examples of this approach include the West African
Rice Development Association, and a proposed UNDP Asian Farm
Machinery Project. Through the Current Agricultural Research
Information System (CARIS) and the International Information
System for Agricultural Science and Technology (AGRIS), FAO is
assisting in the exchange of research information among countries. The United Nations Conference on TCDC, to be held in
August 1978, may be expected to identify further specific areas
for TCDC in food and agriculture, and this subject is also to
be discussed at the 1978 FAO Regional Conference.

                               Forestry

The consumption of major forest products has been growing much
more rapidly in the developing countries than in the world as a
whole, and this trend is likely to continue and even intensify.
Growth has been particularly rapid for paper, paperboard and
wood-based panels, which are products where economies of scale
have been important in determining the feasibility of establishing production capacity. International markets for these
products are seriously disrupted by alternating periods of
shortage or surplus as demand varies with the economic situation. This points to the need for intensified monitoring of
market developments in order to ascertain the appropriate
timing of mill construction. International assistance is also
required for the transfer and adaptation of technology, the
training of skilled manpower, the design of efficient smaller
mills, and the provision of investment capital.
    A major objective is to raise the value of exports from
developing countries, rich in tropical hardwoods, through
greater processing at the source. Except in a few countries,
exports have predominantly been in the form of unprocessed logs,
because of the past lack of adequate local markets to justify
domestic processing, and the limited availability of infrastructure, technical knowledge and skills, as well as the nature of
concession agreements for wood removal rights, often made without full realization of ultimate wood product values. The market for these exports has fluctuated widely as requirements for
wood, especially for construction, have varied with erratic
economic growth and changing policies for housing construction.
The disruptive effects of this instability on exporting coun-

tries should be countered through the further development of
domestic markets for processed goods, improved concession
agreements, and international commodity arrangements. As
noted later, tropical timber is one of the commodity groups
covered by the UNCTAD Integrated Programme for Commodities.

In tropical forests, the frequent market-oriented pattern
of harvesting select quality material has often led to the degradation or even loss of the forest area. An intensification
of international assistance for work on extending the utilization and marketing of the less accepted qualities and grades is
essential.

Of particular concern is the extent to which both the
planned and unplanned destruction of forest cover for agricultural settlement or shifting cultivation is taking place on
soils which are not sufficiently fertile to sustain crop production, or in places (such as steep slopes) unsuited to cultivation. The consequent destruction of biological capital
through erosion, flooding and drought threatens agricultural
productivity over a much wider area than that immediately affected, sometimes in adjoining countries. In particular it has
aggravated flood problems in some densely populated areas of
Asia already suffering from severe food shortage.

In areas poorer in natural forests, the continuous and
increasing need for fuelwood has also frequently led to the
marked reduction or disappearance of the limited wood resources.
A major effort is needed to improve both the supply and the
efficiency of use of the wood and other organic fuels on which
upwards of 1,500 million people depend for cooking their food,
with little scope for substitution by other fuels in the foreseeable future.

The establishment of forest plantations is a solution for
the rehabilitation of degraded forest areas, as well as for
meeting the critical needs for fuelwood in many areas. The
United Nations Conference on Desertification recommended increased international financial and technical support for the
establishment of plantations in dry lands. Despite much
progress in the development of planting methods and in basic
research on genetic improvement and nutrient requirements,
further efforts are required. However, securing investment
funds for the effective establishment of plantations is usually
the major problem.

The apparently rapid shrinkage of the tropical forests is
seldom well monitored at the national level, so that attempts
at regional or world appraisals are extremely difficult. Although FAO and UNEP are undertaking considerable resource
monitoring work, it urgently needs to be greatly intensified if
this serious problem is to be adequately appraised. The inter-
facing of agriculture and forestry in the supply of food and
fibre and in their competition for land and investment funds
also calls for a major international effort to resolve con-

flicts in choosing and implementing alternative land uses and
even more to develop methods for the joint production of trees,
crops and animals.

Recently FAO and the World Bank have re-emphasized forestry's economic and social role in improving the well-being of
the rural poor through a programme of Forestry for Local Community Development. This programme concentrates on the reorientation of policies and institutions to bring about communal action for supplying the whole range of goods and services
required from local forests and other tree resources.

Fisheries

The new legal regime of the oceans which is emerging from the
successive sessions of the United Nations Conference on the Law
of the Sea is a development with far-reaching effects on world
fisheries. By extending their national jurisdictions over exclusive economic zones, generally of 200 miles from the base-
lines of territorial seas, many coastal States have already
assumed rights over the responsibilities for resources previous-
ly regarded as common property. Non-coastal States are thereby
denied access to these resources, except under conditions prescribed by the coastal States.

The primary effect of such extended jurisdictions is to
increase greatly the coastal State's power to determine the
utilization of the resources, and to give it a more secure base
for planning the development of its fisheries. At the same
time, the exercise of expanded rights over resources brings
with it the acquisition of new responsibilities by coastal
States for the optimum utilization and proper management of the
resources. Many of these States are confronted with a serious
task of adjustment to the new opportunities and responsibilities.

Special issues emerge when important migratory stocks of
fish are shared by two or more coastal States. They will be
obliged in their own interest, as well as expected by the international community, to reach agreement on appropriate means
for the conservation and joint use of the resource. In the
past the application of such systems has generally been attained
through multilateral negotiations involving all interested
parties. The effect of the extension of national jurisdictions
is to concentrate the responsibilities in this regard, and to
increase the number of cases where only two or a few coastal
States will negotiate the sharing and conservation of a resource.

The seventy-fourth session of the FAO Council in November
1978 endorsed the recommendations of the Committee on Fisheries
(COFI) regarding the comprehensive medium-term programme being
formulated by FAO to assist developing coastal States, upon
request, in managing and developing fisheries in their ex-

clusive economic zones (EEZ). It agreed that the highest
priority should be given to this programme, and recognized that
its implementation would entail the need for financial assistance from the UNDP and other funding agencies, in addition to
support from FAO's Regular Programme.

None of the technical problems is in principle new. What
is new is the urgency for particular countries to seize new
opportunities and assume new responsibilities, for regional
bodies to provide assistance, services and fora for collaboration between contiguous States sharing the same resources, and
for the world as a whole to avoid a temporary fall in production
during the period of adjustment. It will not be possible to
meet the expected increase in the demand for fish as food without sound management of the resources of conventional species
of fish, whose further potential for exploitation is in many
case limited. At the same time, concerted efforts will be necessary for the effective utilization of species at present
deemed of little commercial value, and for substantial reduc-
tions in losses at all stages of the handling, processing and
distribution chain. The developing countries particularly require increased access to market intelligence and to improved
technology for fish processing. Another crucial area is the
expansion of production in inland waters and from aquaculture
in general, on which assistance is provided through the FAO/UNDP
Aquaculture Development and Co-ordination Programme.

Economic Co-Operation Among Developing Countries

Since agriculture is the most important sector in the economy
of most developing countries, it has formed part of the objectives and programmes of many of the schemes for regional and
subregional economic integration and co-operation among these
countries. In some cases, it is covered within an over-all
framework for economic co-operation, while in others specific
provisions for food and agriculture (for example in the field
of trade) have been included in the agreements for economic
co-operation. However, the experience so far has made it clear
that, at least in the agricultural sector, co-operation cannot
be confined to trade, but must be based on the joint planning
of the future expansion of production, including the common
development of infrastructure and resource use.

The introduction of the concept of collective self-reliance
in the Declaration and Programme of Action on the Establishment
of a New International Economic Order has made economic co-
operation among developing countries (ECDC) a major area of
concern and action. Efforts to promote ECDC in more specific
areas have also been stimulated by the difficulties encountered
in the wider schemes for economic integration and co-operation.
UNCTAD has recently established a Standing Committee on ECDC.

The resolutions of the General Assembly concerning TCDC have
stressed its vital role in promoting and supporting ECDC.
    Some general areas for ECDC are identified in the action
programmes for food and agriculture adopted by the Third Ministerial Conference of the Group of 77 (Manila, February 1976),
the Fifth Conference of Heads of State or Government of Non-
Aligned Countries (Colombo, August 1976), and the Conference on
ECDC (Mexico City, September 1976). FAO will be convening a
Technical Consultation of Government Experts on ECDC in Food
and Agriculture in mid-1979, which is expected to review
progress and identify more specific ways in which such co-
operation could be strengthened and in which FAO and the international community could provide further support.

                Flow of Resources for Agricultural Development

FAO estimates of the investment requirements for increasing the
food production of the developing countries at a rate that would
match the annual increase of 3.6 percent in demand projected in
1974 indicated that total investment (excluding fertilizer
plants and other agro-industries, rural communications and
transport, and multipurpose river basin projects) would have to
be doubled, to reach an annual level of $US 18,000 to 20,000
million in 1975-80. The external assistance (excluding private
flows) needed to support this level of investment was places at
just under a third of the total, or $5,000 to 6,000 million at
1972 prices, of which a large part would be required on concessional terms.
    The FAO Guidelines on International Agricultural Adjust-
ment include the target of at least $5,000 million a year of
external assistance in 1975-80. Adjusted by the United Nations
index of the unit value of manufactured exports $5,000 million
at 1972 prices would amount to somewhat more than $8,000 mil-
lion at 1975 prices) as the annual target by 1980, of which
$6,500 million on concessional terms.
    Revised estimates indicate that official commitments of
external assistance to agriculture from all sources except the
socialist countries under the OECD "narrow" definition of agriculture* rose from $US 3,390 million in 1976 to $4,980 million
in 1977, or by 35 percent in real terms. There is likely to
have been a further large rise in 1978. Loans and credits for
food production approved by the Work Bank and the International
Development Association (IDA), which are the major sources of

---

*Roughly equivalent to food production, and excluding rural de-
velopment and rural infrastructure, agro-industries, fertilizer
production, and regional and river basin projects.

external assistance for agriculture, increased from $1,945 million in 1977 to $3,052 million in 1978.

There was still a shortfall in 1977 of about $3,750 (at 1975 prices), or 45 percent below the World Food Council (WFC) target of $8,300 million by 1980. The shortfall from the target of $6,500 on concessional terms was about $3,500 million, or 54 percent. The poorest developing countries, particularly those in the densely populated areas of Asia, have continued to receive less external assistance for agriculture, on a per caput basis, than those with higher incomes. Commitments in 1977 under the OECD "broad" definition were only $1.8 per caput in the countries with per caput GNP of $250 or less, as compared with $3.2 in the higher-income developing countries. The poorest countries did better with commitments on concessional terms, however, and received $1.6 per caput as against $1.3 in the others. Moreover, per caput commitments to the poorest countries rose twice as fast as those to the others in 1974-77, and the difference was even greater for concessional commitments.

The major prerequisite for bridging this gap is a substantial expansion of external assistance to all sectors. If the Development Assistance Committee (DAC) of the OECD increased their commitments of official development assistance (ODA) on concessional terms to the IDS target of 0.7 percent of GNP (about double the current proportion), then the target of $6,500 million at 1975 prices on concessional terms for agriculture in 1980 would represent no more than 15 percent of total ODA commitments. If, however, ODA commitments stayed at the current proportion of GNP, this target would be 30 percent of the total, as compared with agriculture's actual share of 10 percent in 1976. In any case, in addition to a substantial increase in over-all development assistance, it would be necessary for more bilateral donors to follow the example of the World Bank in giving much greater priority to agricultural and rural development. The replenishment of IFAD's resources, as the only major financing institution created exclusively for agriculture, should also receive priority attention during 1979-80.

Expanded external assistance for the food and agricultural sector, directed increasingly to small-scale programmes and projects in favour of small farmers, will require a considerable increase in local financing. This may involve changes in the traditional system of appraising and monitoring externally financed projects, with greater reliance on decentralized local institutions. Such changes would greatly accelerate the utilization of external assistance for food and agricultural projects. A major problem in many developing countries, especially the poorest, will remain the need for assistance (including training) in the identification and preparation of investment programmes and projects, and FAO is giving increased emphasis to assistance of this kind.

A paramount need is for considerably expanded external
assistance on concessional terms for the agriculture of the
poorest of the developing countries. The MSAs have so far
received much less assistance for agriculture per head of their
population than the other developing countries. IFAD plans
that the largest proportion of its resources should go to the
poorest developing countries on highly concessional terms, but
much more will be needed.

Main Areas Requiring National and International Action

There is no doubt that the most pressing need as already identified in the IDS for DD2, remains a massive acceleration of
the increase in food and agricultural production in the developing countries. More recently it has become clearly apparent
from their lagging production and deteriorating nutritional
situation that it is in the poorest developing countries (of
which the MSA countries are a representative sample) that the
greatest acceleration is needed.

A faster increase in production implies higher priority
for agriculture in the domestic investment programmes of the
countries concerned. But it also implies a considerable expansion in development assistance on concessional terms for the
agriculture of the developing countries, and an even larger
increase for the poorest of them. Even if over all development
assistance for all sectors were raised to the IDS target, a
larger share for agriculture would still be required. Most
developing countries will also need more assistance (including
training) in the identification and preparation of investment
programmes and projects. At the same time, new approaches to
financial assistance are required if external assistance has to
play a greatly expanded role in financing small-scale, labour-
intensive projects in the food and agricultural sector.

For production to be increased sufficiently rapidly, there
are a number of specific areas that require special emphasis
both by the developing countries themselves and in development
assistance. Particularly large investments will be needed for
land and water development, the more so if greater regard is to
be paid in the future to environmental aspects such as soil
degradation and the loss of forest cover. It is of crucial
importance to ensure that the developing countries can obtain
adequate supplies of the improved seeds, fertilizers and other
inputs essential for raising production. Investment in fertilizer production capacity in these countries will contribute
not only in this regard but also to the achievement of the Lima
industrialization target. In the meantime, one of the most
pressing needs is for greatly increased international assistance
to enable developing countries short of foreign exchange to
import their requirements of fertilizers and other essential

inputs. A reorientation of assistance is needed for the adjustment of fishery programmes to the extended jurisdiction
acquired over exclusive fishing zones, and in order to avoid a
fall in production during the adjustment period. Another new
area for assistance is in Forestry for Local Community Development. A major effort now has to be made to strengthen national agricultural research systems in the developing countries, in part so that they can take better advantage of the
recent large expansion in research at the international level.
Improved technology has to be developed for small farmers, and
a better feedback between farmers and researchers established,
so that their needs are more fully reflected in research
programmes. Closely allied to increasing production is the
need for a substantial reduction in the huge avoidable food
losses in the developing countries.

If the increase in food and agricultural production in the
developing countries can be accelerated in these and other ways,
and if it can be supplemented by a reduction in food losses,
this will be a big step towards the enhanced self-reliance of
these countries and the narrowing gaps between rich and poor
countries envisaged under a New International Economic Order.
But, essential as it is, it will not by itself be sufficient
for the eradication of hunger and malnutrition. For this to be
achieved will also entail the reduction of poverty, as well as
special nutritional measures.

A key element in the reduction of poverty is that most of
the production increase should come from the small farmers and
landless labourers who constitute the vast majority of the rural
poor. They thus need adequate access to land and other productive resources, as well as suitable institutions not only
for the effective delivery to them of the necessary technology
and physical inputs, and of the price incentives and credit
they need to apply them, but also for their full participation
in development. Education and training, particularly at the
grass-roots level, are essential factors in such a concept of
rural development, and represent an area where greatly increased
international assistance could be particularly fruitful. In
most countries the new international consensus on the need to
integrate women in training and other development programmes
has yet to be effectively followed up at the national level.

Apart from a direct assault on poverty, of which nutrition
is a principal indicator, special nutritional measures will
continue to be necessary, especially for vulnerable groups such
as women and children. This is an area where increased national
emphasis and international assistance are particularly desirable.
Nutrition is so important a component of basic needs that it is
necessary to evaluate the impact of development programmes and
projects on nutritional status, and as far as possible to incorporate nutritional considerations at the formulation stage.

In most of these areas discussed above there is already
full agreement on what is required, but in many cases there is
still a deplorable shortfall in the national and international
action taken so far. Many of them also represent promising
areas for ECDC and TCDC, where a main need appears to be the
identification of more specific areas for co-operation. Finally, there are a number of important areas, namely world food
security, food aid, and international trade, where it is very
largely international action that is required. Here too there
is a consensus on the measures that are required, but little
has been achieved so far.

The first main requirement for world food security is the
faster increase in production already emphasized. The second
is to seize the opportunity provided by the present high level
of cereal stocks to establish the system of internationally
co-ordinated stocks envisaged in the International Undertaking
on World Food Security. It is urgent that progress here should
not be held up by delays in negotiations on wider issues of
international trade. Although it is essential to conclude a
formal international grains arrangement as quickly as possible,
Governments should already begin voluntarily to implement the
stock provisions of the International Undertaking. In addition,
greater assistance is required for developing countries implementing national food security schemes for the acquisition
of stocks, and establishing related facilities, including
storage, marketing and transport.

Food aid remains essential as an interim measure until
production can be increased sufficiently in the developing countries. The conclusion of a new and enlarged Food Aid Convention
is similarly held up by the failure to reach agreement on an
international grains arrangement. If necessary, a new convention should be concluded as a separate instrument. Consideration should also be given to a higher target for food aid in
cereals than the minimum agreed at the World Food Conference,
which has still not been met. The provisional pledges to the
WFP should be reconsidered, with a view to meeting the pledging
targets for both 1977-78 and 1979-80. Governments should be
urged to meet without further delay and on a continuing basis
the annual target for the International Emergency Food Reserve.
Guidelines for improved food aid policies should be agreed as
soon as possible, particularly concerning forward planning,
greater multilateral channelling, and better integration with
other forms of aid.

The solution of the long-standing problems of international
trade in agricultural products, which is central to the establishment of a New International Economic Order, continues to
prove particularly intractable. While the main thrust must
continue to be in the negotiations on UNCTAD's Integrated
Programme for Commodities, it is necessary at the same time to
expedite the conclusion of liberalized general compensatory

financing schemes, and of stabilization arrangements for those
individual commodities on which early agreement appears likely,
to mitigate the effects of protectionist measures through
further extentions of the GSP and greater concessions in the
GATT Multilateral Trade Negotiations, and to stimulate research
and development measures to enhance the competitiveness of the
agricultural exports of the developing countries. The developed countries should recognize that adjustments in their
domestic agricultural economies and policies would bring benefits to them as well as to the developing countries.

National and international action is urgently required in
all of the main fields summarized above, as well as in many
other related ones. On a longer-term basis, it is also essential that the necessary action should be fully integrated in a
new IDS for the next decade and beyond, which aims, within the
framework of a New International Economic Order, at the eradication of poverty and of the hunger and malnutrition that are
among its worst effects.

WORLD FOOD SECURITY

World Food Security

Most of the issues so far discussed involve increased action at
the national level in the developing countries, supported by
international assistance, mainly designed to accelerate the
increase in production. There remain some major issues, concerning world food security, food aid, and trade, commodity
and adjustment problems where rather specific international
action is required. On many aspects of these issues there is a
high degree of international consensus, but it has not yet been
fully implemented.

FAO's International Undertaking on World Food Security has
now been endorsed by 72 Governments and the EEC. Its main aims
are to ensure continuous consultations among Governments on
food security problems; to establish a global food information
system; to provide special assistance for the production and
stock programmes of developing countries; and to establish an
internationally co-ordinated system of national food reserves
at adequate levels.

Progress has been made towards some of these objectives.
Regular intergovernmental consultations are held by the FAO
Committee on World Food Security (CFS), established in 1975 as
a standing committee of the FAO Council. The Global Information and Early Warning System, set up in FAO with the participation of 90 countries, alerts the international community to
threats of severe shortage or emergency. However, it is still
handicapped by inadequate data in some countries, and by the

non-participation of several major food producing countries, notably Brazil, China and the USSR. FAO has established a Food Security Assistance Scheme, to help developing countries to draw up national food security programmes, including food reserve targets, and to mobilize bilateral or multilateral assistance to implement them. The resources available to the scheme are small, and require to be substantially increased. Bilateral programmes could also co-operate by using the scheme as a clearing-house for information on projects, and food aid should be provided for building food reserves in interested developing countries.

The FAO Food Security Assistance Scheme (FSAS) has so far received contributions totalling $27 million and has already allocated more than $17 million to assist food security measures in nine developing countries. FAO has recently issued an appeal for additional financial support for this scheme.

FAO now forecasts that total carry-over stocks of cereals (excluding China and the USSR) will rise by a further 26 million tons, or 15 percent, to reach 203 million tons by the close of the 1978-79 crop seasons. They would thus represent 21 percent of annual consumption in the countries concerned. While this is above the 18 percent estimated by FAO as the minimum required for world food security, the stocks are unevenly distributed geographically and remain inadequate in most developing countries. Stocks of wheat and coarse grains are increasingly concentrated in a narrow belt of North America, where, if considerable additional supplies had to be shipped to meet crop failures in 1979, difficult logistic problems might arise as a result of the already strained rail and port facilities.

However, no progress has been made so far in negotiations for the establishment of internationally co-ordinated food security reserves, which are being carried out within the broader framework of the negotiations concerning a new international grains arrangement. Following preparatory discussions for two years under the auspices of the International Wheat Council, UNCTAD convened a negotiating conference in February 1978 to replace the International Wheat Agreement of 1971, but this was inconclusive, and the former agreement was extended by protocol for a further year to 30 June 1979. The main areas of disagreement in the negotiations include the nature and function of the price provisions, the size and distribution of the reserve stock, whether coarse grains should be included, and the assistance to be given to developing countries in establishing reserve stocks. The international grains negotiations were adjourned on 14 February 1979 without agreeing on the formal establishment of the internationally co-ordinated system of national reserve stocks called for in FAO's International Undertaking on World Food Security.

The third session of the CFS in April 1978 stressed the
pressing need for the early conclusion of an international
agreement, and recommended that the Governments participating in
the negotiations should give special consideration to the following aspects, so that the new agreement would make a meaningful contribution to world food security: in determining the
size of reserve stocks, to bear in mind the objective of ensuring adequate world supplies at all times, so as to avoid
acute food shortages in the event of widespread crop failures
or natural disasters; adequate provision for special international assistance to developing countries assuming stock-
holding obligations for the acquisition of stocks, meeting
carrying charges, and establishing storage facilities for national reserves, and full consideration to the proposal of the
developing countries concerning a Reserve Stock Financing Fund;
in determining the price range, to bear in mind both the need to
ensure that the developing countries would be in a position to
satisfy their import requirements, and the need to assure an
adequate return to producers; and in periods of global food
shortage, to bear in mind the need to enable developing countries to meet their essential consumption requirements. The
CFS also made recommendations concerning a new Food Aid Convention (FAC), which are discussed below.

Pending the conclusion of these formal negotiations, major
exporting and importing countries should be urged to fix and
announce cereal stock targets voluntarily, and to follow the
guidelines contained in the International Undertaking for the
release and replenishment of stocks.

The third session of the CFS also expressed concern at the
implications of the lag of rice production behind demand,
especially in the Far East, for the food security of developing
countries. It emphasized the need for increased financial and
technical assistance for rice production programmes in developing countries, the provision of adequate incentives and resources for rice production by the developing countries themselves, and strengthened international research on rice varieties with higher resistance to pests and drought.

Prevention of Food Losses

In addition to the need to accelerate the expansion of production in developing countries, it is of the utmost importance to
increase the available supplies of food by reducing avoidable
losses. Pre-harvest losses due to pests are estimated to
average 20 to 40 percent of global production. Post-harvest
losses of cereals from mechanical causes range from 5 to 10
percent, and those from biological causes are of the order of
10 percent. The reduction of such losses could considerably
diminish the rising food import requirements of the developing
countries.

The seventh special session of the General Assembly called
for the reduction of post-harvest losses by at least half by
1985. The nineteenth session of the FAO Conference in 1977
established an Action Programme for the Prevention of Food
Losses, to be financed from a Special Account, based on voluntary contributions, with a target of $20 million. The pro-
gramme will focus particularly on the prevention of losses at
the farm and village level, and will seek to help countries
obtain the very substantial external financial assistance that
will be required. While cereals and other staple food crops
have been selected for priority action, it is hoped later to
include animal products and other perishable foods in the
programme.
     Contributions of $14.3 million have so far been received
towards the Special Account, based on voluntary contributions,
of the $20 million Action Programme for the Prevention of Food
Losses established by the nineteenth session of the FAO Conference in 1977. Project requests amounting to $14.4 million
have been received, and 28 projects costing $5.7 million ap-
proved. A major problem that has emerged is a serious shortage
of the experts required for the various aspects of the prevention of food losses.
     There were substantial food losses in 1978 as a result of
renewed invasions of desert locust in wide areas of Africa and
Asia. In spite of intensive control operations, the infestation spread to many countries. While every effort is being
made to control the situation, ecological conditions continue
to be favourable for breeding in most of the areas concerned,
some of which are inaccessible to control teams. Thus the
desert locust continues to be a major threat to food production
in many countries in 1979. In addition to sums provided immediately from FAO's TCP and Working Capital Fund, it was possible to mobilize voluntary contributions of $1.6 million for
emergency assistance in control operations. At the end of 1978
the European Economic Community (EEC) allocated a further $1.8
million for this purpose.

FOOD AID

Food Aid

During the interim period while production is increased sufficiently in the developing countries food aid plays a vital
role in providing emergency relief combating hunger and malnutrition, and promoting economic and social development. It
called for a minimum food aid target of 10 million tons of
cereals a year. Subsequently the seventh special session of
the General Assembly recommended the establishment of an International Emergency Food Reserve of at least 500,000 tons of

cereals designed to increase the capacity of the United
Nations/FAO World Food Programme (WFP) to meet emergency
situations.

Shipments of food aid in cereals are estimated to have
increased slightly to 9.4 million tons in 1977-78. Allocations
for 1978-79 so far amount to 9.5 million tons, as against the
minimum target of 10 million tons set by the World Food Conference. The international grains negotiations failed to reach
agreement on a new and enlarged Food Aid Convention (FAC) designed to meet this target. The negotiating conference recommended that the former FAC should be prolonged by protocol "in
the light of the negotiations".

There is a consensus among participating Governments in
the international grains negotiations that the main objective
of a new FAC should be to ensure the annual availability of not
less than 10 million tons of cereals as food aid. However, the
failure so far to reach agreement on the trade and other issues
has prevented the conclusion of a new and enlarged FAC. Many
delegates at the third session of the CFS therefore urged that,
if these differences were to persist, a new FAC should be concluded as a separate instrument at the resumed negotiating conference. The CFS stressed the need for donor countries to make
all efforts to raise food aid to the levels necessary to
achieve the objective of not less than 10 million tons of
cereals under a new FAC, and to channel a more significant proportion of food aid through the WFP. Many delegates also urged
the negotiating conference to consider favourably the proposal
to meet large-scale emergency needs by increasing food aid in
years of substantial shortfalls in food production.

It is also necessary to review the adequacy of the food
aid target in the light of actual requirements. Based on FAO's
latest commodity projections and taking account of the limits
to absorptive capacity, the time needed to launch projects, and
some improvement in the commercial import capacity of recipient
countries, an interim report presented to the fifth session of
the WFP Committee on Food Aid Policies and Programmes (CFA) in
April 1978 suggested that 15 to 16 million tons a year would be
a reasonable estimate of food aid requirements for cereals by
1985, 300,000 tons for vegetable oils, and 250,000 tons for
dairy products. There was a general consensus in the CFA that
these estimates provided useful indications of likely requirements, but it stressed that it would be useful to review them
periodically in the light of actual developments.

The Mexico Declaration of the fourth session of the WFC
recommended that the International Emergency Food Reserve
(IEFR) of 500,000 tons of cereals should be established as a
continuing reserve with yearly replenishment to be placed at
the disposal of the United Nations/FAO World Food Programme
(WFP), and that reserves not called upon in one year would be
carried over into the next. Contributions to the IEFR more

than doubled in 1978, but at 348,000 tons they still fell far
short of the target. By the end of the year, 293,000 tons had
been utilized, and only a few new commitments have so far been
made for 1979.

The activities of WFP have been limited by inadequate resources. If it had sufficient resources, it could meet commitments for new projects at the rate of $500 million a year on
the basis of requests that are already in the pipeline. Insufficient resources for the Programme are in striking contrast to
the mounting surpluses of livestock products in Europe and the
ample cereal stocks in North America. The WFP emergency allocation of $45 million was quickly exhausted and had to be
raised by $10 million at the sixth session of the Committee on
Food Aid Policies and Programmes (CFA) in November 1978.
Pledges to the WFP for 1979-80 so far amount to only $695 mil-
lion in comparison with the target of $950 million. Other
problems include the composition of the WFP's "food basket"
(particularly a shortage of dairy products, pulses and rice),
and a likely future shortage of cash contributions in relation
to commodity contributions.

As regards the implementation of the other aspects of improved food aid policies called for by the World Food Conference,
the CFA should be urged to complete its work as soon as possible
on guidelines and criteria for food aid. In spite of some improvements in food aid policies, there are several aspects,
such as forward planning, the expansion of multilateral channelling (including a greater role for exports from developing
countries), the terms of food aid, and its better integration
with other forms of assistance, where more progress is still
required.

AGRICULTURAL TRADE

Trade, Commodity and Adjustment Problems

Although developing countries are much more dependent on agriculture for their export earnings than are developed countries,
their share of world agriculture trade fell from 46 percent in
the mid-1950s to 38 percent in the early 1960s and only 30 percent in the mid-1970s. Since the early 1960s the value of
their agricultural exports had doubled to $40,000 million,
while that of their agricultural imports, chiefly food, has
trebled to $27,000 million. The prices of agricultural com-
modities exported by developing countries have risen less
rapidly and have been much more volatile than the prices of
those exported by the developed countries. Their over-all export earnings (including those from non-agricultural products)
also affect the agricultural sector, because of the need to pay

for imports of food and of the capital goods and inputs to increase domestic agricultural production.

There was a slight recovery in 1977, for the second year
in succession, in the share of the developing countries in
world exports of agricultural products. This appears, however,
to represent only a temporary reversal of the longer-term downward trend. The recovery in the agricultural terms of trade of
these cereal imports reached the record level of 66 million
tons in 1977-78 and the FAO Commodity Projections indicate that,
if past trends continued, they would exceed 90 million tons by
1985.

The World Bank has estimated that the complete elimination
of tariff and non-tariff barriers in the developed countries
could raise the export earnings of the developing countries
from 37 primary and semi-processed agricultural products by
nearly $6,000 million in 1985 at 1975 prices, which is almost
double the current level of commitments of development assistance for agriculture. However, only a limited degree of
liberalization of imports from developing countries has so far
been achieved. The implementation of the Generalized System of
Preferences (GSP), agreed at the second session of UNCTAD in
1968, has been limited in its commodity coverage, although it
has gradually been extended to additional commodities and countries. Most of the growth which can be attributed to it has
been in exports from a small number of beneficiaries. In the
seventh round of the GATT Multilateral Trade Negotiations
(MTN), begun in 1975, the only tangible (though limited) results so far have been in tropical products.

Levels of protection in existing and potential import
markets therefore remain high. They are compounded by the widespread use in the developed countries of support measures which
favour domestic production, and by competition from synthetics.
For processed agricultural commodities trade remains even more
severely restricted, except for the products of industries
which have already declined in the developed countries, such as
jute goods, coir products, and rough-tanned or finished leather.
Whereas imported raw materials are generally admitted into the
industrialized countries free of tariff or at very low duties,
products manufactured from the same raw materials bear moderate
to high duties, the rate rising with the degree of processing.
Trade in processed agricultural commodities also continues to
be subject to non-tariff restrictions, particularly quotas and
"voluntary" export restraints, which (as in the case of tex-
tiles) have been widely invoked since the beginning of the economic recession.

Further extension of the GDP and greater concessions in
the MTN are required, in order to mitigate the growth of protectionist measures in developed countries. In addition, however, new approaches are necessary. Concern at the slow
progress that has been achieved with traditional approaches to

these problems has led to their reappraisal and to the development of a number of new policy proposals. The principal objectives and policy guidelines for a new approach to trade
problems are set out in the Declaration and Programme of Action
on the Establishment of a New International Economic Order, and
in the Resolution on Development and International Economic
Co-operation adopted by the seventh special session, and need
not be repeated here. They have mainly led so far to the discussions and negotiations on an Integrated Programme for Commodities, which have been a major focus of UNCTAD since its
fourth session in May 1976.

The Integrated Programme covers 18 commodities of export
interest to developing countries, of which the following 13 are
agricultural products (including processed products) or re-
quisites: bananas, cocoa, coffee, cotton and yarn, hard fibres
and products, jute and products, meat, phosphates, rubber,
sugar, tea, tropical timber, and vegetable oils and oilseeds.
It aims to stabilize the conditions of world trade for these
commodities, to improve and sustain the real incomes of developing countries through higher and more stable export earnings,
and to improve market access and the reliability of supply. So
far, two sessions of the negotiating conference on a common
fund to finance the Integrated Programme have been held, but
they have not yet succeeded in reconciling the different views
on the financing and operation of the fund. The Secretary
General of UNCTAD has recently carried out a series of consultations with Governments with a view to resuming the negotiations but differences on the main issues remain.

Under the Integrated Programme, preparatory meetings on
eight individual agricultural commodities have also been held,
with close technical support from FAO, but only those on rubber
have yet made substantial progress towards the negotiation of
an international agreement. A negotiating conference on a
natural rubber agreement convened in November 1978. The FAO
Intergovernmental Group on Tea agreed in January 1978 on the
framework of a possible international agreement, and the first
preparatory meeting under the UNCTAD Integrated Programme decided to work towards the negotiation of an agreement as soon
as possible.

International agreements already exist for three of the
agricultural commodities listed under the Integrated Programme,
namely cocoa, coffee, and sugar. However, the economics provisions of those for cocoa and coffee are not operative at
present. Negotiations regarding an agreed price range that
would bring into force the economic provisions of the International Coffee Agreement are under way in the International
Coffee Council. A Preparatory Committee of the International
Cocoa Council met in late 1978 to prepare a draft of the Third
Agreement, which is currently under negotiation. Market prices
for coffee are higher than the relevant prices referred to in

the agreement, which are at present being reviewed. The new
International Sugar Agreement which entered into force provi-
sionally on 1 January 1978, represents a major achievement, and
includes the novel feature of a levy on members' exports to and
imports from the free market to provide financial assistance to
exporting members holding special stocks, as well as a number
of special provision in favour of developing countries. However, heavy stocks overhang the market, and prices are still
well below the established range, pointing to the urgent need
for enlarged participation in the agreement. Moreover, the
absence of the EEC from the Agreement and the fact that it has
not yet been ratified by the United States and some other countries means that no practical results have taken place yet.
The current state of the negotiations for a new international
grains arrangement has been discussed in the earlier sections
of this document concerning world food security and food aid.

Through a number of Intergovernmental Commodity Groups FAO
is engaged in the improvement of information required for
policy decisions at national and international level, the attainment of consensus among exporters and importers, and the
achievement of more orderly marketing, including appropriate
stabilization and trade measures. The work of the FAO Intergovernmental Group on Bananas on the elements of an international agreement is expected to result during the second half
of 1978 in a working draft which could form the basis for
negotiations in UNCTAD. Informal price stabilization arrangements for jute, sisal and henequen are operated by FAO Intergovernmental Groups, and provision has also been made for consultations should abaca prices move outside an indicative range.
Other FAO Intergovernmental Groups, such as those on meat and
rice, provide mainly for consultations on policy changes.

There is a growing consensus, both in UNCTAD and in FAO,
on the need for research and development measures to make the
agricultural products of developing countries more competitive
in international markets. Several schemes to achieve this end,
notably those proposed for jute, sisal coir and cotton, have
been held up by problems regarding sources of finance, the
degree of participation by interested countries and related
issues, as well as by delays in the establishment of the common
fund, especially its "second window".

The limited progress towards the trade objectives of a New
International Economic Order is due partly to the sluggish
growth of the world economy in recent years, which has inevi-
tably slowed the pace of adaptation to changing conditions.
However, it also reflects the reluctance of the developed countries to make domestic adjustments to shifts in international
comparative advantage, especially for processed products. A
neglected aspect of International Agricultural Adjustment is
that these countries, in spite of their employment problems,
might pay more attention to the possible beneficial effects of

trade liberalization on their other main problem of inflation.
Combined with increased development assistance, trade laterali-
zation could lead to accelerated growth in the developing countries, which would in turn expand the demand for the exports of
the developed countries and ease their adjustment problems.
The developed countries should be urged to draw up programmes
of phased adjustment in both agriculture and processing industries, in order to allow progressively freer access to their
markets for the exports of developing countries. Meanwhile,
they should take steps to extend the GSP to a wider range of
agricultural commodities, including processed products, and to
provide increased technical assistance to enable developing
countries to take full advantage of any concessions.

AGRICULTURE AND INDUSTRY

Agro-Industries

The Lima Declaration and Plan of Action on Industrial Development and Co-operation, adopted by the Second General Conference
of UNIDO in 1975, called for the share of the developing countries in world industrial production to reach at least 25 percent by the year 2000. It emphasized the need to promote an
integrated industrialization process, "with the objective of
achieving the highest degree of interaction between industry
and other sectors of the economy, in particular agriculture by
setting up agro-industrial research centres, developing new
agricultural areas, and introducing new crops for industrial
purposes." The achievement of the Lima target will involve a
substantial expansion of agro-industries, both those processing
agricultural products and those producing inputs for agricultural production. The Declaration requested a continuing system of consultations on specific industries to identify possible areas of co-operation between developed and developing
countries, in order to raise the latters' share of production.
In the agro-industrial field, such consultations have so far
been held on fertilizers, leather and leather products, and
vegetable oils and fats, and preparations are under way for a
consultation on agricultural machinery in 1979.
    Concerning fertilizer industries, the FAO/UNIDO/World Bank
Working Group on Fertilizers periodically reviews the development of production capacities, with particular attention to
plant location and the possibilities for regional and cooperative ventures. The share of the developing countries in
the world production of nitrogen and phosphate fertilizers is
expected to rise from 11 percent in 1975-76 to 20 percent in
1981-82 and more than 25 percent by the year 2000, but the
achievement of self-sufficiency in these fertilizers would require an even greater expansion.

RURAL DEVELOPMENT

Human Resources and Rural Institutions

Since small farmers are responsible for so much of the agricultural production of the developing countries, the investment
flows, land and water resources, inputs and technology discussed above must reach them if production is to be increased
and poverty reduced. The majority of the rural poor (small
farmers and landless labourers) can improve their employment,
incomes and nutrition only if they have adequate access to land
and other productive resources. This implies structural
changes in the ownership of assets in many countries, and the
development of institutions for the mobilization of their productive potential. FAO has a number of programmes in this
field arising from the World Land Reform Conference of 1966,
and (with the United Nations and ILO) monitors progress in land
reform in a biennial report ECOSOC.
     Suitable institutions have to be built up for the ef-
fective delivery to the majority of producers of the necessary
technology and physical inputs, and of the means to apply them
through price incentives and credit. Innovative approaches are
particularly needed in the extension, credit and marketing services of the developing countries if they are effectively to
reach the mass of small farmers. The establishment of co-
operatives and farmers' associations may often provide a solution, as well as the opportunity for greater people's participation in the development decisions that affect them. FAO is
associated with the United Nations, ILO and non-governmental
organizations in the Committee for the Promotion of Aid to Co-
operatives (COPAC), which co-ordinates assistance for cooperative development in the developing countries. In the
field of agricultural credit, an important initiative in co-
operation among developing countries is the recent establishment
of three regional agricultural credit associations, in response
to a recommendation of the World Conference on Credit for Farmers in Developing Countries, held in 1975.
     Education and training are essential factors in the devel-
opment of human resources. There is a massive need for training
at the grass roots level, aimed at the small farmers and rural
women and youth, through a network of activities covering both
formal and informal types of training. Some of the main requirements were identified by the First World Conference on
Agricultural Education and Training, held in 1970. FAO is re-
orienting its training programmes in order to make them more
effective in meeting the needs of the majority of the rural
people, but this is an area where a very large increase in international assistance would be particularly fruitful.

The past neglect of the need for the integration of women
in development has at last been overcome at the level of the
international consensus on development requirements and strategies. This is apparent not only in the World Conference of
International Women's Year, held in 1975, but also in other
recent international conferences on development. National action has, however, been slow. In most developing countries it
is still necessary to integrate women more effectively in
training and other development programmes, especially those
concerning food and agriculture, in view of the important role
of women in food production, processing and utilization.   In
common with other international agencies, FAO has established a
system for the review and monitoring of its agricultural and
rural development programmes and projects in order to ensure
that the participation of women is specifically included
wherever feasible.

Land and Water Resources

Most estimates agree that the world's arable land area could be
somewhat more than doubled. However, the unused land that remains is increasingly costly to open up and enormous investments will be required for its exploitation. FAO is at present
engaged in a study of agro-ecological zones, to assess the amount
of land suited to rainfed crop production and the likely yields
of major crops. Because soil resources are very unevenly distributed in relation to population as regards both quantity and
quality, agricultural production has had to be expanded into
marginal areas, resulting in the degradation and even the loss
of soil resources. Such environmental problems will have to be
taken much more seriously into consideration in the future expansion of production. Among a large number of FAO projects
carried out in collaboration with UNEP is the first comprehensive appraisal of actual and potential soil degradation. A
World Map of Desertification was prepared by FAO, UNESCO and
WMO for the United Nations Conference on Desertification, held
in 1977. The Plan of Action adopted by this conference calls
for increased assistance to countries suffering from desertification.
      About half of the total investment requirements for agri-
culture referred to above would be for water development. Estimates prepared by FAO for the United Nations Water Conference,
held in 1977, indicate the need for a total investment of the
order of $97,000 million at 1975 prices in 1975-90 in order to
extend the irrigated area of the developing market economies by
22 million hectares (24 percent), to make improvements on existing irrigation systems, and to improve drainage. Following a
request of the United Nations Water Conference, the Secretary-
General of the United Nations has initiated a study of mechan-

isms to increase the flow of financial resources for water development and management. For land and water development together, the earlier FAO estimates indicated the need for external assistance (adjusted to 1975 prices) of $3,200 to 4,000
million a year in 1975-80, but commitments in 1974 and 1975
averaged only $886 million a year, mostly from multilateral
agencies.

Livestock Resources

The livestock sector still tends to be neglected in many developing countries. Very little has been done to improve grazing
lands, or to make efficient use of by-products and waste as
livestock feed. Because of the long-term nature of the expansion of ruminant production, attention should be given to
poultry meat, eggs, and (where acceptable) pigmeat, which can
be increased much more rapidly. In the longer run, some shift
may be expected from cattle fed on high-priced cereals in developed countries to roughage-fed cattle in Africa and Latin
America, provided disease problems and trade barriers can be
overcome.
    The International Scheme for the Coordination of Dairy
Development and the International Meat Development Scheme are
operated by FAO with the support of Trust Funds. There has
been difficulty in attracting sufficient financial support for
projects under these schemes in developing countries, and it is
recognized that these countries themselves will have to play a
more active role in seeking finance in the future. FAO's Ar-
tificial Insemination and Breeding Development Programme is
closely linked with these schemes.
    A second consultation on the FAO Programme for the Control
of African Animal Trypanosomiasis took place in December 1978.
It endorsed the plans and management structure for the programme
proposed by FAO.
    African swine fever was confirmed in March 1978 in Malta
and in Sardinia (Italy), and in June 1978 in Brazil. Initial
attempts to contain it were unsuccessful, and by August it had
spread to 11 states of Brazil and also threatened the pig populations in the neighbouring countries of Argentina, Bolivia,
Paraguay, Peru, Uruguay and Venezuela. In July 1978 it was
confirmed in the Dominican Republic, where it also spread
rapidly. In order to meet the serious threat to the income and
nutrition of small farmers posed by this disease, FAO organized
a number of emergency consultations and training courses. The
FAO Technical Co-operation Programme (TCP) proved particularly
useful and speedily provided $1.1 million for control and pre-
vention to establish an African Swine Fever Control Fund of
about $2 million. On a wider front, it is planned to discuss
measures to improve the international system for animal disease

control, to cope with emergency situations created by known or
unknown diseases.

Considerable efforts are still required for the control of
many other major diseases. The continuous search for improved
methods of disease surveillance, and investigations of the economics of disease control are other important problems in the
field of animal health.

NUTRITION AND THE ERADICATION OF MALNUTRITION

Nutrition

FAO's newly published Fourth World Food Survey estimates that
dietary energy supplies per head (the principal global indicator of nutritional levels) in the developing countries as a
whole increased by 7 percent between 1961-63 and 1972-74. In
the latter period, however, they were still 4 percent below
average nutritional requirements. Moreover, in the MSA countries they actually decreased, so that in 1972-74 they were as
much as 10 percent below requirements, whereas in the other
developing countries they approximately met requirements. Allowing for the highly unequal distribution of the available
food supplies within countries, the survey estimates that the
number of undernourished people in the developing market economies rose by almost 15 percent between 1969-71 and 1972-74,
or considerably more than the growth of population. The figure
of 455 million in 1972-74 amounts to a quarter of the total
population of these countries. Two thirds of the undernourished people lived in the MSA countries and more than half
in the densely populated Far East. Virtually all of the
increase between 1969-71 and 1972-74 was in the MSA countries
in Africa and the Far East.

The improvement of nutrition requires not only increased
production and the reduction of poverty, but also specific nutritional programmes. These include food and nutrition intervention programmes and special feeding programmes for vulnerable groups, nutrition surveillance, and intersectoral food and
nutrition planning, as well as appropriate price and distribution policies. The newly established ACC Sub-Committee on Nutrition is engaged in the stimulation and harmonization of the
necessary programmes within the United Nations system, but
greatly increased international assistance is still needed in
all these fields. It is also necessary for nutritional considerations which are so important, in the improvement of over-
all health conditions, to be incorporated in wider development
programmes and projects, and the nineteenth session of the FAO
Conference in 1977 called for "a review of FAO's programmes to
assess their impact on the nutritional status of the urban and
rural poor."

Partial data indicate that per caput dietary energy supplies in the developing market economies fell back in 1975 to
below the 1973 level, but recovered in 1976 to the peak reached
in 1971. Since per caput food production in these countries
failed to rise in 1977 for the second year in succession, there
is unlikely to have been much subsequent improvement. Per
caput food production in Africa in 1977 was 10 percent less
than in 1969-71.

The ACC Sub-Committee on Nutrition, which held its fifth
session in February 1979, is proving an important stimulus to
increased and better co-ordinated effort by the United Nations
system in this field. FAO has provided nutrition planning support to a number of countries and work has begun on the evaluation of the nutritional impact of agricultural and rural development projects, and on the introduction of nutritional criteria in the preparation of such projects. The seventy-fourth
session of FAO Council in December 1978 expressed the hope that
more resources could be made available for nutrition under
FAO's Regular Programme, as well as those being sought from
extrabudgetary sources. The next session of the Council in
June 1979 will consider arrangements for intergovernmental consultation on technical and policy issues concerning nutrition.

3 The Record of Action: Reports of the Specialized Agencies

THE MEXICO DECLARATION OF THE WORLD FOOD COUNCIL

The preamble of the Mexico Declaration adopted at the sixth meeting of the fourth ministerial session of the World Food Council, records action to that point in time.

We, the Ministers and Plenipotentiaries of the World Food Council attending the fourth session in Mexico City in June 1978, have studied the present world food situation and the progress achieved since 1974 in attaining the goals of the World Food Conference. For this purpose we have reaffirmed the resolutions of that Conference* and given particular consideration to the responsibilities of this Council, which deals with all aspects of world food problems, to implement further the Manila Communique of the World Food Council: A Programme of Action to Eradicate Hunger and Malnutrition.**

The Programme of Action we adopted during our third session was unanimously endorsed by the Economic and Social Council in its resolution 2114 (LXIII) of 4 August 1977 and adopted in full by the General Assembly in its resolution 32/52 of 8 December 1977, in which the Assembly called on all Governments, specialized agencies, organs and other bodies within and outside the United Nations system dealing with food, agriculture and human nutrition to implement the Programme of Action fully and as a matter of urgency.

---

* See Report of the World Food Conference, Rome, 5-16 November 1974 (United Nations publication, Sales No. 75.II.A.3), part one, chap.II.
** Official Records of the General Assembly, Thirty-second Session, Supplement No. 19 (A/32/19), para. 1.

The positive attitude demonstrated by the Economic and Social Council and the General Assembly has contributed to the important activities of the World Food Council and we believe that the initial efforts of Governments and agencies demonstrate progress in implementing the Programme of Action and the resolutions adopted by the World Food Conference.

The Council, in pursuance of its mandate from the World Food Conference and the General Assembly, has:

(a) Promoted the establishment of the International Fund for Agricultural Development, which approved its first food projects for developing countries in April 1978;

(b) Stimulated contributions to the international emergency reserve of 500,000 tons of cereals to rise from 82,000 tons to more than 425,000 tons;

(c) Promoted machinery to accelerate action in the field of nutrition within the United Nations system;

(d) Encouraged the initiation of food and nutrition strategies for specific developing countries;

(e) Stimulated actions to eradicate hunger and malnutrition through the adoption of the Manila Communique.

These are positive achievements in the direction of fulfilling the goals set by the World Food Council. However, closer examination of the present world food situation shows that the rate of progress in solving fundamental food problems is far too slow. Employment and income opportunities of the rural poor lag seriously behind population growth and the rate of growth in agricultural production.

Favourable weather and vigorous action by Governments and agencies spurred by the world food crisis made it possible for world food production to increase rapidly in 1975-1976. However, less favourable weather and reduced concern had serious consequences in 1977 - production increased by barely 2 percent, and by only 1 percent in the developing countries. In Africa and Latin America there was no increase at all, and in the Near East production declined.

Food prices, especially of cereals for human consumption, have risen significantly since our third session. This is creating difficulties for consumers, especially in food priority countries. In some cases, however, current prices remain lower than production costs, so price increases represent an incentive for producers.

Progress has been slow in negotiating a new international wheat agreement, despite generally abundant supply and stock conditions.

Thus, Governments and international organizations did respond to the 1972-1974 food crisis, although limitedly and unevenly. This inadequate response gives rise to the present unstable situation and our grave concern for the future. Had the important immediate objectives of the World Food Conference been achieved, this current uncertain situation could have been

avoided. Had the fundamental changes the Conference called for
been effectively and adequately initiated, we would not fear
for the future.

REPORT BY THE EXECUTIVE DIRECTOR OF WFC (A/AC.191/35)

The WFC background document concisely reports on recent decisions of the WFC.
In compliance with the request of the Committee, the Executive
Director submits the following report as a summary of the recent
decisions of the World Food Council, and the actions taken in
pursuance of those decisions. The conclusions of the Council's
1978 Meeting, particularly its Mexico Declaration, are before
you.* They constitute the latest report of world food problems
and actions by the Ministerial body specifically chartered for
that purpose by the United Nations. The Council was created by
the General Assembly to follow up the proposed strategy of the
1974 World Food Conference, based on three main objectives of:
    Increasing food production in countries where it is most
    needed;
    Broadening the effective distribution of food through mea-
    sures for improving trade, consumption and nutrition; and
    Providing a better system of world food security.
As a unique overview body, the World Food Council was given the
heavy responsibility of mobilizing the political support needed
to achieve these objectives, and to exercise a continuing role
in reviewing the adequacy and coherence of policies and programmes related to food.
    At its third session in Manila in 1977, the World Food
Council sharpened the focus on issues related to overcoming
widespread malnutrition and hunger in a call to action known as
the Manila Communique which was strongly endorsed by the Economic and Social Council and the General Assembly, and contributed to a growing awareness of the problems of hunger and malnutrition.
    Last year's meeting in Mexico was concerned with reviewing
progress, further building understanding and political support,
and devising concrete steps to translate policy into action.
The General Assembly, in resolution 33/90 of 15 December 1978,
adopted the Mexico Declaration and called for its full and complete implementation.
    In reviewing progress on world food matters on the basis
of the report of the World Food Council, the General Assembly,
in the same resolution, expressed its deep concern at the lack

---

*Official Records of the General Assembly, Thirty-third Session,
Supplement No. 19 (A/33/19).

of progress in solving the fundamental food problems facing the
developing countries, in particular the food priority countries
and other developing countries who have large food deficits,
and whose food production situation is still deteriorating.

The General Assembly had good reason to express concern.
From one point of view the progress of the past year and a half
is significant. Good harvests have contributed to a currently
improved world food situation. The International Fund for Agricultural Development (IFAD), proposed by the World Food Conference in 1974, has begun operations. Contributions have approached the 500,000 ton target of the Emergency Grain Reserve
called for by the seventh special session of the General Assembly. Steps are being taken in the United Nations to improve
nutritional levels, and there is growing awareness throughout
the world of the need for stepped-up action to eliminate hunger
and malnutrition.

Statement by Mr. Maurice J. Williams of WFC

Mr. Williams updates the work of the WFC and puts it in the
perspective of world agro-economic conditions.
That resolve was articulated at the World Food Conference in
1974. The Conference, meeting under the pall of dire fears
that a crowded world would be unable to feed its growing population, adopted objectives for cooperative global action. Taken
together, they constitute a comprehensive world food policy.
Specifically, the Conference adopted resolutions to:

- safeguard populations affected by drought and dis-
  aster;

- increase food production in countries where it is
  most needed;

- broaden the effective distribution of food by improving trade, consumption and nutrition; and

- build a better system of world food security to prevent another crisis like that of 1972-1974.

To meet the food needs of poorer people, the Conference
called on developing countries to give higher priority to food
production, with increases of at least 4 percent annually.
Successful development was linked, in effect, to the levelling
off of high population growth; the Conference endorsed programmes "to achieve a desirable balance between population and
food supply." It emphasized the role of women as partners in
food production and improved nutrition and in decisions on the
size of families.

None at the World Food Conference disputed the assertion
that eliminating the appalling misery of hunger was the responsibility of the world as a whole. Unanimously, the Conference called on developed countries to increase their assistance to low income countries, not only by effective financial

and technical aid but by a re-direction of economic and trade policies. In the past, such policies had tended to depress development in economically weaker countries; restrictions against exports and policies for disposing of food surpluses had the effect of depressing production in developing countries. In effect, the developed countries agreed that their economic and technical strength should underpin the food security of poorer countries to help them increase food production and the pace of development.

Thus, the World Food Conference dealt with the fundamentals of a multi-dimensional world food strategy and produced a consensus on most of its major elements. This strategy is aimed at closing the double food gap of developing countries in their growing imports of food, on the one hand, and of their increasing numbers of malnourished people, on the other hand. Most of the specifics of how these policy objectives were to be achieved were left to future negotiations and decisions. The Ministerial-level World Food Council was envisaged as a new institutional means for mobilizing support, for monitoring policies and programmes, and generally for ensuring the coherence of overall efforts in the food field.

Established in 1975, the World Food Council is made up of 36 Member States elected on a three-year rotating basis and representing the interests of countries from all continents - rich and poor, food exporting and food deficit, free market and centrally planned economies - in brief, a food security council with representative membership and wide responsibility for all aspects of the world food problem. Its role is that of advocate, catalyst and coordinator - stimulating governments and international agencies to adopt essential policies and programmes to alleviate hunger and malnutrition.

Progress Since the World Food Conference

Since the World Food Conference, there has been progress in many areas. But these advances, while important, have not been adequate to reverse the double food gap. The world must mobilize to feed an additional 72 million people every year. This is an unremitting pace, both in terms of increasing numbers of people, and of the imperative for improved consumption. In this regard, it can be seen as an advance - although far from adequate - that for MSA countries the average annual growth rate in food production per capita increased from minus 1.7 percent during 1970-1974 to plus 1.0 percent in 1974-1978 and the annual rate of per capita food production in all developing countries changed from minus 0.2 percent in 1970-1974 to plus 0.7 percent in 1974-1978.

But 1974 was a poor year for food production and hence misleading as a base for measuring progress. It is essential to keep in view that most MSA countries did less well in food

production in the 1970s, with annual increases of 2.2 percent
compared with 2.6 percent in the 1960s - whereas in other developing countries food production rose slightly from 3.1 percent to 3.2 percent annually in the same period.

Among the areas of welcome progress is the evidence that
an increasing number of countries recognize that food, and food
sector management, require special policy attention within the
context of overall developing planning. No longer can the food
needs of people be regarded as essentially "self-solving" -
rather they are emerging as major concerns of governmental policy. These concerns have resulted in increased investment in
food production in developing countries, but the efforts to
date are still far less than adequate to the needs.

We can also take some encouragement from the growing effectiveness of international institutional arrangements. New
programmes such as FAO's Global Information and Early Warning
System and the International Fertilizer Supply Scheme have been
launched. Agricultural research, especially as it relates to
developing country institutions and the needs of the poor, has
drawn new interest and increased assistance. FAO, the World
Bank, the Regional Banks in Asia, Africa and Latin America, the
new International Fund for Agricultural Development recommended
by the World Food Conference, and the United Nations system as
a whole - all are increasingly responsive to the development
needs of hungry, poor and malnourished people.

The flow of development aid to agriculture has doubled in
real terms from $2 billion in 1973 to about $4 billion in 1977.
Most of this increase has been through the programmes of the
international organizations, particularly the World Bank. Far
too little has been contributed by national bilateral aid programmes which still represent 70 percent of total development
assistance, although some of the smaller developed countries
have demonstrated that very rapid increases in assistance to
food production can be achieved.

Efforts to increase production, even when they are effective, will not help the hungry unless they are accompanied
by improvements in food distribution. Basically, the problem
of meeting the nutrition needs of large populations is one of
poverty or lack of effective demand. By effective demand is
meant the ability of consumers to pay for food. To market food
at prices which cover adequately the costs of sustaining higher
levels of production is, at the same time, the necessary incentive for farmers. A long-term solution consequently must be
sought in development policies which increase employment for the
rural landless and the urban poor, and which increase production by small subsistence farmers.

There is increasing recognition of a need for measures
which will effectively bridge the gap between a long term development solution, which cannot effectively reach the great
majority of those suffering from hunger and malnutrition for
many years, and the immediate but relatively limited impact of

nutrition intervention programmes. Such programmes have high
administrative and personnel constraints and require for
their success adequate social infrastructure and health services. However, the development of primary health care, which
governments strongly supported in Alma-Ata in 1978, opens up
new opportunities for simpler, less expensive delivery of a
package of basic health and nutrition services. The idea of
more consumer or demand oriented food planning is relatively
new and as yet not fully developed. This will be one of the
major topics for consideration by the World Food Council at its
Fifth Session in Ottawa, Canada, next September.

The problems encountered demonstrate that as the international community has moved beyond broad generalizations and
urgent exhortation about world hunger, it has encountered the
complex and resistant situations in which hungry people exist.
Tested at that more concrete level of priorities and policies,
political action has been faltering. Nor has the most effective
combination of mutually reinforcing actions among countries and
international agencies been achieved.

It is against the background of the deteriorating food
situation for poor countries and peoples that the World Food
Council, at its 1978 meeting in Mexico, proposed a programme of
urgent consultations among various groups - developing countries, developed countries, aid donors and the major international development agencies - to identify the major obstacles
to increased food production and improved nutrition and to work
out specific agreements to overcome them. The first round of
consultations have been initiated. Representatives of various
groups are invited to participate with the World Food Council
in developing action proposals which will have the commitment
of all those involved and which should lead to more effective
efforts to give priority to food production and nutrition and
reverse the deteriorating trend of increasing hunger and malnutrition in low income regions.

What we seek to achieve from these consultations is to
break out of the present impasse and misunderstandings which
impede food production and nutrition improvement in the developing countries. Each group presently appears to have dif-
fering explanations for the relative lack of progress, and
there is a tendency to place responsibility on others. For
example, developing countries draw attention to inadequate increases in development assistance, overly rigid aid procedures
and reluctance by developed countries to consider policy adjustments in such areas as trade. Developed countries, for
their part, claim that governments of developing countries have
given inadequate priority to food and agriculture and are slow
to consider the necessary internal policy adjustments. International agencies have been inclined to assert that they are
already doing everything possible within the limits of the resources available and that, in any case, they are responding to

the demands and priorities of member countries. These implied
misunderstandings, in which everyone feels they are doing reasonably well and no one assumes responsibility for the overall
inadequate results, are a major problem impeding adoption of
more adequate efforts to alleviate the world food problem.

Our objective must be to achieve a framework of understanding which will promote mutually reinforcing national and
international action in a global commitment to overcome hunger
and malnutrition.

The problems which are being encountered do not invalidate
the Conference's vision and its principal conclusions. Its 20
resolutions concerning food and development issues remain re-
markably pertinent and, taken together, they constitute a valid
world food strategy for the eradication of hunger and malnutrition, the unfinished agenda for the 1980s. The question is
where do we stand on that agenda and where is there most need
to galvanise progress.

STATEMENT BY MR. S. AZIZ OF IFAD

Mr. Aziz reports on the establishment of the International Fund
for Agricultural Development and structural reform since the
World Food Conference in 1974.
A careful analysis of the progress reports on follow-up of the
World Food Conference will show that the overall progress in
attaining the essential objectives has been essentially marginal. The results are particularly disappointing in terms of
bringing about the structural reforms mentioned above. It is
also clear that the international community cannot fulfill its
commitment to abolish malnutrition within the foreseeable
future if this objective remains secondary to their domestic
agriculture policy or other national objectives.

We in IFAD are primarily concerned with the objective of
increasing food production and improving its distribution, and
in mobilizing additional resources for these purposes. I will
therefore briefly refer to the problem and prospects in these
two areas.

If the long-term food and nutrition problem is to be
solved, the developing countries must increase their total food
output by at least 4.0 percent per annum on a sustained basis.
Even this will be a major challenge, particularly for those
countries in which the availability of cultivable land is relatively limited. In 55 developing countries, the average availability of arable land for each rural inhabitant is less than 1
hectare; in 30 of them it is less than half a hectare. The
cost of increasing production through the use of marginal
lands is becoming excessive.

The importance of physical and ecological constraints on food production cannot be undermined, but many constraints are in essence man-made. The issues of food shortages and poor nutrition are generally the outcome of development policies which for long have stressed overall economic growth and the maximization of certain economic aggregates, rather than emphasizing the equitable distribution of the gains from development. The result has been further deviation from an equitable pattern of food consumption as reflected in urban-rural differences as well as imbalances within the agricultural sector itself. Accordingly, many of the current food issues are inherently related to development policies and not so much, as generally believed, to ecological conditions.

The only important area in which notable progress has been made is in the flow of external resources to agriculture. The flow of external assistance has increased from $2.0 billion in 1973 to $6 billion in 1977 (or $4 billion in real terms). Most of the increase has come from the World Bank, which has expanded its lending to the agriculture sector from less than $1.0 billion in 1973 to $3.0 billion in 1978 (in current prices). Bilateral aid programmes which still account for 70 percent of development assistance have contributed very little to this increase.

Perhaps the most significant outcome of the World Food Conference has been the creation of the billion dollar International Fund for Agricultural Development (IFAD). The Fund, which started its operations in December 1977, not only provides a new low cost mechanism for channelling larger resources exclusively to agriculture and food production, but also constitutes an important example of structural change in international institutions for development assistance. With OPEC countries providing 43 percent of total resources and with the total voting power divided equally between developed countries, OPEC countries and developing recipient countries, IFAD is the first financing institution in which developing countries have two-thirds of the voting power in the governing bodies.

This increased availability of external resources for agricultural development in developing countries is certainly encouraging but the level of such assistance is still below the target suggested at the World Food Conference ($5.0 billion in 1973, $8.4 billion in 1976 or $10 billion in 1978 prices). Even more serious, the acceleration in the flow of external assistance is not yet reflected in a corresponding improvement in the growth of food production.

Statement by Mr. Montague Yudelman of the World Bank

Mr. Yudelman reports on the Bank's activities in funding agriculture and food production over the past five years.
The World Bank has responded to the food crisis of the early
1970s in a very positive way. The World Bank and its affiliate
the International Development Agency have given agriculture and
food production high priority over the past five years. The
Bank is now by far and away the largest single source of external funding for this purpose; according to FAO we provide
over 40% of all official commitments to agriculture. Over the
last five years Bank lending for agricultural development has
grown from $1.4 billion per year to $3.3 billion in 1978, totalling $10 billion over this five year period. As a percen-
tage of total lending it has increased from 22% of the total in
1973 to 39% in the year just ended. Since each dollar invested
by the Bank is supplemented by local investment the total value
of Bank projects in the last five years exceeds $24 billion, a
figure which represents anywhere from 15-25% of total public
investment in agriculture in the developing world. Over 75% of
this investment is oriented towards increasing food production
and it is our expectation that at full development, Bank projects may well contribute as much as a third of the annual increase in food production in developing countries.
    Bank lending for agriculture and rural development has
been predicated upon the realization that this sector has been
relatively neglected, and of the importance of growth in this
sector for balanced development. In many regions the scale of
new investment has barely matched the rate of physical depreci-
ation for irrigation works, soil erosion and related capital
investments. Domestic policies, often oriented towards building up indigenous manufacturing, resulted in large transfers of
capital out of agriculture to be used for investment in other
sectors. Under-capitalizing agriculture in rural areas has
contributed to the emergence of the food and productivity gaps
noted above. A recent study sponsored by the Trilateral Commission dramatically illustrated the capital requirements of
increasing agricultural output. It was estimated that $3 bil-
lion a year - double present expenditures - would be required
to improve and expand irrigation systems so as to double rice
production in Asia by 1995. The World Bank's experience indicates that this figure may well be too conservative an estimate and be excessively optimistic regarding capabilities to
implement such a program.

4 The Documented Record: Implementation of International Decisions by FAO

FAO reported to the COW in technical document A/AC.191.34 on the progress it had made in implementing decisions on international action in food and agriculture, contained in resolutions of the General Assembly (GA), World Food Conference (WFC), World Food Council (WFCC), FAO Conference (FAOC) and FAO Council (FAOCL). The report is reproduced in its entirety, but in reorganized form: the contents are grouped around five of the seven sections headings in the Agreed Conclusions of the Committee of the Whole. Note that the Agricultural Trade and Agriculture and Industry sections are absent.

Decisions	Implementation

FOOD AND AGRICULTURAL PRODUCTION IN DEVELOPING COUNTRIES
AND THE FLOW OF EXTERNAL RESOURCES

Increasing Food and Agricultural Production

Decisions	Implementation
FAO in consultation with UNDP and other organizations to formulate programmes and projects for additional food production and indicate ways and means for carrying them out. (WFC I, para. 9; GA 3362 (S-VII), V. para. 1)	Country and regional level studies have identified development alternatives and helped Governments to formulate development project proposals for financing by potential donors or lenders. FAO's Present and Potential Land Use Project commenced in September 1976 is to provide first approximation of areas

DECISIONS	IMPLEMENTATION

variously suited to rain-fed production of food crops. Programmes and projects have also been formulated for more intensive land use, more efficient utilization of existing irrigation facilities and improvements thereof. Special efforts are being made in the area of fertilizers, and improved seeds which are the core of more productive modern agricultural technology. UNDP and FAO in cooperation have undertaken a number of programmes for the prevention of the deterioration of basic natural resources for agricultural forestry and fishery production, viz. land and water. Attention is also given to accelerating the production of fish and other aquatic products through aquaculture, and a programme is being formulated to assist developing coastal states in exploiting living marine resources in the extended areas of national jurisdiction.

CGFPI to quickly identify developing countries with potentials for more rapid and efficient increase of food production, potential for such expansion in other developing countries, especially those with food deficits.
(GA 3362 (S-VII), V. para. 4)

While CGFPI has been wound up, FAO, UNDP and the World Bank continue to assist countries, in formulating and implementing specific programmes and projects for increasing food production. Four food priority developing countries. Sudan, Senegal, Bangladesh and Honduras, had submitted their food plans in 1977, the first three with FAO's substantial support. Further assistance

DECISIONS	IMPLEMENTATION

| | has been provided to the Sudan in the identification and formulation of specific investment projects and to Bangladesh in the formulation of a UNDP financed project to assist the Government in the strengthening of its own capabilities in the fields of agricultural planning and project analysis. FAO, in cooperation with ECA and Member States, has prepared the Regional Food Plan for Africa. The Tenth FAO Regional Conference for Africa, 18-29 September 1978, endorsed in general the findings and recommendations of the Regional Food Plan. An Inter Departmental Task Force in FAO is drawing up an advisory programme for national action on rice production in South and South East Asia. |
| FAO, World Bank, UNDP and CGFPI and regional banks to cooperate with 'food priority countries' in early determination of measures and programmes to increase food production to at least 4 percent per annum within a feasible time period. (WFCL – Second session recommendations) | For programmes and projects in food priority countries the observations under WFC I, para. 9, are also relevant. As regards financial assistance, World Bank loans and credits to 'food priority' countries for agricultural projects on the 'narrow' OECD definition i.e. mainly food production, rose from $447 million in 1974 to $546 million in 1975, $771 million in 1976, $1067 million in 1977 and an estimated $1789 in 1978. Financial assistance by regional development banks for |

DECISIONS	IMPLEMENTATION

food production in these
countries has also increased
substantially. The Asian and
African Development Banks
together committed $72 million
in 1974, $139 million in 1975,
$95 million in 1976 and an-
other $192 million in 1977.
The Inter-American Bank committed $20 million in 1976 and
$136 million in 1977. In the
5-year period 1974-78, the FAO
Investment Centre assisted
'food priority' countries to
prepare projects on the OECD
narrow definition of agriculture with total investment
costs of approximately $3337
million.

Increased Financial Resources for Food Production in Developing Countries

World Bank, regional banks,
UNDP, FAO, UNIDO and other
international agencies to
substantially increase their
assistance for agriculture and
fisheries, giving priority to
programmes for poorest groups
of population.
(WFC I, para. 10; GA 3362
(S-VII), para. 2)

World Bank lending in the OECD
'narrow' definition for agriculture in developing countries (including IDA Credits)
increased from $1080 million
in 1974 to $1306 million in
1975, $1294 million in 1976
and $1945 million in 1977.
There was a further large
increase in 1978 to an estimated $3052 million. A con-
siderable part of all this
lending was for projects
benefiting the rural poor.
Lending for food production by
regional banks also showed
increases from $325 million in

DECISIONS	IMPLEMENTATION

1974 to $409 million in 1975,
$440 million in 1976 and $653
million in 1977. Arab funds
too, are providing assistance
for food production.
FAO is continuing to assist
Governments to prepare investment projects and, in 1978,
was responsible for preparing
food production projects with
total investment costs of an
estimated $3407 million,
compared to $1344 million in
1974, $717 million in 1975,
£1096 million in 1976 and
$2257 million in 1977. The
FAO Technical Cooperation
Programme committed $16
million to assistance for
food production in 1977 and
$14 million in 1978.

Although there are indications
that UNDP has been devoting
an increasing share of resources
to projects in agriculture
and the rural sector, FAO's
percentage share of the UNDP
programme dropped in 1977 to
26.6 percent from its 1976
figure of 29.2 percent, the
actual expenditure dropping
from its 1975 level of $119.6
million to $115.2 million in
1976 and $88.4 million in
1977. Estimated expenditure
in 1978 was $104 million. At
the same time, expenditure
under the Trust Fund pro-
grammes has increased from
$32.1 million in 1975 to
$42.8 million in 1977.

DECISIONS	IMPLEMENTATION

The international community effectively and substantially to increase its official development assistance (ODA) level to food and agriculture production in order to achieve, as soon as possible, at least a 4 percent sustained rate of growth of food production in developing countries.
(WFCL - Manila Communique, para. 3; WFC, para. 3)

Commitments of official development assistance (ODA) from all sources (except countries with centrally planned economies) for activities covered under the OECD 'broad' definition of agriculture rose from $2893 million in 1974 to $3429 million in 1975, $3310 million in 1976 and to an estimated $3742 million in 1977. At 1975 prices, ODA commitments amounted to $3251 million in 1974, $3429 million in 1975, $3277 million in 1976 and to an estimated $3402 million in 1977.

The estimate of $US 8.3 billion in external resources on an annual basis (of which about $6.5 billion is estimated to be on concessional terms) is a necessary element for achieving this 4 percent rate of growth.
(WFCL - Manila Communique, para.3)

FAO estimates of $8.3 billion (in 1975 prices) minimum external resources needed by developing countries to sustain a 3.6 percent annual increase in food and agricultural production, presented to the World Food Conference are more closely related to the 'narrow' OECD definition of agriculture. On this basis, official commitments of assistance were $3110 million in 1974, $3313 million in 1975, $3423 million in 1976 and an estimated $4142 million in 1977. ODA commitments on this basis, however, at 1975 prices, were $2111 million in 1974, $2137 million in 1975, $2439 million in 1976 and an estimated $2640 million in 1977.

All developed countries take urgent steps to reach the official development assistance target of 0.7 percent of GNP 1/ bringing the overall grant element of the official development assistance to at least 86 percent. Bilateral donors and international and financial institutions should take urgent steps to provide the external resources needed to reach at least 4 percent annual growth in food production, which had been estimated on an annual basis of US$ 8.3 billion in 1975 prices of

DECISIONS	IMPLEMENTATION

which $6.5 billion should be concessional. Consequently it urges all donor countries to increase effectively and substantially their commitments for food production, particularly to food priority countries, so that noticeable progress can be reviewed at the Fifth Ministerial Session. Such additional external assistance should be combined with essential internal efforts in developing countries in order to achieve as soon as possible, the growth rate of at least 4 percent in food production in developing countries. (WFCL, Mexico Declaration, para. 1)

World Soil Charter and Land Capability Assessment

FAO, UNESCO and UNEP, in accordance with WMO, and other competent international organizations, and in consultation with Governments concerned, prepare without delay an assessment of the lands that can still be brought into cultivation, taking proper account of forestry for the protection of catchment areas of land required for alternative uses.
(WFC VI, para. 2; GA 3202 (S-VI) para. 2 (b))

Activities in pursuance of this resolution comprise of (i) soil survey, soil correlation and the Soil Map of the World; (ii) assessment of world land resources by agroecological zones; (iii) standardization of a methodology for land evaluation; and global assessment of soil degradation.

The map and soil data collected during its compilation are now being used to assess the world's land resources available for agricultural extension.
Work is actively pursued on Latin America and South Asia and an assessment of the land resources of developing coun-

DECISIONS	IMPLEMENTATION

tries will be available
before the end of the year.

From the study on agro-
ecological zones, high
potential areas for both
rain-fed and irrigated
agriculture will be selected
for more detailed assessment.
In addition a broad based
study of the population
supporting capacities of
developing countries at
regional levels will be
undertaken with the financial
assistance from UNFPA.
The FAO/UNEP project for a
global assessment of soil
degradation has produced a
draft map of soil degradation
and degradation hazards for
Africa north of the Equator
and the Middle East. A
follow up of this project
will be the launching of an
International Action Pro-
gramme for Soil Conservation
and Organic Wastes recycling,
which has been submitted to
UNEP for financial support.

All efforts should be made to
undertake concrete and speedy
measures with a view to ar-
resting desertification. (GA
3202 (S-VI), para. 2 (c))

A World Map of Desertification was prepared by FAO,
UNESCO and WMO as part of the
documentation of the United
Nations Conference on De-
sertification held in August-
September 1977. The Plan of
Action adopted by the Conference has recommended the
following objectives for
international action:
(a) Increased flows of
     multilateral assistance
     programmes to countries
     suffering from desertifi-
     cation.

DECISIONS	IMPLEMENTATION
	(b) Pooling of resources of the United Nations system in launching the Plan and carrying out an integrated and world-wide programme of development, research and application of science and technology to solve the special problems of desertification.
	(c) Utilization and strengthening of national capabilities in science and technology with particular attention to planning and management for the rational use of resources as well as the conditions which will lead to adequate international flows of technology to the developing countries.
Food and Agriculture Organization of the United Nations select the most appropriate ways and means to establish a World Soil Charter. (WFC VI, para. 3)	The eighteenth session of the FAO Conference (November 1975) did not recommend that additional resources be made available for the drawing up of a World Soil Charter.

Food and Agricultural Research, Extension and Training

FAO undertake the systematic collection, and dissemination of data on current research. (WFC IV, para. 9 (i))	The Current Agricultural Research Information System (CARIS) aims at the development of basic agricultural research based on a global scale. In 1978 three volumes of Agricultural Research in Developing Countries have been published. Information is available from 60 countries and 8 international institutes

DECISIONS	IMPLEMENTATION
	which covers a total of 2027 research institutions, 9913 research workers and 3310 programmes. So far 92 countries have agreed to establish CARIS liaison offices.
Resources of the Consultative Group on International Agricultural Research, co-sponsored by FAO, UNDP and the World Bank be substantially enlarged to enable it to augment the number of scope of international and regional research programmes in and for the developing countries. (WFC IV, para. 9 (ii))	During 1978, financial resources of the CGIAR system were increased even further. The estimated net budget requirement for the nine International Agricultural Research Centres (IARCs) including WARDA and IBPR for 1979 is $103.355 million. The operational budget for the centres in 1979 will be $97.758 million. The new IARCs, namely ILCA, ILRAD and ICARDA are now operational.
FAO, UNDP and the World Bank to consider establishing a coordinated programme for the improvement of extension systems. (WFC IV, para. 9 (iii))	FAO, UNDP and the World Bank continue to work closely in developing extension systems, improving training of extension personnel and in the evaluation of technical assistance efforts in this common interest. No formal machinery has been set up as FAO work by its nature ensures close cooperation. An evaluation exercise in a number of countries is being developed by FAO and UNDP, using professionals from both organizations and UNDP providing the funds.

DECISIONS	IMPLEMENTATION

Increased Input Material Supplies and Technical Assistance

To support increased food production efforts of developing countries, particularly food priority countries:
Immediate steps be initiated by Governments together with appropriate international agencies to determine a minimum package of agricultural inputs in support of the expanded programmes of food priority countries to achieve a minimum rate of food production (including livestock and fisheries) of 4 percent per year. Those parts of this minimum package of inputs, to be provided by donor countries and international agencies on concessional terms to food priority countries, should include fertilizers, pesticides, high-yielding varieties of seeds which are pest and disease resistant, improved breeds of livestock, credit to small farmers, irrigation equipment and selective and appropriate implements for mechanization. Other developing countries will be provided with similar assistance on terms appropriate to their economic circumstances.
(WFCL Manila Communique, para. 4 (a); WFC III, para. 2; GA 3362 (S-VII), para. V.5)

The determination of a minimum package of agricultural inputs will be undertaken within the framework of the FAO Study on Agriculture Towards 2000 (AT 2000) which aims, inter alia, at identifying input and investment requirements related to different rates of growth for agriculture. A provisional report on the Study will be discussed by the FAO Conference in 1979 and the final report will be ready in mid-1980. Indications for the African region and sub regions have been given in the report on the Africa Regional Food Plan which FAO prepared in collaboration with ECA and which was submitted and discussed at the FAO Regional Conference for Africa in September 1978.
See also action under WFC Res. 1, para. 9.

DECISIONS	IMPLEMENTATION

Agricultural Adjustment

FAO to take full account of discussions and decisions of the World Food Conference in formulating and implementing the proposed strategy of international agricultural adjustment.
(WFC XIX, para. 12; FAOC – 9/75)

FAO Conference resolution 9/75 has laid down a strategy including 11 guidelines for International Agricultural Adjustments as a global policy framework and has urged member Governments and Executive Heads of other international and regional agencies to take these into account in the formulation and implementation of their policies and programmes.

FAO should continue to monitor progress towards international agricultural adjustment. The monitoring should be based on the existing guidelines which still reflect the consensus of member Governments.)
(FAOC Decision, para 59)

A report on progress towards international agricultural adjustment will be submitted to the FAO Conference in 1979 along lines similar to the report to the last FAO Conference in 1977 taking into account the suggestions made in the Report of the Conference in 1977.

FAO to review from an agricultural standpoint the relationship between prices of agricultural products and other commodities and industrial products, in particular how to achieve greater price stability and improved access to agricultural commodities markets by exports of developing countries. (FAOC – 3/75, para. 2)

A report was presented to the nineteenth session of the FAO Conference in November 1977, within the framework of FAO's work on international agricultural adjustment. Detailed studies of Terms of Agricultural Trade, 1969–1976, Vol. I Commodity Analysis and Vol. II –Country analysis have been prepared which are under consideration for publication.

DECISIONS	IMPLEMENTATION

Special Measures for Least Developed, Land-Locked, Island and Most Seriously Affected (Developing) Countries

International organizations and bilateral aid agencies significantly intensify their efforts to meet the needs of developing countries, particularly the least developed and those most seriously affected by economic crisis, through increased material and financial support to the International Fertilizer Supply Scheme and by stepping up bilateral efforts, so as to bridge the gap in supply as estimated by the Scheme from time to time. The estimated needs of MSA countries for fertilizer nutrients in 1975/76 were estimated at 1 million tons. (WFC III, paras. 1 and 2; GA 3362 (S-VII), V, para. 10; WFCL - Manila Communique, para. 4 (d))

The total supply of fertilizer on either grant or concessional terms to developing countries in nutrient terms declined from 570,000 in 1974/75 to 540,000 tons in 1975/76, 430,000 tons in 1976/77 and 400,000 tons in 1977/78.
Of these supplies to MSA countries through the International Fertilizer Supply Scheme amounted to about 40,000 tons in 1974/75, 93,000 tons in 1975/76, 31,000 tons in 1976/77 and 21,000 tons in 1977/78 as against their estimated requirements of about 1 million tons in 1975/76.

Food aid to least developed countries should be essentially on a grant basis. (WFCL - Manila Communique, para. 9)

With the exception of United States and Japan, member countries of the Food Aid Convention provide all their food aid on a grant basis.
In some cases, donors have made agreements with recipients of grant aid and about the use of counterpart funds obtained from local sale of commodities supplied as food aid.
The grant element in United States' food aid is also expected to go up with implementation of the recently added Food for Development section (Title III) in PL

DECISIONS	IMPLEMENTATION

which authorizes the use of
resources provided by concessional sales of agricultural
commodities for agricultural
and rural development in
recipient countries, including
voluntary family planning, and
health and nutrition pro-
grammes. Under this provision
the United States has now
agreed to provide 800,000 tons
of wheat to Bangladesh, valued
at $96.8 million, to be de-
livered over the next three
years. Of this 400,000 tons
will be sold in the open
market in Bangladesh, 200,000
tons will be distributed to
poor rural consumers, and the
remaining 200,000 tons held in
reserve. The United States
has also agreed to provide
85,000 tons of wheat, valued
at US$ 10.8 million, to
Bolivia, while an agreement
with Honduras is under consideration.

Developed countries and the
international organizations
concerned to maintain and
expand their support for
economic cooperation among
developing countries.
(WFC XIX, para. 15)

To maintain continuity of work
in the United Nations system,
UNCTAD has been designated the
focal point for support to
ECDC and ACC has set up an
Inter-Agency Group on ECDC.
FAO and other agencies are
providing support to various
cooperation groupings through
Regular and Field Programmes.
These are given in detail in
ECOSOC document E/AC.51/90/
Add. 1 (Part I) and (Part II).
FAO is convening a Technical
Consultation among Developing
Countries in Food and Agri-
culture to be held from

DECISIONS	IMPLEMENTATION

25 June to 6 July 1979. The Consultation will review problems, assess progress and prospects and make recommendations on priorities for economic cooperation among developing countries in food and agriculture including for support and assistance by FAO.

WORLD FOOD SECURITY

World Food Security

All countries concerned to adopt objectives and main elements of the International Undertaking on World Food Security.
(WFC XVII, para. 1; FAOCL L/64, paras. 1-4; GA 3362 (S-VII), para. 12; FAOC 2/75, paras. 2 and 3; WFCL Manila Communique, para. 6)

As of December 1978, 75 countries and the EEC had subscribed to the International Undertaking on World Food Security. Implementation and other follow-up action is monitored by the Committee on World Food Security.

These objectives and main elements should be appropriately reflected in the provisions of a new International Grains Arrangement which should pay particular attention to safeguarding the special interests of developing countries and envisage an adequate reserve as well as appropriate price and supply commitments.
(WFCL Manila Communique, para. 6)

The reconvened session of the Conference convened by UNCTAD to negotiate an international arrangement to replace the International Wheat Agreement, 1971 as extended, was suspended on 24 November 1978. It is scheduled to be reconvened from 22 January to 9 February 1979, to finalize the new international agreement.

DECISIONS	IMPLEMENTATION

Negotiations proceed as rapidly as possible to establish, within the framework and as one of the important features of a new International Grains Arrangement, an international system of nationally held reserves, sufficient to ensure adequate supplies of food grains for importing countries as well as to contribute to price stability. A new food aid convention should be negotiated in connexion with a new international grains arrangement to ensure continued availability of food grains for food-aid needs. All efforts should be made to conclude this arrangement by June 1978.
(WFCL Manila Communique, para. 5)

To contribute to world food security, especially safeguarding the interests of developing members is one of the agreed objectives of a new international grains arrangement.

Early completion by FAO bodies of operational and other practical arrangements required for implementation of the proposed international undertaking, including examination of practical economic and administrative problems involved. (WFC XVII, para. 2; GA 3362 (S-VII), para. 12)

The FAO Conference in November 1975 established a Committee on World Food Security as a standing committee of the FAO Council charged with the functions suggested in resolution XVII. It has so far held three sessions: the fourth session is scheduled for 5-11 April 1979.

DECISIONS	IMPLEMENTATION
Governments and concerned international and regional organizations to provide necessary technical, financial and food assistance in the form of grants or on specially favourable terms to develop and implement appropriate national food stocks policies in developing countries. (WFC XVII; para. 4; FAOCL 1/64, para. 5; FAOC 2/45, para. 3; WFCL Manila Communique, para. 7).	The FAO Food Security Assistance Scheme, launched in 1976, continues to assist developing countries in the formulation of food security policies, identification and preparation of long-term projects relating to food security, and programming and implementation of national food security projects.

The FAO Food Security Assistance Scheme, launched in 1976, continues to assist developing countries in the formulation of food security policies, identification and preparation of long-term projects relating to food security, and programming and implementation of national food security projects.
While the earlier activities of the scheme centred on the preparation of country surveys, with the availability of extrabudgetary funds, emphasis shifted to project preparation in 1977, and to implementation in 1978.
Future action under the Scheme will centre on the development of storage capacity and related infrastructures, and on stock operations. At the same time, it is planned to strengthen the programming, coordinating and advisory functions of the Scheme at the country and regional levels, in so far as this meets the wishes of the countries concerned.
Progress since the inception of the Scheme, and plans for future action were reviewed by the Committee on World Food Security at its third session in April 1978.
As at the end of December 1978, a total of US$ 27 million had been contributed by donors to support the scheme and finance the different food security projects in the field. Nevertheless, donations still fall considerably short of the amounts required to finance new projects, and

DECISIONS	IMPLEMENTATION
	this has prompted the Director-General of FAO, in August 1978, to request all Governments and international organizations in a position to do so to extend more contributions in support of the Scheme.
Intensive work should be continued on a priority basis in the World Food Council and other appropriate forums in order to determine, inter alia, size of the required reserve, taking into account among other things the proposal that components of wheat and rice in the total reserve should be 30 million tons. (GA 3362 (S-VII), para. 12)	The question of the size of the reserve required for world food security has been under discussion in various fora, notably the FAO Committee on World Food Security, IWC and UNCTAD. The Committee on World Food Security agreed, pending further examination, with the FAO secretariat's estimated figures of the minimum safe level of carry-over stocks as a reasonable basis for its assessments. (The FAO secretariat has estimated the minimum safe level of world carry-over stocks for cereals to be between 17 to 18 percent of world consumption; of this total, "reserve" element would amount to 5 to 6 percent, the rest being "working" or "pipe-line" stocks.) It also recom-mended in April 1977 that the objectives and main elements of the international under-taking on world food security should be appropriately re-flected in the provisions of a new International Grains Agreement.

DECISIONS   IMPLEMENTATION

Post-Harvest Food Losses

Further reduction of post-
harvest food losses in developing countries should be undertaken as a matter of priority,
with a view to reaching at
least a 50 percent reduction
by 1985. All countries and
competent international organizations should cooperate
financially and technically in
the effort to achieve this
objective.
(GA 3362 (S-VII), para. 3)

The FAO Conference at its
nineteenth session in November
1977 approved an Action Programme for the Prevention of
Food Losses which lays down a
strategy for loss prevention
activities in developing
countries to be carried out by
member countries, FAO and
other agencies. It decided,
by resolution 3/77, to establish a Special Account for the
programme with an invitation
to Member Nations of FAO and
other contributors to make
contributions amounting to at
least $20 million to the
Special Account. Contributions and pledges for the
Action Programme as at 31
December 1978 amounted to US$
14.5 million.

Programmes should be supported
by appropriate international
agencies and bilateral donors
to reduce harvest and post-
harvest losses, and to this
end FAO's activities in these
areas should be substantially
strengthened. (WFCL Manila
Communique, para. 4 (b); FAOC
3/77)

The Action Programme concentrates in the initial phase on
reducing post-harvest losses
of staple foods, i.e. food
grains, roots and tubers, and
priority is given to LDCs,
MSAs and food priority countries and within these countries to the rural poor.
Emphasis is on immediate
actions to reduce losses at
the farm and village level.
As at 31 December 1978, 60
project requests have been
received from Member Governments covering projects which
would have a total FAO contribution of approximately $12.5
million. Thirty-seven of
these requests are presently

DECISIONS	IMPLEMENTATION

| | being evaluated and 23 have been approved by the Director-General for a total amount of $4.875 million. Twenty-five of the above requests came from the Africa region, 14 from Asia and the Far East, 13 from Latin America and 8 from the Near East. |

FOOD AID

Increased and Improved Food Aid

DECISIONS	IMPLEMENTATION
Need for continuity of a minimum level of food aid in physical terms, in order to insulate food aid programmes from the effects of excessive fluctuations in production and prices, and all donor countries, traditional and potential, to make all efforts to provide commodities and/or financial assistance that will ensure in physical terms at least 10 million tons of grains as food aid a year starting from 1975 and also adequate quantities of other food commodities, to ensure that the minimum target is reached by 1977/78. (WFC XVII, paras. 1 and 2; GA 3362 (S-VII), para. V.8; FAOC 2/75, para. 4; WFCL Manila Communique, para. 9).	The flow of food aid in cereals has increased since the World Food Conference. Food aid shipments have risen from the low of 5.6 million tons in 1973/74 to 9.5 million tons in 1977/78. Preliminary food aid allocations in cereals for 1978/79 have reached the minimum target of 10 million tons of food aid in grains set by the World Food Conference, but it is not certain that these preliminary allocations will be fully translated into actual shipments. Aid in non-cereal food has also increased.
All donor countries accept and implement the concept of forward planning of food aid, and those which have not yet done so should make every effort to ensure as soon as possible the forward planning	Some progress in this direction has been made. But a large part of total food aid still lacks continuity and several donors have yet to adopt the practice of forward planning explicitly.

DECISIONS	IMPLEMENTATION

of food aid supplies. (WFC
XVIII, para. 2; WFCL Manila
Communique, para. 9).

All countries also accept the principle that food aid should be channelled on the basis of objective assessment of requirements in the recipient countries. In this respect all countries are urged to participate in the global information and early warning system on food and agriculture. (GA 3362 (S-VII), para. V.8)	The Committee on Food Aid Policies and Programmes, at its fifth session in April, 1978, considered an interim report on the assessment of food aid requirements and targets. The Committee noted that a quantity of 15-16 million tons would be a reasonable first estimate of the food aid in cereals required by 1985, and accepted these figures as a useful basis for assessing food aid requirements. It recommended that the estimates should be reviewed periodically in the light of actual developments.
Interested cereals-exporting and importing countries as well as current and potential financial contributors meet as soon as possible to take cognizance of the needs and to consider ways and means to increase food availability and financing facilities during 1975 and 1976 for the affected developing countries and, in particular, for those most seriously affected by the current food problem.	An urgent consultation on cereals supplies and ways of meeting the short-term requirements of developing countries, particularly those most seriously affected, was convened by the Director-General of FAO on 29 November 1974. The findings of the consultation were transmitted to the Secretary-General and the UNEO contributed a substantial portion of its total emergency assistance to MSA countries in 1974 and 1975 for food imports.
All donor countries to (a) channel a more significant proportion of food aid through the World Food Programme, (b) consider increasing progressively the grant component in their bilateral food aid	(a) The amount of food aid passing through multilateral channels increased sharply in 1975 and more slowly in 1976 and 1977. The share of multilateral aid in total

DECISIONS	IMPLEMENTATION

programmes (c) consider contributing part of any food aid
repayments for supplementary
nutrition programmes and
emergency relief, (d) provide,
as appropriate additional cash
resources to food aid programmes for commodity purchases from developing countries to the maximum extent
possible.
(WFC XVIII, para. 4; GA 3362
(S-VII), para. V8.

food aid rose to 17
percent in 1975 but fell
to 15 percent in 1976.
According to available
information, it has
probably increased again
in 1977.

(b) With the exception of
United States and Japan,
the member countries of
the Food Aid Convention
provide all their food
aid on a grant basis. In
some cases, donors have
made agreements with
recipients of grant aid
about the use of counter-
part funds obtained from
local sale of commodities
supplied as food aid.
The proportion of total
food aid given as grants
increased from 25 percent
in 1976 to 31 percent in
1977. In the case of the
United States, the grant
component of food aid is
expected to go up, due to
recent amendments in PL
480 relating to Title II
and the introduction of a
new Title III on Food for
Development (see (c)
below).

(c) The United States Public
Law 480, as amended in
December 1975, provides
that currencies acquired
from loan repayments
under Title I can be used
for assistance to meet
emergency or extraordin-
ary relief requirements.
The recently introduced
TITLE III in PL 480 on

DECISIONS	IMPLEMENTATION
	Food for Development authorizes the use of such funds also for agricultural and rural development in recipient countries.
	(d) In response to this recommendation, Saudi Arabia pledged $50 million in 1975/76 and also again in 1977/78. No other country has yet come forward with an additional cash contribution to the Programme for this purpose.
World Food Programme and other international organizations concerned to give priority to use of cash resources available for multilateral or bilateral food aid for purchases in developing countries at competitive world market prices and terms. (WFC XIX, para. 17)	WFP made purchases of commodities for food aid worth about $31 million in 1975, $23 million in 1976 and $15.3 million in 1977, of which $9.3 million came from its own regular cash resources and the balance was on account of other United Nations agencies and bilateral donors. Total purchases in 1978 are estimated at $31.3 million, of which $18.0 million come from the WFP's regular cash resources and the balance on account of other United Nations agencies and bilateral donors. The purchases made in developing countries from the cash resources of WFP programmes increased from 91 percent of all commodity purchases in 1976 to 94 percent in 1977 and an estimated 97 percent in 1978.

DECISIONS	IMPLEMENTATION
Donor countries which provide food aid on a credit basis should increase the element of concessionality in their aid and substantially enlarge the proportion of food aid given on a grant basis, especially to developing countries in serious economic difficulties. (FAOC 2/75, para. 5; WFCL Manila Communique, para. 9)	See above under WFC XVIII, para. 4.
Intergovernmental Committee of the World Food Programme, reconstituted as recommended, be entrusted with the task of formulating proposals for more effective coordination of multilateral, bilateral and non-governmental food aid programmes and of coordinating emergency food aid. (WFC XVIII, para. 5)	On coordination of emergency food aid, the WFP has taken over the task of coordinating emergency operations in the Sahel. A study on multi-lateral emergency food aid was considered by the Committee of Food Aid Policies and Pro-grammes at its sixth session in October 1978. On coordina-tion of other types of food aid, the Committee is continu-ing to examine various aspects of the question and some related studies are in prepara-tion.
A Food Aid Convention be negotiated as an element of a new International Grains Arrangement with a view to contributing to the attainment of the target agreed upon in the World Food Conference; and negotiations cover provisions for movement of a larger amount of food through the World Food Programme. All efforts should be made to conclude this Arrangement by June 1978. (WFCL Manila Communique, para. 10).	There was agreement at the negotiations held in February-March 1978 that the objective of a new FAC should be to carry out a programme of food aid ensuring the availability of not less than 10 million tons of wheat and other grain suitable for human consumption annually to developing coun-tries. So far, only the United States and Canada have made specific offers of in-creased food aid and commit-ments under the new FAC, provided that agreement is reached on a Wheat Trade Convention.

DECISIONS	IMPLEMENTATION

The Committee on Food Aid Policies and Programmes intensify its efforts, on a priority basis, to develop and implement an improved policy framework for food aid by including guidelines and criteria for multilateral emergency food aid as well as expanded and improved food aid programmes to advance food production, support other development efforts, assist in developing and maintaining food reserves, and augment food supplies for malnourished people; to ensure that food aid does not retard efforts to increase food production in recipient countries or distort commercial trade flows. (WFCL Manila Communique, para. 11)

Some progress has been made toward implementation of an improved food aid policy. In particular, positive steps were taken to direct food aid to the neediest countries and to promote nutrition improvement and agricultural production and employment in rural areas. Steps were also taken to improve arrangements for meeting emergency needs. However, there remain several aspects on which further action is needed, in particular on rising cereal import requirements of several LDCs and MSA countries; covering the gap between the volume of current food aid in grains and the minimum target of 10 million tons, explicit adoption by several donor countries of the practice of forward-planning food aid; the grant aid component of food aid; the small share of multilateral food aid in total food aid; the gap between contributions made to the International Emergency Food Reserve and the target of 500,000 tons; and the need to increase the participation of developing countries in food aid programmes through the use of triangular transactions. Guidelines and criteria for expanded and improved food aid programmes were considered by the Committee on Food Aid Policies and Programmes at its fifth session in April 1978. The matter will be considered again at the Seventh session of the Committee in May 1979.

DECISIONS	IMPLEMENTATION

International Emergency Food Reserve

The General Assembly establish the International Emergency Food Reserve of 500,000 tons of cereals as a continuing reserve with yearly replenishment determined by the Committee on Food Aid Policies and Programmes and placed at the disposal of the World Food Programme. Reserves not called upon in one year will be carried over into the next year. Governments should indicate the amounts of cereals or cash they are prepared to place at the disposal of the World Food Programme up to the level of 500,000 tons, such amounts should preferably be indicated for more than one year in advance. The Committee on Food Aid Policies and Programmes (CFA) should examine the procedures and modalities governing the International Emergency Food Reserve to improve the effectiveness of its operations including securing its continuity and its ready availability. All countries able to contribute to the International Emergency Reserve, who have not yet contributed should do so in order to ensure that the target of 500,000 tons of cereals is achieved in 1978 and maintained thereafter.
(WFC, Mexico Declaration, paras, 30-33).

In line with the recommendations of the WFC, the Committee on Food Aid Policies and Programmes, at its sixth session, agreed on the revised modalities for the operation of the International Emergency Food Reserve, although some delegations concurred only in principle.

DECISIONS	IMPLEMENTATION
All potential donors pledge support to the International Emergency Reserve of 500,000 tons of cereals by the end of 1977, on the basis of the modalities agreed to in the Committee on Food Aid Policies and Programmes, and inform the World Food Programme as soon as possible of their contributions. (WFCL Manila Communique, para. 8)	During 1977 the International Emergency Food Reserve (IEFR) became an operational reality as a result of contributions by Australia, the EEC, the Federal Republic of Germany, the United Kingdom and the United States, in addition to those made by the original participants, Norway and Sweden. Total annual contributions rose from 81,462 tons of food grains in 1976 to 141,672 in 1977 and 315,215 tons in 1978, as against the annual target of 500,000 tons recommended by the Seventh Special Session of the United Nations General Assembly in 1975. The quantity utilized until the end of November totalled 277,265 tons. For 1979, a contribution of 125,000 tons of food commodities valued at US$ 27 million has been announced by the United States and one of Ł2 million ($3,960,396) by the United Kingdom, subject to parliamentary approval. The General Assembly intended that the IEFR should function as a contingency fund and CFA subsequently confirmed this (see above). Therefore, if the reserve is to operate effectively, it is essential not only to achieve the target of not less than 500,000 tons, but also to maintain it at this level through annual replenishments by the participating governments.

DECISIONS	IMPLEMENTATION
International guidelines for emergency stocks be developed as a part of the proposed undertaking to provide for an effective coordination of emergency stocks and to ensure that food relief reaches the neediest and most vulnerable groups. (WFC XVIII, para. 6)	Following a preliminary discussion at its second session, the CFA will be considering emergency food aid questions, including guidelines and criteria for emergency food aid and the International Emergency Reserve, at its seventh session.

Global Information and Early Warning System on Food and Agriculture

A Global Information and Early Warning System on Food and Agriculture be established and FAO is the most appropriate organization to operate and supervise the System. (WFC XVI, para. 1)	The FAO Council, at its sixty-fourth session in November 1974 agreed that the System should be established in FAO, incorporating in it related FAO activities already existing in this field.
FAO, in cooperation with other concerned international organizations particularly the International Wheat Council, formulate arrangements necessary for the establishment of the System, and submit them for final approval by Governments participating in the System. (WFC XVI, para. 2)	All member States of FAO and the United Nations were invited to join. So far 92 Governments, the EEC, and the Permanent Secretariat of the General Treaty on Central American Economic Integration (SIECA) have agreed to participate in the System. Close cooperation has been established with IWC, UNDRO, WFP and WHO and other international organizations concerned.
All Governments participate in the System and extend full cooperation, on a voluntary and regular basis, by furnishing as much current information and forecasts as possible, initially on basic food products, including partic-	The number of participating Governments supplying to the System information on staple food products has increased steadily but there is still need for improvement. Assistance is being given to strengthen the national early

DECISIONS	IMPLEMENTATION

ular, wheat, rice, coarse grains, soybeans, and live-stock products and, to the extent practicable, other important food products and other relevant aspects. (WFC XVI, para. 3; FAOC 2/75, para. 7)

warning and crop forecasting systems of developing countries.

Governments take steps to amplify and improve their data collection and dissemination services in these fields; and FAO, WMO, WHO, the Inter-governmental Bureau for Information and other multilateral and bilateral sources urgently assist interested governments with technical and financial assistance, and coordinate this action with that of the World Food Council. (WFC XVI, para. 4)

FAO sent missions to 15 drought-prone developing countries which reviewed existing country information systems on food crops and advised Governments on the improvement or establishment of such systems with particular reference to early forecasting of their crop production. Attention of Governments was focused on the need for coordinating the early warning system with the regular statistical services of the country; and for strengthening these services where necessary. Follow-up action is now being taken on requests for technical assistance for establishment of national early warning systems which have already been received from some countries.

Information thus collected be fully analysed and disseminated periodically to all participating Governments, and for their exclusive use; it being understood that, where requested, certain information provided by Governments would be disseminated in aggregate form particularly in order to avoid unfavourable market repercussions. (WFC XVI, para. 5)

Global food outlook reports are issued monthly, and are now available for general distribution following the decision of the Committee on World Food Security at its Third Session. A network of reporting officers gives early warning of worsening crop conditions and possible food shortages in individual countries. Special missions are sent whenever necessary

DECISIONS	IMPLEMENTATION

to assist governments in the
assessment of possible emergency needs. News of potentially critical situations is
immediately telexed to
donors, and summary country
reports are contained in
"Foodcrops and Shortages"
issued monthly to partic-
ipants. Up-to-date FAO/IWC
estimates of the uncovered
cereal import requirements of
developing countries are
issued periodically in a
Special Report.

World Meterological Organization in cooperation with FAO
(a) provide regular assess-
ments of current and recent
weather on the basis of information presently assembled
through the World Weather
Watch; (b) expand and establish joint research projects
to investigate weather/crop
relationships; (c) strengthen
present global weather monitoring systems at national and
regional levels; and (d)
encourage investigations on
assessment of probability of
adverse weather conditions
occurring in various agricultural areas, and on a
better understanding of causes
of climatic variations.
(WFC XVI, para. 6)

FAO has been making, since
1976, an assessment of climatic conditions for agriculture in the 6 countries of
the Sahelian zone. This
exercise has been extended to
the 14 countries of the
African semi-arid belt. FAO
is also officially associated
with the UNDP/WMO programme
in the Sahel.
The 19th FAO Conference has
adopted a resolution for
increased cooperation between
FAO and WMO in the field of
agricultural meterology.
WMO has developed a system
for the exchange of agro-
meteorological information
for the specific requirements
of agriculture. This system
has been experimented in the
summer 1978 on a pilot basis
in West Africa. The information will be provided to FAO.

FAO has already taken with
WMO appropriate steps for a
better monitoring of meteorological conditions in the
desert locust infestation
area in relation with locust
monitoring and control
operations.

DECISIONS	IMPLEMENTATION

Food Aid to Victims of Colonial Wars in Africa

The Director-General of FAO and the Executive Director of WFP to take immediate action to intensify food aid to the populations of Guinea Bissau, Cape Verde, Mozambique, Angola, Sao Tome and Principe. (WFC XV, para. 1)	No longer relevant as these are all independent countries.
The Secretary-General of the United Nations and all the executive heads of organizations within the United Nations system to take all necessary measures to assist the national liberation movements or the Governments of these countries to formulate a comprehensive plan of national reconstruction. (WFC XV, para. 2)	The measures taken to assist national liberation movements or the Governments of those countries are reported in the annual report of the Secretary-General, prepared in compliance with General Assembly resolution 32/36 on "Implementation of the Declaration on the Granting of Independence to Colonial Territories by the specialized agencies and the international institutions associated with the United Nations."

RURAL DEVELOPMENT

Women and Rural Development

Integration of Women in Agricultural and Rural Development and Nutrition Policies

FAO Council supports the necessary approach to the development of food production, food availability and utilization and the improvement of the quality of rural family life through the full integration of women in rural	Increasing support is being given by FAO to member governments in the development of institutional programmes for training those who work with rural families and rural women, to help enhance their contribution to food produc-

DECISIONS	IMPLEMENTATION

development.
(Resolution FAOCL 2/66, para.
1; FAOC 10/75, para. 1 (a))

The Director-General of FAO to
ensure that current programmes
and projects in nutrition,
agriculture (including fisheries and forestry) and rural
development be reviewed by all
Departments and Divisions
concerned with these activities with a view to the incor-
poration of a suitable component benefiting women.
(FAOCL 2/66, para. 4; FAOC
10/75, paras. 4 (a), (b)
and (c).

The Director-General of FAO to
assure the integration of
women in all FAO programmes
and projects by directing all
Departments and Divisions
concerned with these activities to investigate, design,
plan, implement and review, on
a regular basis, all proposed
projects and programmes in
order to establish a measure
of progress in assuring the
important participation of
women as equal partners with
men in the total development
process, it being understood
that wherever possible women
should be directly engaged in
the planning, decision-making
implementation and evaluation
of FAO projects and programmes.
(FAOCL 2/66, para. 5; FAOC
10/75, para. 1(b))

tion, food utilization and
improving overall quality of
family life. LDC's in all
regions are given priority.

The FAO Inter-Divisional
Working Group on women in
development (FAO)/IDWG/WID)
established in April 1976
continues to be active,
coordinates FAO activities,
and plays a catalytic role
within FAO for integrating
components to benefit rural
women and families in all food
and agriculture activities.
A similar group has been
established in three of the
Regional Offices.

Based on replies from 246
projects in 55 countries to
the FAO Guidelines for the
Integration of Women in Agricultural and Rural Development
Projects, an analysis has been
completed by country, region,
funding source and technical
area. This analysis has
assisted in the identification
of countries and FAO projects
for a concentration of efforts
within FAO's assistance and
approaches in working on the
country and sub-regional basis
for the development of programmes benefiting women in
the agricultural sector.
Continuous follow up is being
done on a systematic basis and
a monitoring system developed.

DECISIONS	IMPLEMENTATION

All Member States of the United Nations and its specialized agencies to support measures ensuring that women share in the rural sector, particularly through the recognition of their full legal equality and the adoption of measures implementing such equality.
(FAOC 10/75, para. 2)

The FAO had a strong joint population/better family living programme with African Training and Research programme for Women in UN/ECA – Addis with itinerant training activities for rural women in most countries of Africa. FAO participates actively in Inter-Agency Group on WID, and will contribute to preparatory meetings and documentation for United Nations Decade on Women; also there are plans for preparing information materials based on WCARRD results.

FAO Director-General include in the major items for discussion by World Conference on Agrarian Reform and Rural Development, the growing role of women in all aspects of rural development including policies and means required to ensure their full participation on an equitable basis in policy making, planning and implementation of agrarian reform and rural development.
(FAOC 14/77, para. 1)

The theme on the role of women in development has been included as a separate item in the provisional agenda of the WCARRD Conference under the title "Integration of Women in Development". It will deal with all aspects of women in development such as their equal access to resources, employment, education and organizational opportunities.

FAO Director-General, within the framework of the preparations for the Conference, takes steps to have a systematic analysis made of the situation of rural women and of the role they play in rural activities, with particular emphasis on food production, and submit the results of this analysis, including measures for achieving the full incor-

A series of regional and national papers were commissioned by FAO on this subject, and the systematic analysis has been included as a chapter in the background document "Review and Analysis of Past Developments and Policies on Agrarian Reform and Rural Development since the mid-1960's", to the WCARRD Conference. The Conference

DECISIONS	IMPLEMENTATION

poration of women in social and economic development processes in their respective countries, to the Conference for review and consideration. (FAOC 14/77, para. 2)

working papers on the Agenda item will contain a suitable analysis and recommendations to get Government commitments on practical steps to bring rural women into the main-stream of rural development.

Agriculture and Rural Development

Priorities for Agricultural and Rural Development

UNDP, IBRD, FAO and other international and bilateral agencies to review their criteria for financial, technical and other assistance for integrated rural development; to give greater importance to social criteria so as to implement broader and longer-range programmes of rural development; and if necessary improve their technical and administrative capacity for implementing these programmes. (WFC II, para. 5)

An Inter-Agency Task Force has been established to examine the practical applications of a poverty-oriented approach to rural development to organize field activities in a co-ordinated interagency pro-gramme in a few selected countries and to establish amongst the agencies common procedures for evaluation, monitoring, research, staff training, and other coordinating activities.

Governments, UNDP and other international and bilateral agencies to cooperate in accelerating the planning and implementation of integrated rural development programmes and to devote greatly expanded resources to these activities. (WFC II, para. 6)

A World Conference on Agrarian Reform and Rural Development has been approved by the FAO Conference and ECOSOC to be held from 12 to 17 July 1979 in Rome, with the purpose of providing the opportunity for member countries to assess their experience and consult together in order to improve their own performance, evalu-ate issues of policy at coun-try and international levels, and enhance the role of rural people's representative bodies in agrarian reform and rural

DECISIONS	IMPLEMENTATION

development. This Conference
is being organized with the
full cooperation of all the
agencies in the United Nations
system. The practical implications of an integrated
approach to rural development
oriented towards the rural
poor has been discussed in a
series of regional expert
consultations.

The FAO Conference decides
that the World Conference on
Agrarian Reform and Rural
Development will be held in
Rome for eight working days,
beginning 12 July 1979.
(FAOC 13/77)

A rounding-up session to bring
together the views expressed
at these regional consultations was held in September
1977. The Regional Conferences of FAO held in five
regions in 1978, examined the
regional and sub-regional
aspects of the World Conference themes and have made
recommendations to it in four
resolutions. The basic document for the Conference, "A
Review and Analysis of Agrarian Reform and Rural Development in the Developing Countries since Mid-1960's" has
already been prepared in close
consultation with other concerned members of the UN
system, and by utilizing 75
Country Review Papers prepared
by participating Governments,
and over 100 case studies,
organized by FAO and collaborating organizations, on different aspects of the main
themes.

FAO and other United Nations
organizations concerned to
collect, evaluate and disseminate the results and

To disseminate experiences in
rural development among interested countries, at the
initiative of FAO, an agree-

DECISIONS	IMPLEMENTATION

experience from past and ongoing rural development programmes, to determine the suitability of these programmes in bringing about both expanding agricultural production and social integration. (WFC II, para. 7)

ment has been reached to establish the Centre for Integrated Rural Development for Asia and the Pacific (CIRDAP) as an inter-governmental and autonomous organization, with a network of national institutes. It is expected that funds would be provided by - besides FAO - several donor and member countries. Its primary purpose will be to promote and assist national action for integrated rural development in the region. A similar Centre is expected to be set up in Africa.

Agencies substantially increase their efforts in rural development within the framework of agency responsibilities for specific activities, as indicated by resolution II of the World Food Conference and within the framework of the coordinating mechanism established by the Administrative Committee on Coordination (ACC). (WFCL Manila Communique, para. 21)

United Nations agencies have substantially increased their efforts in rural development particularly within the framework of the ACC Task Force on Rural Development. The FAO Conference held November/December 1977 in Rome noted that the poverty-oriented approach to rural development advocated by the ACC had already been adopted in respect to the World Conference on Agrarian Reform and Rural Development and other FAO activities in this field. During 1977, FAO participated in four out of five inter-agency exploratory missions fielded by the ACC Task Force on Rural Development, to discuss with Governments their policies, programmes and approach towards planning and implementation of rural development. It is too early

DECISIONS	IMPLEMENTATION

to determine the results of
these activities which are
continuing.
FAO has participated in two
other major areas of work
initiated by the ACC Task
Force. In the first, monitoring and evaluation of poverty-
oriented rural development
activities, FAO has produced
an inventory of its rural
development activities, and
is developing its approach
through work on the monitoring of project intent for
design purposes, as a lead
into elaboration of performance evaluation. In the
second, harmonization of
programme proposals, FAO has
contributed, through a small
interagency team, to innovate
thinking on institutional
development and popular
participation. Efforts will
be made to produce a concise
document on United Nations
agencies' programmes for
rural development in 1980/81.
FAO assumed leadership of
this Inter-Agency Task Force
on 1 January 1978.

Major support be provided by
Governments and international
agencies towards the implementation of the basic needs
approach as endorsed by the
ILO World Employment Conference.
(WFCL Manila Communique,
para. 22)

Considerable emphasis has been
placed in the State of Food
and Agriculture (SOFA) and
other FAO situation and outlook reports on the relationship between food availability
and the satisfaction of basic
nutritional needs, and to the
analysis of food consumption
and nutrition as a contribution towards the identification of basic needs, and the

DECISIONS	IMPLEMENTATION

requirements for their satisfaction in developing countries. Adoption of resolution 8/77 on nutrition and action being taken to implement it, emphasize FAO interest in the basic needs approach.
The Fourth World Food Survey (1977) provides, among other things, an analysis at the country level of nutrition intake among different groups of people, paying particular attention to the most vulnerable groups, and lays special emphasis on the nutritional situation in MSA and LDC countries. It discusses the dimension of undernourishment in the world and estimates the number of people with food intake below minimum limits within regions. FAO is collaborating with the U.N. and its specialized agencies in the development of the National Household Survey Capability Programme in developing countries for the promotion of the collection of data needed for assessing the social conditions and for monitoring progress in the nutritional status of the population of these countries.

Fertilizers

International agencies and donor countries concerned should, on a voluntary basis, extend their financial and technical assistance to

Bilateral fertilizer assistance to developing countries, according to information available by the end of December 1978, was as follows:

DECISIONS	IMPLEMENTATION

developing countries, to encourage their self-reliance through the installation of new fertilizer and pesticide capacities and by improvement in the operation of existing facilities. To the fullest extent practicable, measures should also be taken to reduce undue fluctuations in the price and supply of agricultural inputs in international markets.
(WFCL Manila Communique para. 4 (d); WFC III, paras. 1 and 2; GA 3362 (S.VII), para. V.5)

Bilateral fertilizer aid (in terms of fertilizer material

(metric tons)

1974/75	1975/76
1,305,000	1,098,000
1976/77	1977/78
969,000	944,000

Since developing countries, particularly the MSA countries, would still have difficulty in obtaining adequate supplies of fertilizers in spite of relatively lower prices in the international market, the FAO Commission on Fertilizers at its fourth session in September 1977, endorsed the proposal of the Director-General that IFS be continued during the next biennium.

FAO, UNDP and World Bank to jointly organize a programme to assist developing countries to improve the efficiency of their fertilizer plant operations.
(WFC III, para. 3; GA 3362 (S-VII), para. V.5)

As requested by the FAO Commission on Fertilizers, FAO/UNIDO/World Bank in cooperation with ESCAP, ECLA, ECA, and IDCAS are investigating and promoting further expansion of fertilizer production capacity in developing countries, giving particular attention to plant location and the possibilities for cooperative ventures.

International institutions, developed countries and others in a position to do so to provide financial assistance, technical assistance, technology and equipment on favour-

The FAO/UNIDO/World Bank Working Group on Fertilizers is surveying continuously development of fertilizer production facilities in developing countries. A

DECISIONS	IMPLEMENTATION

able terms, to build required additional fertilizer production capacities in appropriate developing countries with storage facilities, distribution services and other related infrastructures.
(WFC III, para. 4)

concept for a regional approach to fertilizer production and supply has been worked out in cooperation by FAO, UNDP, and the Economic Commission for Latin America. FAO, UNIDO, and IDAS are cooperating in the Near East for better coordinated development of fertilizer production capacities, including more rational use of available raw materials. The FAO Fertilizer Programme field projects include increasing assistance in improvement of infrastructure for fertilizer distribution and credit.

FAO in collaboration with other international organizations, such as UNIDO and the World Bank, and Governments to undertake analysis of long-term fertilizer supply and demand aimed at ensuring adequate supply at stable and reasonable prices in order to provide the elements of a world fertilizer policy.
(WFC III, para. 6)

The FAO Commission on Fertilizers, at its Fourth Session in September 1977, reviewed the current and longer-term fertilizer supply and demand position, and considered a number of possible price stabilization measures. Further work on these measures, requested by the Commission, Council and Conference is in progress in FAO. These include an option proposal with the general objective of ensuring fertilizer import needs of developing countries, particularly the MSA countries, at prices equivalent to domestic prices in developed countries, and introducing an element of stability in international prices for fertilizers. Arrangements for making the system operational will be considered by the Commission

DECISIONS	IMPLEMENTATION

| | on Fertilizers at its Fifth Session in January 1979 since commitments in principle have been received from manufacturers in developed countries amounting to the minimum target figure of import requirements of the MSA countries required to make it operational. |
| Intensification of international efforts in the transfer of technical knowledge, particularly on the intermediate level, in order to increase production and to make more effective use of fertilizers, including the improvement of extension services and training of farmers in all countries. (WFC III, para. 8) | FAO's Fertilizer Programme has the objective to promote fertilizer use at the farmers' level. Training activities in fertilizer use development at different levels have been intensified through regional and national seminars, with emphasis on Africa and Asia. As a continuing process over years, and per year, the FAO Fertilizer Programme is running on average the following training activities: |

1 - at small farmers' level 11,000 fertilizer and related inputs demonstrations and trials and 11,000 farmers' field days with 160,000 participating farmers;

2 - at district level - 200 technical courses for extension supervisors;

3 - at national level - 20 management courses for counterpart staff.

The FAO Fertilizer Programme is also running per year on average 28 pilot schemes for improved fertilizer distribution and credit with 12,000 participating farmers in eight countries.

DECISIONS	IMPLEMENTATION

A UNEP supported project on nitrogen biological fixation in Africa and Latin America, has been initiated. FAO's assistance in more rational use of organic materials as fertilizers has been intensified. FAO/SIDA Regional Workshops on Organic Fertilizers in Asia, Latin America, Africa and the Near East have been conducted.

Technical advice on the improvement of fertilizer use, marketing and credit has been provided through FAO/UNDP projects in six countries; short practical training seminars have been organized in three countries. Unfortunately, assistance to fertilizer use development, given with UNDP support, had to be reduced to a certain extent in 1976, as a result of financial difficulties. A detailed analysis of fertilizer marketing and credit systems in developing countries has been made through a series of more than 40 case studies and conclusions of this analysis have been published in several reports widely circulated.

Seeds

Developing countries be supported through bilateral programmes or contributions on a voluntary basis to the FAO Seed Industry Development Programme in an amount of at least $US 20 million.
(WFCL Manila Communique,

By December 1978 the FAO Seed Improvement and Development Programme (SIDP) assisted 22 Governments in the formulation of national seed programmes and relatex projects with a total identified aid requirement of US$ 39 million of

DECISIONS	IMPLEMENTATION
para. 4 (c); FAOC 4/77; WFC XII, para. 3)	which US$ 27 million could be committed or are under negotiation. In 1978, the Programme provided technical support to 54 field projects with 102 expert posts. 20,000 seed samples were shipped to 120 countries for experimental purposes, 500 tons of seeds were supplied to 13 countries for further increase and assistance was given in emergency seed supply of 1,300 tons to six countries. 12 countries have been assisted in the establishment of national seed production and training centres through the supply of specific equipment. During 1978, 125 intermediate and lower level staff have been trained in national courses, and 20 senior and intermediate level staff attended one regional training course in seed technology. During 1979, it is planned to conduct 17 national training courses for 350 intermediate and lower level staff, and two regional workshops on seed technology activities for 40 senior and intermediate level staff. Thus it can be expected that during 1978/79 more than 500 persons will be trained in various seed activities.

Water

International institutions and bilateral and multilateral aid agencies to provide substantially increased external assistance to enable the

Total official commitments of capital assistance for water development (including irrigation, land reclamation and drainage, dams, barrages and

DECISIONS	IMPLEMENTATION
developing countries to undertake rapid action set out under paragraph 1. (Para. 1 deals with urgent action on technical measures which Governments and international agencies such as FAO and WMO were requested to take, and paras. 3 and 4 with the urging of Governments and international agencies to make appropriate arrangements for meeting energy requirements for irrigation and to strengthen research in all aspects of water technology.) (WFC VII, para. 2)	river development but excluding rural water supply) amounted to $812 million in 1974, $866 million in 1975, $840 million in 1976 and a preliminary figure of $1483 million in 1977. Over the four-year period, 1974-1977, the World Bank committed $2246 million or 56% of the total. Multilateral agencies taken as a whole contributed $295 million for water development over the four-year period, or 73.5% of the total.

Pesticides

FAO in cooperation with UNEP, WHO and UNIDO to convene an ad hoc consultation, including member Governments and industry to recommend ways and means to give effect to the intentions of the resolution on pesticides. (WFC X, para. 4)	The FAO Conference at its eighteenth Session in November 1975, supported the recommendation of the "Ad Hoc Government Consultation on Pesticides in Agriculture and Public Health", which had been convened in April 1975 in response to this Resolution. However there have been some shifts in emphasis since, due to world-wide developments characterized by adequate availability with minor exceptions, of key agricultural pesticides at persistently higher prices. Efforts were undertaken to collect information on the pesticide supply and demand situation, but this matter proved so complex that no satisfactory results were achieved. Also in view of the current lack of interest in the matter, this activity will

DECISIONS	IMPLEMENTATION

not be pursued. There are
also serious problems of
inadequate trained manpower,
infrastructure and hard cur-
rency resources, especially in
MSA countries, to use pesticides efficiently and in
conjunction with other appropriate plant protection measures.

As a further follow up of
these activities, an intergovernmental ad hoc consultation on the official registra-
tion of pesticides was held in
Rome in October 1977, which
was attended by some 50 countries, representatives of
United Nations agencies and of
industry. The consultation
accepted that there was a need
to support technical services
behind the use of pesticides
and to strengthen the arrangements in developing countries
for supervision of their
introduction and use.

The requested action pro-
grammes for (1) the development and application of integrated pest control in agriculture and (2) the international programme on horizontal resistance, are actively implemented. Field projects are established in
Brazil, Zambia, Ethiopia, East
Africa, and the Near East, and
are in an advanced stage of
negotiation in the Sahelian
zone and South East Asia.

DECISIONS	IMPLEMENTATION

Programme for Control of African Animal Trypanosomiasis

FAO in cooperation with the Government of the countries concerned, interested international organizations and specialized research institutes and with the support of bilateral and multilateral assistance agencies, launch as a matter of urgency a long-term programme for the control of African animal trypanosomiasis as a project of high priority.
(WFC XI, para. 1)

The Second Consultation of Experts from African Member Nations, attended also by observers from international and regional organizations and assistance agencies, was convened in December 1978 to plan further implementation of the Programme and advise on its management.
Cooperation has been developed with the Organization of African Unity/Scientific, Technical and Research Commission (OAU/STRC) through reciprocal participation in technical meetings and planning of joint action, carried out to advise Governments on the establishment of national control services and to assist in the preparation of control programmes in Benin, Cameroon, Ethiopia, Guinea, Malawi, Mozambique, Niger, Sudan, and Zambia.

Immediate establishment of a small coordinating unit at FAO headquarters to start the first phase of the programme devoted to training, pilot field control projects and applied research, in preparation for future large-scale operations.
(WFC XI, para. 2)

A Coordinating Unit has been established at FAO headquarters, with an outposted officer in the FAO Regional Office for Africa. Courses and seminars for training have been organized in cooperation with WHO, OAU and French, German and British assistance. The preparation of training manuals has been initiated. An information and news service on tsetse sponsored by FAO, WHO, OAU and the Government of the United Kingdom commenced at the end of 1978.

DECISIONS	IMPLEMENTATION

FAO take immediately the necessary steps to mobilize the funds and services required for the programme. (WFC XI, para. 3)

Research contracts have been granted to various African applied research institutes and special efforts have been made to improve exchange of information among all international and national organizations and institutes interested in trypanosomiasis research particularly, WHO International Atomic Energy Agency, International Laboratory for Research on Animal Diseases, International Livestock Centre for Africa, International Centre for Insect Physiology and Ecology, Centre for Overseas Pest Research (Overseas Development Ministry, UK), Institut d'Elevage et de Medecine Veterinaire des Pays Tropicaux (France), University of Wageningen in the Netherlands and the German Agency for Technical Cooperation (GTZ). A tsetse control pilot scheme is in implementation in Niger. Preparatory surveys have been initiated in Mozambique and Ivory Coast. Interested assistance agencies have been approached through personal visits and participation in the meeting of the European Donor Agencies, especially devoted this year to trypanosomiasis control. A meeting of representatives of assistance agencies interested in trypanosomiasis is planned to be convened in 1979 to discuss the funding and management of the programme.

DECISIONS	IMPLEMENTATION

NUTRITION AND THE ERADICATION OF MALNUTRITION

Policies and Programmes to Improve Nutrition

That FAO, in cooperation with WHO, UNICEF, WFP, IBRD, UNDP and UNESCO, assisted by PAG, prepare a project proposal for assisting Governments to develop inter-sectoral food and nutrition plans. (WFC V, para. 2)

Following meetings in 1975, an Interagency Working Session on Country Action and Priorities in Relation to Nutrition Planning Support was held in Rome in June 1976, which identified a number of countries as suitable points for concentration and integration of interagency efforts. Activities in 1976-78 involved application of the new approach to nutrition improvement when providing nutrition planning (NP) support to countries as part of sectoral and overall national development plans, formulating the nutrition components of these plans and training of national personnel in 10 countries. A sub-regional seminar on food Economics and Nutrition Policy for countries of French speaking Africa was held in Senegal in October 1978.

Through bilateral and multilateral action, in particular by FAO, WHO, WFP, UNICEF, UNDP, the World Bank and IFAD, developing countries be assisted upon request to develop and implement nutrition plans and policies and practical programmes and projects, if necessary through an increased priority on the part of the agencies. (WFCL Manila Communique, para. 13)

The ACC Sub-Committee on Nutrition has taken this as its first main task; different concerned agencies and organizations of the United Nations system aim to develop a consistent approach in their response to requests from developing countries. The Sub-Committee will prepare a statement as the common approach that could be used by all agencies. In this context FAO Conference Resolution (8/77) on Nutrition

DECISIONS	IMPLEMENTATION

| | places emphasis on assisting developing countries in planning and implementing nutrition projects, more especially as part of agricultural and rural development. Assistance has been focussed on the building up or strengthening of national capacity to formulate and carry out their own programmes for improving nutrition. Twelve countries have been given assistance and there is evidence that requests from a number of additional countries will be received in 1979. |
| Within the Framework of agency responsibilities for specific fields indicated by resolution V of the World Food Conference and within the framework of any new coordination mechanism that the Economic and Social Council may decide upon, the agencies mentioned in that resolution and ILO, should develop their capacity to respond to requests by Governments for nutrition improvement programmes to provide direct and speedy assistance to the populations in greatest need and these agencies through the new institutional arrangements, inform the World Food Council at its fourth session of the action they have undertaken. (WFCL Manila Communique, para. 14) | In response to the recommendation of its ad hoc Committee on Food and Nutrition Policies, FAO has introduced nutrition in the terms of reference of the Working Group on Rural Development in order to systematically take nutrition into consideration when planning agricultural and rural development. Additional funds were made available directly from the regular programme and also from TCP to allow timely response to requests for assistance. |

DECISIONS	IMPLEMENTATION
FAO, UNICEF, WHO, WFP, UNESCO, The World Bank, in cooperation with bilateral and non-governmental agencies in developing and developed countries prepare a systematic evaluation of the experience gained in the field of nutrition intervention programmes, identifying opportunities for immediate and future action to advance nutrition, the findings and action proposals emerging from this evaluation to be presented to the World Food Council at its fourth session. (WFCL Manila Communique, para. 15)	The ACC Sub-Committee on Nutrition, together with its Advisory Group on Nutrition, considered a useful report by a consultant. The next step would be to obtain the views of national planners, administrators and managers of nutrition programmes, as to what level of cooperation they hope to receive from the United Nations system, as well as on nutrition planning and inclusion of nutritional objectives in agricultural and rural development.
FAO, in close collaboration with other concerned United Nations Agencies, through the new institutional arrangements, formulate programmes and projects for international cooperation in the field of nutrition and report to the World Food Council at its fourth session for further consideration. (WFCL Manila Communique, para. 16)	The ACC Sub-Committee on Nutrition, in its recommendations to the World Food Council for possible actions by Governments to improve nutrition, has observed that such improvement depends primarily on policies and programmes of each country, and external agencies can do little by themselves. The agencies have no executive powers and cooperate with countries in the framework of country programming. The Sub-Committee has therefore recommended illustrative types of action that need to be taken at country level as the first essential step. As the next step, the Sub-Committee has decided to study realizable goals in nutrition that could be useful to countries setting their own goals as well as to the inter-

DECISIONS	IMPLEMENTATION
	national community. It will continue to examine what can be done to overcome the main constraints on more rapid improvement of the nutrition situation.
International organizations and bilateral donors assess the nutritional impact of their existing development programmes and incorporate nutritional considerations into their planning and programme preparation. (WFCL Manila Communique, para. 17)	The ACC Sub-Committee on Nutrition has already focussed attention on this recommendation. At its third meeting, an FAO paper "Towards Criteria and Practical Procedures for Systematic Introduction of Nutrition Considerations in the Preparation and Appraisal of Agriculture Projects" was discussed. At its fourth meeting FAO presented a draft for field testing of "Guidelines for the Introduction of Nutrition consideration into Development Projects". FAO jointly with WFP has initiated impact evaluation studies on food for work and supplementary feeding projects in Egypt and Lesotho.
FAO review its present programmes to assess their impact on the nutritional status of the rural and urban poor and suggest methods for ensuring that nutritional considerations are included in FAO's programmes and projects. (FAOC 8/77)	The FAO Conference in 1977 passed a resolution 8/77 on Nutrition which requires (a) nutrition impact evaluation of FAO on-going field projects (b) the development of methodology for integrating nutrition considerations in agriculture and rural development programmes and (c) establishment of a mechanism in FAO for explicit inclusion of nutrition objectives in appropriate FAO programmes. Action taken in 1978 were desk studies on nutrition impact evaluation of

DECISIONS	IMPLEMENTATION

| | 40 projects in 9 countries; in-depth studies of projects in 2 countries; preparation of draft guidelines for integrating nutrition considerations in agriculture projects, and; initiation of activities towards (a) field application of guidelines, (b) assistance to Ministries of Agriculture and (c) training in this important activity. A study kit for training in this subject was prepared by FAO jointly with the Nutrition Planning Unit of the London School of Hygiene and Tropical Medicine. Training packages on nutrition programme management were developed and a nutrition training course for field-level agricultural staff was organized in Africa, to assist countries in planning and implementing nutrition activities within agricultural programmes. |
| That the international agencies, non-governmental agencies and countries which are in a position to provide funds and foods for this purpose, should provide assistance to Governments who will request such aid in order to introduce in the period 1975-76, emergency programmes for supplementary feeding of a substantial number of the malnourished children with due attention to basic health and other essential services for the welfare of all children at risk. (WFC V, para. 8) | As of 30 September 1978, beneficiaries actually reached through ongoing vulnerable group feeding projects in 1978 amounted to about 15 million, as compared to about 8.3 million in 1976 and 12 million in 1977. FAO is assisting developing countries in the formulation of their nutrition programme for the International Year of the Child. |

DECISIONS	IMPLEMENTATION
That FAO, in association with other international and non-governmental organizations concerned, undertakes an inventory of vegetable food resources other than cereals, such as roots, tubers, legumes, vegetables and fruits, including also those from unconventional sources, and that it studies the possibility of increasing their production and conumption, particularly in countries where malnutrition prevails. (WFC V, para. 10)	Work on the elaboration of a matrix giving specific information on fruits and vegetables has been completed. Arrangements to hold technical meetings and develop projects at subregional and regional levels to intensify their production and utilization, genetic improvement, and economic importance, have been made. An Expert Consultation on Grain Legume Processing was organized which assessed available technologies for their utilization in developing countries with a view to reducing post-harvest losses, increasing milling yields and improving manufacture of legume-based products. An Expert Consultation on Food Legume Production and Improvement will be held in February 1979.
That Governments take action to strengthen and modernize consumer education services, food legislation and food control programmes and the relevant aspects of marketing practices, aiming at the protection of the consumer (avoiding false and misleading information from mass-media and commercial fraud, and that they increase their support of the Codex Alimentarius Commission. (WFC V, para. 11)	FAO has been engaged on a number of activities to strengthen national food control capabilities to better protect consumers from food hazards and commercial fraud, and to develop food industry and trade in developing countries. These include advice and assistance on updating food legislation, training of food-control administrators, inspectors and analysts, strengthening food control laboratories and advice on organization of food control infrastructure. Assistance and advice have been given to decrease contamination of foods by mycotoxins and other

DECISIONS	IMPLEMENTATION

<table>
<tr><td></td><td>contaminants in production, processing and marketing, and jointly with WHO the safety-in-use evaluation of food additives and contaminants including pesticides has been continued and expanded. The Codex Alimentarius Commission has 117 Governments as members. Regional Codex Co-ordinating Committees for major developing areas have been established to assist harmonization of food legislation regulations.</td></tr>
<tr><td>That the joint FAO/WHO food contamination monitoring programme, in cooperation with UNEP, be further developed in order to provide early information to the national authorities for appropriate action. (WFC V. para. 12)</td><td>The programme has completed its preparatory phase to select priorities and develop a data system to handle food contaminant monitoring information. A number of developed and developing countries have agreed to participate, collaborating centres have been designated and a control management unit set up at WHO headquarters. Pilot operations were started in mid-1977 and a guideline is in final stages of preparation which will enable participation by developing countries. To complement this effort, preparatory work is under way to develop the programme for monitoring of contamination of animal feed.</td></tr>
<tr><td>That a global nutrition surveillance system be established by FAO, WHO and UNICEF to monitor the food and nutrition conditions of the disadvantaged groups of the</td><td>WHO is the lead agency in Nutrition Surveillance which is being developed in a number of countries through different approaches. FAO's efforts include cooperation with WHO</td></tr>
</table>

DECISIONS	IMPLEMENTATION

population at risk, and to provide a method of rapid and permanent assessment of all factors which influence food consumption patterns and nutritional status.
(WFC V. para. 13)

in providing technical expertise in areas of food consumption, socio-economic and agricultural indicators and relating these to nutritional status. FAO in 1978 further clarified its priority to include assistance to governments in NS as an integral part of (a) the monitoring of agriculture and rural development programmes and (b) national nutrition policy projects. Agreement was reached on the inclusion of a nutrition module in future national agriculture statistics projects as an approach to NS; a draft manual on NS in transmigration projects was prepared.

That Governments consider establishing facilities and funds for applied nutrition research related to economic, cultural, social and medical aspects of production, processing, preservation, storage distribution and utilization of food and that FAO, WHO and UNICEF arrange for an internationally coordinated programme in applied nutritional research including establishing priorities, identifying appropriate research centres and generating the necessary fundings.
(WFC V, para. 14)

An interagency meeting on applied nutrition research in December 1975 identified some priorities in this field and formulated a proposal for interagency machinery for implementation of this decision. No further action was taken pending the setting up of new institutional machinery for nutrition in the United Nations system, viz. the ACC Sub-Committee on Nutrition which will need to locate resources to undertake this research.
The Advisory Group on Nutrition of the Sub-Committee at its first session has drawn an over-all programme including priorities for research in nutrition.
Economic aspects of human

DECISIONS	IMPLEMENTATION

| | lactation were reviewed on the basis of field investigations conducted in Ghana and Ivory Coast. |

ARRANGEMENTS FOR FOLLOW-UP ACTION INCLUDING APPROPRIATE MACHINERY

FAO establish a Committee on World Food Security as a standing committee of the FAO Council. The Committee should submit periodic and special reports to the World Food Council. (WFC XXII, para. 5)	The FAO Conference at its eighteenth session in November 1975 established the Committee on World Food Security as a Standing Committee of the FAO Council charged with the functions suggested in the resolution.
FAO to initiate urgent steps, through its Commission on Fertilizers, for following up on Conference resolution III on Fertilizers, and to take appropriate initiatives with respect to fertilizers, pesticides, fungicides and herbicides, working in close cooperation with UNIDO and IBRD, and other agencies. (WFC XXII, para. 9)	See above under Fertilizers.
FAO to examine its ability to follow up on Conference resolution XVI on the Global Information System and Early-Warning System in Food and Agriculture with a view to recommending to the FAO Council, at its sixty-fourth session in 1975, any new arrangements which may be necessary. (WFC XXII, para. 10)	See above under Global Information and Early Warning System.

DECISIONS	IMPLEMENTATION

Economic and Social Council to consider on an urgent basis, and make recommendations, whether or not rearrangements in the United Nations system or new institutional bodies may be justified in order to ensure effective follow up on Conference resolution V on nutrition.
(WFC XXII, para. 11)

An ACC Sub-Committee on Nutrition has been established in compliance with this resolution. (See above in the section on Nutrition).

The Consultative Group on International Agricultural Research (CGIAR) and the Technical Advisory Committee to assume leadership in following up on the research aspect of Conference resolution IV on research.
(WFC XXII, para. 12; FAOC 4/75)

Each of the co-sponsors of the CGIAR viz. FAO World Bank and UNDP, has its own unique role in the field of international agricultural research which each is pursuing vigorously in addition to their continuing joint activities through the Group itself.

FAO, IBRD, UNDP and other relevant international organizations and interested Governments to investigate the desirability of introducing an organizational approach, along the lines of the Consultative Group - Technical Advisory Committee for Agricultural Research, for other sectors such as extension, agricultural credit and rural development.
(WFC XXII, para. 13; FAO 4/75)

For agricultural extension, education and training, FAO, ILO and UNESCO, have established a Working Group on Agricultural Education, Science and Training which considers all questions relating to research evaluation and policy developments in these areas with the help of a Joint Advisory Committee. This Working Group also considers problems of organizational approaches in these fields. A Task Force on Rural Development has been created by the ACC to deal with matters concerning rural development on an interagency basis. In the field of agricultural credit and banking, FAO has set up a Scheme for Agri-

DECISIONS	IMPLEMENTATION

cultural Credit Development (SACRED) under which FAO has established consultative relationships with financial institutions in the developed countries. At the same time, FAO has supported the organization of four Regional Agricultural Credit Associations with membership extended to all the financial institutions in developing countries including central banks. FAO arranges ad hoc consultations on SACRED wherein other international organizations, together with national institutions from both developed and developing countries have an opportunity to redirect their policies and programmes.

The IBRD, FAO and UNDP to organize a Consultative Group on Food Production and Investment in Developing Countries (CGFPI), to be composed of bilateral and multilateral donors and representatives of developing countries, chosen as in the case of the CGIAR, to be staffed jointly by the IBRD, FAO and UNDP. (WFC XXII, para. 14)

The FAO Council at its sixty-fourth session in November 1974, approved the participation of FAO in an appropriate capacity in organizing the Consultative Group on Food Production and Investment. During January and February 1975, the representatives of the three sponsoring agencies, viz. FAO, IBRD and UNDP, met in Washington to develop general operating procedures of the CGFPI. The first session of the CGFPI was held in July 1975, the second in February 1976 and the third in September 1976.

The main functions of the CGFPI should be (a) to encourage a larger flow of external resources for food production,

At the fourth session of the CGFPI, held in Washington in September 1977, it was agreed that the three co-sponsors of

DECISIONS	IMPLEMENTATION

(b) to improve the coordination of activities of different multilateral and bilateral
donors providing financial and
technical assistance for food
production and (c) to ensure a
more effective use of available resources.
(WFC XXII, para. 15)

the CGFPI, namely FAO, UNDP
and the World Bank, would
evaluate the activities of the
CGFPI before the end of 1977.
The evaluation report concluded that the terms of
reference of the CGFPI are so
wide as to be unattainable
given the Consultative Group's
resources, and it must rely on
the co-sponsors or other
agencies to carry out much of
its work, and can have only
marginal influence on the
decisions of the Governments
of developing and donor countries, or of multilateral
agencies, about the levels and
kinds of investment in food
production and nutrition.
Assistance to Governments
wishing to develop investment
strategies to increase food
production and to improve
nutrition can be provided
through established channels
by other agencies including
FAO, UNDP, the World Bank and
other development banks, IFAD
and bilateral donors. It
would be neither practicable,
nor in accordance with the
wishes of most participants,
to increase the budgetary and
staff resources of the CGFPI
sufficiently to permit it to
have a decisive impact, and to
do so would lead to duplica-
tion with the work of the
organizations mentioned. The
report therefore recommended
that the CGFPI be disbanded,
with appropriate arrangements
to ensure an orderly phasing

DECISIONS	IMPLEMENTATION

out of its activities.
The executive heads of the
three co-sponsors have endorsed the above recommendations, and have taken the
necessary steps to wind up the
CGFPI (also see above under
Increased resources for food
and agricultural production).

5 Current Efforts—
Progress Reports

The World Food Council, the International Fund for Agricultural
Development, the United Nations Development Programme and a
number of States report on current actions in progress to
eradicate hunger and to assist agricultural development, internationally and domestically.

REPORTS OF THE SPECIALIZED AGENCIES

Report of the World Food Council (A/AC.191/35)

In its Mexico Declaration, the World Food Council sought to
address the problems of hunger and inadequate action to overcome it in the most effective way possible. Bearing in mind
the Secretary-General's emphasis that the search for a meaningful and positive consensus among Governments is at the heart of
its work, the Council of 36 ministers and plenipotentiaries
exerted itself strenuously to find agreement which really had
the assent of its member Governments, and consequently represented a realistic and practicable approach to action.
     The Council turned its first attention to the problem of
increasing production in the developing countries as a whole,
which is universally agreed to be the basis of a solution to
the world food problem. In addressing this problem, the Council noted that developing and developed countries tend to have
different explanations for the slow progress in improving food
production. Developing countries tend to focus on inadequate
support from the developed countries. Developed countries, on
the other hand, maintain that the fundamental cause is to be
found in inadequate commitment and action by developing countries. International agencies point out that their priorities

are determined by member countries and that the agencies are
doing what they can within the resources available to them.
Thus, we have a situation in which all participants see themselves as doing not too badly and yet the over-all results are
less than adequate to the food needs of hundreds of millions of
people. In an effort to overcome these difficulties and reach
common agreement on the necessary action, the Council called
for a series of meetings between developing countries in regional groupings, donors both new and old, and international
agencies.

These consultations are under way. Representatives of
various groups are invited to participate with the World Food
Council in developing action proposals which will have the commitment of all those involved and which should lead to more
effective efforts to give priority to food production and reverse the deteriorating trend of increasing hunger and malnutrition in low-income regions. Especially, the consultations
include:

> Meetings of developing countries which will take place in
> three regional groupings - Africa, Asia and Latin Amer-
> ica - in co-operation with the development banks and the
> United Nations regional commissions. These consultations
> have been scheduled in Manila, Philippines (27-29 March),
> Abidjan, Ivory Coast (5-7 March) and Port-of-Spain,
> Trinidad and Tobago (19-20 February). The Economic Com-
> mission for Western Asia will also make a contribution;

> The Development Assistance Committee of the Organization
> for Economic Co-operation and Development (OECD) discussed
> the issues in Paris at the end of January;

> The secretariat of the Special Fund of the Organization of
> Petroleum Exporting Countries (OPEC) will co-ordinate the
> views of the OPEC countries at meetings in January and
> March;

> The Executive Director of the World Food Council will seek
> the views of the major development financing institutions,
> the Food and Agriculture Organization of the United Na-
> tions and the United Nations Development Programme, in a
> meeting at the World Bank in late February;

> The Governments of China and the socialist members of the
> World Food Council - the USSR, the German Democratic Re-
> public, Poland, Yugoslavia - have been asked for their
> views and recommendations on the world food problem.

The views of the various group consultations will be brought
together at a meeting to be held at Bellagio, Italy, in early
April. On the basis of this meeting, it is hoped to develop
constructive proposals on which the Council can reach agreement
at this year's Fifth Ministerial Session, to be held from 4 to 7
September at Ottawa.

Effective action must take place at the country level.
The Council therefore called for the development of specific
food production and improved nutrition plans by food-priority
countries. These countries will need assistance both in formulating and implementing such plans. For this they look to
the major international agencies and to bilateral donors: the
Council stands ready to help when called upon.

Increased food production in the developing countries will
not be enough unless it is accompanied by improvements in food
distribution and actions to ensure that food reaches those who
need it most. The Council, with this in mind, has asked that
the United Nations system make the eradication of hunger and
malnutrition a major objective.

The Council also asked the ACC Sub-Committee on Nutrition
to prepare a programme of work identifying the resources and
mechanisms necessary for a more effective attack on malnutrition.

The Council also asked Governments to accept the goal of
eradicating, within a decade, severe vitamin A deficiency,
which causes blindness in 100,000 children every year, and endemic goitre which affects 200 million people. It asked the
World Health Organization to put forward specific proposals for
an international effort to this end.

The President and the Executive Director of the World Food
Council have discussed this recommendation with the Director-
General of the World Health Organization (WHO), Dr. Mahler, who
welcomed the WFC initiative and described as "scandalous" the
continuing existence of endemic goitre as a major nutri-
tion/health problem affecting 200 million people, while effective low-cost means are available to control this nutritional deficiency within a few years. Early this year the Executive Director of the United Nations Children's Fund (UNICEF),
Mr. Labouisse, publicly referred to endemic goitre as a problem
"so easy to prevent that it is a crime to let a single child be
born mentally handicapped for that reason".

Seeing a lack of commitment to major action as the most
important constraint to progress in goitre control, Dr. Mahler
agreed that WHO would take the lead role in an international
effort to stimulate government action and co-operate with countries in programmes aimed at eradicating goitre within a
decade.

Dr. Mahler and the WFC Executive Director agreed on the
first phase of the international goitre effort: a three-
pronged approach by WHO, UNICEF and WFC to 19 countries having
a major goitre problem will endeavour to build broadly based
political support for goitre action at country level. Dr. Mahler
wrote to ministers of health; Mr. Labouisse to ministers of
planning; and President Arturo R. Tanco of WFC to ministers of
agriculture, or, in some cases, Heads of State or Government.
President Tanco's letter emphasized the unique opportunity for

Governments and the world community to demonstrate that they can deal with an important aspect of malnutrition, and indicated the possibility that a successful attack on endemic goitre could lead the way to new approaches to international co-operation in dealing with other, more complex food and nutrition problems. On the basis of the response to this first step, WHO, in co-operation with WFC, will develop a detailed international action programme.

The World Health Organization is also undertaking a further study of the problems of overcoming vitamin A deficiency, which require some further examination in detail before action is practical.

In relation to issues of food security, food aid and food trade, the Council noted with concern the delay in the negotiations proceeding in other forums. Not wishing to complicate these negotiations, the Council refrained from detailed suggestions but it called on Governments to undertake new initiatives so as to achieve agreement on an adequate system of grain reserves. The Council was also concerned to facilitate the establishment of a new 10 million ton food aid convention. Without an adequate system of grain reserves, and a binding food aid convention, the world lacks food security and millions are exposed to the future risk of starvation.

At the time of writing this report, the outcome of those negotiations is uncertain. While respecting the wish of the Council not to complicate these important negotiations, the President and the Executive Director have taken some important initiatives to assist them.

> When it became apparent that existing donors were unlikely to contribute sufficient grain to a food aid convention to achieve the target of 10 million tons, the Executive Director initiated approaches to a number of OPEC donors, urging them to consider a contribution. This action was in accordance with World Food Conference resolution XVIII, which envisaged contributions to the target in terms of both commodities and financial assistance. The outcome of this initiative is not yet clear, and it may be possible to report further when the Committee meets.

> When the Geneva negotiations reached a critical phase on 9 February, the WFC President cabled the Chairman of the Conference and a number of key Governments, urging them to exert every effort to compromise on an effective world food reserve system while food grain supplies were ample for the purpose, and pointing out that those who refused cooperation would bear a heavy responsibility. The Executive Director supplemented this action by personal consultations in Geneva with a number of representatives of Governments and agencies concerned with the negotiations.

When the Negotiating Conference dissolved without reaching any agreement, the WFC President and Executive Director again called on Governments to review their positions and find a solution. They urged that the developed countries and others in a position to do so should unilaterally commit the higher levels of food aid informally pledged at the Geneva negotiations, and preferably express them as amendments to the 1971 Food Aid Convention. They also called on the wheat-exporting countries to individually establish reserves and maintain production at levels necessary to prevent recurrence of the tragedy experienced by the world in the period 1972-1974.

The Council is now assessing lines of future action urgently to strengthen international means of ensuring food security in order that people in all countries, rich and poor alike, can provide their families and themselves with the food they need at reasonable prices.

The Council also noted that the 500,000 ton Emergency Reserve established by the General Assembly at its seventh special session was originally envisaged as an interim measure pending the establishment of an effective system of world food security. It is now clear, however, that any system of international food security reserves which may emerge will still leave a continuing need for the 500,000 ton Emergency Reserve to provide assistance in emergency situations which do not affect the total international grain system. The Council, therefore, recommended that the General Assembly should now establish this reserve on a permanent basis. The Committee will be aware that the General Assembly approved this recommendation and urged Governments to implement it fully.

At this time which is midway between the fourth and fifth sessions of the Council, it may be useful to the Committee of the Whole to make the following observations on the current situation.

Endorsement of the Mexico Declaration by the General Assembly establishes the basis for a framework of action within which Governments and agencies can renew their efforts to mount a concerted attack on hunger and malnutrition. The consultations on food production which the Council has initiated have a key role in achieving this concerted action. Differences in perception of the problem between developing and developed countries are a significant part of the problem of inadequate priority for food production. These different perceptions lead to misunderstandings and retard progress. The programme of consultations which the Council has initiated aims at building common understanding of the problems and achieving meaningful agreement on the necessary actions to be taken. There is good reason to hope that these consultations will be successful in giving new momentum to the drive to increase food production.

The issue facing the international community is whether the potential for increasing food production in low-income

countries can be realized. The stakes are unmistakably high.
Present trends and policies mean a continuing deterioration of
food security and nutritional standards in many low-income
countries, and especially among poorer millions in these countries. The growing number of hungry and malnourished people,
the vicious inequality and relative neglect, this is a travesty
of the idea of development. A sharp reversal of present trends
is necessary. What is needed is a greater policy commitment by
developing countries themselves and a global marshalling of the
technical, organizational and capital requirements for stepped-
up investment in food production as part of internationally
agreed programmes of development.

It is for the Government of each developing country to
take decisions as to how it will address this problem and the
precise mix of policies and practical measures which are necessary for success in the circumstances of its country. Without the right decisions fully and vigourously applied, success
is impossible; but equally, developing countries on their own
do not have the resources to undertake an adequate programme.
It is in this context that the understanding which the Council
seeks to achieve between donors and developing countries is
crucial.

These measures must be complemented by more determined
efforts to ensure that the additional food produced reaches
those most in need of it. This is the core of the nutrition
problem. While it will be taken up, to some extent, in the
consultations already described, leadership by the United Nations system has a key role in stimulating greater attention
and providing guidelines for action. The report requested by
the Council from the Sub-Committee on Nutrition should provide
a substantial input for effective action proposals to be placed
before the next meeting of the Council.

The achievement of an international system of world food
security is an inescapable imperative to enhance the capability
of all nations to offset weather-induced fluctuations in production through building an internationally agreed system of
reserve stocks and enhancing international trade opportunities.
Many nations are in a position to rely on trade and financial
reserves to meet shortfalls in their food production, providing
there is assurance of access to essential supplies in time of
need. The reduction of trade barriers in a more open world
market system strengthens world food security, but an adequate
system of grain reserves is essential to help avoid wide swings
in prices, which are so disruptive to production incentives on
the down swing, and to the essential needs of consumers when
prices are flagrantly high - and per capita consumption levels
of the poor are forced to adjust downward from already unac-
ceptably low levels.

If the present negotiating framework is unable to achieve
food security, the Council will, reluctantly, be forced to consider whether that objective should be pursued in some other
framework. The Council will, in any case, continue its efforts

to promote the realization of the 10 million ton food aid
target.

The eradication of hunger and malnutrition must be a key
element in the development strategy for the third United Nations Development Decade - indeed, it may well be our central
preoccupation until the year 2000, for success will take time.
This commitment and the mobilization of resources to eradicate
hunger from the face of the globe can be accomplished. There
is a widespread recognition that continuation of the present
situation in which millions live in destitution without hope of
a better future is neither just nor prudent. There is general
agreement that the international community must act to eradicate hunger and malnutrition and overcome poverty. There is a
general understanding of the measures which must be taken both
nationally and internationally to achieve this objective, and
there is a willingness in principle to move in this direction.
What is needed is agreement on the precise measures that have
to be taken to translate willingness in principle into action
in practice.

The World Food Council has a vital role to play in achieving that agreement. The Council, being composed of Governments,
must work by consensus and persuasion. As a specialized body,
standing apart both from operational responsibilities and wider
international concerns, it has the opportunity to encourage
agreement quietly.

Statement by Mr. S. Aziz of IFAD

IFAD began its operations on 13 December 1977, when the Fund's
Governing Council held its first session and the Executive
Board and the first President of the Fund were elected. The
Fund's Executive Board consists of eighteen members and seventeen alternates. The total membership of the Fund has now
reached 126. Of these, 120 states have completed all necessary
formalities and are already members of the Fund. The remaining
states have yet to complete the legal steps necessary to become
members.

The initial resources pledged to the Fund are slightly
more than one billion dollars with 56.5 percent contributed by
developed (OECD) countries, 43.5 percent by developing contributing countries (i.e. the Oil Exporting Countries (OPEC)) and
an additional 2 percent by developing recipient countries.

In 1978 the Fund has committed $117.0 million for 10 pro-
jects in cooperation with other financing institutions.

For 1979, the Executive Board has endorsed a target of
$375 million. this will mean a total commitment level of $500
million in the first two years, or half the Fund's total resources.

According to the Fund's Articles of Agreement, the adequacy of the Fund's resources will be reviewed by the Governing
Council periodically. The first such review is to take place

at the next session of the Governing Council before the end of
1979.
     The contribution which IFAD can make to the resolution of
the world food problem will depend very much on the timing and
level of the replenishment of its resources.

Statement by Mr. Bradford Morse of UNDP

The UNDP has long placed its strongest emphasis on technical
co-operation in the agricultural sector. The percentage of
expenditure at the country level for the agricultural sector as
a whole remains about 30% of the total UNDP commitments and the
Food and Agriculture Organization of the United Nations has
since UNDP's founding been our leading executing agency, ac-
counting for more project expenditure than any other. About
half of this expenditure is directly committed to food and nutrition projects while much of the balance, in such areas as
agricultural research, training, soil surveys and rural development, can be expected to have a major impact upon food production. Activities in other sectors, such as the local manufacture of agricultural implements, production of fertilizers
and pesticides, also contribute directly to food production,
while UNDP-financed assistance also strengthens essential institutions in agricultural planning and marketing. Since the
World Food Conference in 1974 heightened the general appreciation of the urgency for increasing and sustaining food production and distribution, UNDP-supported country programmes
have shown particularly in the food priority countries, an increase in the proportionate share of planned expenditures for
agriculture. UNDP's regional and global programmes have responded rapidly to the call for intensification of efforts on
food and nutrition. In 1978, 54% of our interregional and
global commitment was devoted to agriculture, virtually all of
it directly related to food and nutrition.
     Many UNDP-financed technical co-operation projects are
intended to prepare for investments in food and agricultural
production. Between 1973 and 1977, reported investment commitments in food production and nutrition for which the ground
work was done by UNDP-supported pre-investment activity amounting to $2,110 million. In 26 of the 43 food priority countries
identified by the World Food Council, there appears to be a
substantial shift in investment based on UNDP projects during
the period 1973-1977, reflecting a heightened priority for investment in food and nutrition in these countries. Currently
UNDP is financing some 70-80 projects in 46 countries and regions which are designed to attract further investment to food
production and nutrition. UNDP hopes that multilateral and
bilateral sources, as well as the private sector, will review
these in order to identify investment possibilities.

FAO and UNDP have recently agreed on measures to help increase investment in food production and nutrition improvement
in developing countries. The two organizations intend to devote increased resources to the preparation of sound agricultural projects which will meet the criteria of the various
sources of finance. It is expected that the two organizations
will identify some 10 promising food production projects during
1979, and will subsequently enter into discussions with sources
of finance for follow-up action.

As I noted, UNDP has given particular emphasis to agricultural needs in the food priority countries. A recent survey of
UNDP field offices reported that the majority of developing
country Governments have taken deliberate action to accelerate
food production since the World Food Conference. Such positive
action was reported from 90% of the food priority countries and
75% of the other developing countries. A large number of Resident Representatives reported that bilateral and other multilateral programmes, as well as UNDP, reflected an increasing
emphasis on food production; again, the proportion so reported
was higher in food priority countries than in others.

Special interest exists in the four countries which prepared national food investment strategies under the auspices of
the Consultative Group on Food Production and Investment. Each
of the four countries concerned - Bangladesh, Honduras, Senegal
and Sudan - took a unique approach in preparing its strategy
based upon national needs and resources, and an analysis of
current UNDP-financed projects in these countries shows that
substantial UNDP support is directed towards the objectives
expressed in the national food investment strategy in each
country. In one case, these inputs amount to over half of all
UNDP inputs to the country.

In a related activity in the Caribbean, UNDP is financing
a major planning project executed by the Caribbean Development
Bank and designed to help reduce the dependence of the region
on food imports, which are among the highest in the world,
amounting to $80 per capita. Building on previous and ongoing
UNDP-financed assistance for regional economic integration,
crop and animal production and agricultural training, the project is assisting in preparing a Regional Food Plan with the
objective of expediting implementation of food production projects, contributing to the consolidation and co-ordination of
ongoing projects, strengthening the institutional and management structure of the Caribbean Food Corporation, and developing and disseminating agricultural production technology.
UNDP's contribution is $2,370,000 of which $2 million is
provided by the OPEC Special Fund.

A number of UNDP-supported activities concentrate on the
small producer, both in response to current trends to assist
the poorest segments in developing countries and because
greater increases in food production can often be expected from

such assistance than from strengthening already technically
advanced large-scale agricultural, livestock and fisheries enterprises. In close consultation with FAO and other concerned
agencies, UNDP strives to promote a people-oriented agricultural development strategy with emphasis on self-reliance in
food production. Since women play a significant role in small-
holder crop and livestock production systems, UNDP has strongly
support programmes aimed at enhancing the role of women in
rural communities.

With respect to crop production and protection, UNDP is
supporting efforts at all levels, from fundamental research
through operational production activities to the prevention of
losses after harvest, with current commitments of over $121
million for some 238 projects. Fundamental research is being
assisted through a number of activities in the Global programme, principally with the 11 International Centres of the
Consultative Group for International Agricultural Research.

At the applied agricultural research level, UNDP has developed, in conjunction with appropriate executing agencies and
with the Governments concerned, mechanisms for applied research
networks which maximize the use of existing national institutions and national expertise in pursuing high priority research
goals defined by the participating countries. I believe such
technical co-operation among developing countries to be a
highly effective mechanism for the effective application of a
technology to agricultural needs.

In the field of livestock production and health, over the
last 10 years UNDP has been providing assistance to 95 developing countries at a total amount of about $128 million. This
includes 228 national projects, ranging from a few fellowships
or consultancies in veterinary or animal science to large-scale
integrated animal health and production development schemes.
It includes an additional 18 regional and interregional projects in which UNDP has assisted the joint efforts of several
Governments to increase animal production and to control disease situations; and it includes one global livestock research
project. I should also mention in this connexion the $3.5 mil-
lion committed by the Capital Development Fund (CDF) for the
creation or strengthening of infrastructures and the procurement of equipment required for the implementation of livestock
development programmes.

An important part of the developing world's animal protein
requirements is supplied from the fresh and ocean waters of the
world. UNDP has taken three major steps to ensure continued
use, increased production and decreased waste of the fish products of the globe.

First, in co-operation with FAO, UNDP is revamping its
interregional fisheries development network to help the developing nations obtain greater advantage of the oceans' resources.

Second, UNDP is helping to stimulate a more rapid expansion of aquaculture throughout the world. When one considers that over 7 million tons of fish are now produced annually in fresh waters, it is evident that improved production in such waters can eventually contribute almost as much fish for human consumption as now comes from the sea.

Third, as a specific measure to help Latin American countries market their fish production, UNDP has been supporting an effort in this region that has drastically reduced the loss of fish products through lack of sales opportunities. A little over a year ago, UNDP initiated a regional fish market information service that has helped the region find a market for 100,000 tons of fish worth over $100 million. Producers are getting more for their product and the waste of fish has been virtually eliminated. We hope that the experience gained from this project will be of interest to other regions.

The fundamental importance of the forest to human well-being, in terms of soil and water production and protection, housing and fuel wood products has too often been ignored. From a socio-economic point of view, for the most deprived or poverty-stricken of our fellow human beings who are often located in remote and isolated areas, not only are the wood products of the forest of inestimable value but they also constitute reserves of food, fodder, game proteins, medicinal plants, resins and a variety of other products.

Given the need for energy conservation, increasing attention is also being given to the forestry sector because of the renewable nature of this resource. There are long-term prospects for product substitution which will reduce demands for non-renewable energy resources such as petrochemicals and certain metals. In addition, the problem of ensuring fuelwood supplies for rural populations is a subject of major concern to UNDP. The destruction of forest resources has reached such levels in some countries that millions of people can no longer count on two hot meals a day due to lack of fuelwood. UNDP is helping to investigate methods to improve the manufacture of charcoal, as well as means by which efficient wood-burning stoves can replace openfire cooking, where up to 90 percent of woodfuel energy is wasted.

UNDP is giving greater attention to critical environmental questions involving desertification and availability of water resources. Spreading desertification results from the progressive degradation of forest and shrub resources by man, his animals, and fire. Corrective policies and programmes are now being introduced in several Sahelian countries. The downstream problems of water supply for industrial and agricultural use, as well as for human consumption, are dependent on rational management of the forest resources in the upstream watersheds, and these activities are receiving greatly increased attention.

   The implementation of effective and appropriate agricultural technologies depends not only on making knowledge available to the farmers, but also on providing appropriate inputs
such as fertilizers, pesticides and agricultural machinery.
Currently UNDP is supporting over 90 projects on the production
and use of pesticides and fertilizers in developing countries.
A number of other projects strengthen the capacity of the individual countries and of technical co-operation between developing countries in the testing and local production of appropriate agricultural machinery. Action must also be taken to
ensure that the outputs from agricultural production are appropriately handled. UNDP is currently supporting 28 projects
related to storage of staple foods and a further 80 projects on
the marketing of agricultural products, principally foods. The
end point of all these activities is, of course, the enhanced
nutrition of the population, and to this end UNDP is currently
assisting 46 projects in nutrition policy and implementation.
Total UNDP inputs to these fields of activity exceed $40
million.
   In its approach to the problems of food production and
distribution, UNDP has the advantage of a special perspective.
Our country programming process encourages a comprehensive,
interdisciplinary approach. Our network of field offices provides us with on-the-spot means to help countries meet their
priority needs. Our evaluation studies, several of them closely related to food and agricultural problems draw upon our widespread experience, strengthen our institutional memory and help
to strengthen the capacity of responsible Governmental institutions to undertake their own evaluation efforts. UNDP also
functions as a liaison between Governments of the developing
countries and other Agencies within the UN system. In the case
of the World Food Programme for example, specific instructions
have been issued by the Executive Heads of UNDP and WFP to UNDP
Resident Representatives and to WFP field staff concerning the
co-ordination of UNDP and WFP assistance within the context of
country programming.
   We are seeking to enlarge further the scope and range of
our co-operation with developing countries on issues related to
food production and distribution. We intend to participate
actively in the forthcoming World Conference on Agrarian Reform
and Rural Development, and we will stand ready to assist in any
way we can in the implementation of its recommendations. But I
must stress that despite all that is now being done to assist
the food production efforts of developing countries, those countries will continue to lose ground in the race against hunger
until the practical capacity of technical co-operation to assist
them along the lines I have just described is substantially
strengthened. I believe that this Committee therefore has a
major obligation to identify means for effecting an increased
transfer of resources to meet food production needs so that the

important work of feeding our children and their children after
them can go forward on a new and expanded basis.

REPORTS OF THE STATES

The United States: Ms. Melissa Wells

The United States, in addition to its bilateral and multilateral assistance for food and agriculture development and its
food aid programs, is prepared to participate with other donor
countries and international organizations to assist food-
priority countries in developing food and nutrition strategies.
We also provide appropriate technical assistance to individual
countries in pursuing many of the above objectives. The United
States through its assistance programs, its training and research efforts in colleges and universities -- both in the U.S.
and abroad -- and its support of international agricultural
research centers makes a significant contribution to agricultural research efforts, many of which are particularly relevant
to the needs of developing countries.
     The Institute for Technological Cooperation which President
Carter has proposed, will devote considerable attention to research on food and agriculture problems faced by developing
countries. That the Administration is proposing to Congress
the creation of such an institute in a period of severe budgetary stringency demonstrates clearly the importance it attaches
to increased research on problems affecting developing countries and the application of relevant technology to solving
them.
     The United States notes with satisfaction that many devel-
oping countries have had notable successes in applying appropriate technology to their agricultural sectors. We believe
that this experience is especially useful to other developing
countries. In this regard the United States strongly supports
technical cooperation among developing countries in the food
and agriculture areas.
     The United States has recently completed a major policy
review of its attitude toward TCDC. As a result of this review
of existing U.S. Development policies, we have decided to amend
a number of those policies so that they will be more responsive
to requests from the developing world for TCDC support. The
food and agriculture sector is one which we will be examining
closely for opportunities to increase support for TCDC.
     The United States will continue to make major contribu-
tions to programs designed to foster global agricultural development. Our 1979 bilateral aid program contains abut $685 mil-
lion in food and agricultural development programs. We are
contributing $800 million per year from 1979 through 1980 to

the fifth replenishment of the International Development Association, about 30 percent of whose funds are distributed on a
concessional basis for food and agricultural projects in the
most needy countries, and will take a sizable share of the
sixth replenishment which is currently being negotiated. We
also have participated constructively in negotiations which
resulted in agreements for the replenishments of the resources
of the Inter American Development Bank, the Asian Development
Bank and the African Development Fund. All of these replenishments will allow the respective institutions to increase their
lending in real terms. All of them are devoting increasing
attention to food and agriculture. The United States contributed $200 million to the International Fund for Agricultural
Development.

Our PL-480 program will provide in excess of $1.4 billion
in food aid this year. Our programs are designed primarily to
meet humanitarian and developmental needs and we are working to
strengthen the developmental component of our food aid.

We announced yesterday at the International Wheat Council
meeting in London that, despite the failure of the UNCTAD Conference to achieve a new Food Aid Convention, the United States
will pledge to provide a minimum cereal food aid flow of 4.47
million metric tons per year. We are prepared to conclude a
new Food Aid Convention in June of this year, if other nations
are willing to do so. Regardless of whether a new Food Aid
Convention is achieved, we urge other countries to increase
their food aid pledges or to become new donors so that the
World Food Conference's target of 10 MMT will be reached.

Food security requires that adequate supplies be available
in the event of shortfall in production caused by adverse
weather or calamities. Such reserves should be adequate to
prevent extreme swings in prices that create economic hardship
for the poor in all nations.

The United States already has established a government-
supported, farmer-owned grain reserve. In determining the size
of this reserve, the U.S. takes into account the current and
projected levels of world consumption of grains and other
stocks in the U.S. and abroad. This reserve, which now consists of approximately 11 million metric tons of wheat and 22
million metric tons of coarse grains, constitutes a partial
buffer against world food shortages. Moreover, the Carter Administration is seeking to establish a special government-owned
wheat reserve to ensure that the U.S. will be able to meet its
international food aid commitments even in the event of a substantial shortfall in wheat production. Such a reserve would
be an additional contribution to food security for developing
food-deficit countries. The U.S. hopes that other food-aid
donors will undertake similar measures.

The responsibility for effective global food security must
be shared widely. Therefore, the United States would like to

conclude a new International Wheat Agreement which would include a coordinated system of nationally-held reserve stocks.
We are disappointed that the recent round of UNCTAD negotiations to achieve a new International Wheat Agreement and a new
Food Aid Convention (FAC) were not successful. We urge all
participants in the UNCTAD negotiations to strive to create the
conditions which will permit the negotiations to resume as soon
as possible.

New Zealand: Mr. H. H. Francis

The perception of the importance of agriculture is reflected in
New Zealand's approach to the formulation of a new International
Development Strategy for the 1980s. It has helped to shape our
development assistance policies and programmes in the 1970s.
Almost one-third of New Zealand's bilateral assistance is in
the field of agriculture and related activities. There is a
heavy emphasis on projects intended to increase food production.
These range from seed technology, pasture development and livestock breeding and improvement through food storage and processing to agricultural training, which is provided both in New
Zealand and at third-country institutions. Due account has
been given in New Zealand's aid planning to the shift, since
the 1974 World Food Conference, to broad-based strategies for
rural development directed at increasing the productivity of
the poorest levels of society. In keeping with this re-
direction of rural development strategies, New Zealand strongly
supported the establishment of the International Fund for Agricultural Development. As a founder member of that fund, we
pledged an initial contribution of US$2 million over three
years. Among other multilateral and regional institutions and
programmes which have mandates relevant to our concerns at this
session, New Zealand attaches high priority to the World Food
Programme. Our contribution to the World Food Programme for
1977-78 amounted to NZ$1.4 million, two-thirds being in the
form of commodities. We are this year, for the first time,
taking part as a member in the work of the Committee on Food
Aid. By singling out these organizations for special mention I
do not mean to imply any diminution of New Zealand's interest
in or support for the work of other longer-established bodies.
The Food and Agriculture Organization, the International Development Association, the Consultative Group on International
Agricultural Research and the Economic Commission for Asia and
the Pacific, to name only a few with which we have been closely
involved, remain - and will continue to be - central to New
Zealand's concerns.
    Important as development assistant programmes are, New
Zealand is well aware that they will not by themselves solve
the fundamental problems of developing countries. Nor will

they alone bring about a climate in which developing countries
can achieve, through their own efforts, the substantial measure
of self-reliance for which they strive. Least of all is this
likely in the agricultural sector which in most developing countries provides the means of livelihood for the great majority
of their peoples. For the most part they follow traditional
forms of agriculture on land owned and worked by traditional
methods. This is not to devalue traditional forms and methods.
On the contrary, their very persistence indicates that practical experience over long periods of time has shown them to be
the most suitable responses to particular conditions and resource levels. But it does emphasize that the task of devising
appropriate and effective rural and agricultural development
strategies at the national level is a very complex one, im-
pinging on virtually every sector of economic activity, which
demands the highest degree of commitment from governments.

The international community can support these efforts,
through development assistance programmes and through special
forums such as the forthcoming World Conference on Agrarian
Reform. It can also help to create more favourable conditions
for the success of developing country efforts by tackling fundamental problems in international economic policy, including
trade liberalisation, the maldistribution of surpluses, indebt-
edness and commodity issues. On many of these questions, particularly those relating to improved conditions for commodity
trade, New Zealand, as a primary-producing nation which suffers
from a high degree of instability in export earnings, shares a
common interest with developing countries.

For that, among other reasons, we have taken full part in
the recent negotiations for the establishment of a Common Fund
and the related negotiations to establish international agreements on individual commodities. We have pressed as hard as we
could, in many international forums, for much greater liberalisation and stabilisation of agricultural trade. We have also
argued for increases in relative prices for primary products as
a necessary condition for a more equitable international economic order. We have argued, for example, that OECD proposals
for a transfer of resources from surplus economies to developing countries ought to be set firmly in the context of rising
real export incomes. We have deplored the tendency in international trade negotiations to gloss over the problems of both
the developing and the developed countries whose economies, like
New Zealand's, are dependent on agriculture. And we emphasised,
at the first session of this Committee as well as in other
forums, that improved access to markets is just as vital for
agricultural or primary products as it is for manufactured goods.
We were therefore pleased to note in documentation prepared for
this meeting, and in the statement of the Assistant Director-
General of the Food and Agriculture Organisation, a clear and
unambiguous acknowledgement that the problems of protectionism

and non-tariff restrictions are not confined only to trade in
manufactured goods but are directly relevant to the concerns of
this Committee in its work at the present session.

New Zealand's current economic difficulties testify to the
importance of these issues. After a precipitous decline in
1974, New Zealand's terms of trade have continued at historical-
ly-low levels, some 25 percent below the average for 1962-72.
The balance of payments deficit reached 15 percent of GNP in
1974/75 and has continued at lower but still serious levels
since then. Domestic economic activity has been severely de-
pressed with unemployment rising to its highest levels since
the depression of the 1930s. Substantial overseas borrowing
has been necessary to offset the effects of the external sector
on domestic production and employment. In a report on the New
Zealand economy, issued in January of this year the OECD ex-
plicitly recognised

> that part of the New Zealand terms of trade deteri-
> oration is attributable to the exclusion of New Zea-
> land products from markets which they otherwise
> would have enjoyed had trading relations been based
> on purely rational comparative cost considerations.
> In the interests of maximising world real income, it
> would clearly be preferable for this part of the
> adjustment process to be done by other countries
> rather than New Zealand. While New Zealand can at-
> tempt to improve market access by trade negotiations,
> or at least maintain what it now has, its bargaining
> power in this area is obviously limited. It would
> seem ironic if New Zealand, which already has such a
> large adjustment problem to surmount without the
> additional burden imposed by exclusion from markets,
> should be left to shoulder this as well.

It should be readily apparent therefore that New Zealand
does indeed have common cause with developing countries on commodity trade and access questions.

For New Zealand progress in these areas will have ramifications beyond our own economy and society. Our capacity to
play a full part in the international development effort, and
in negotiations towards the establishment of a new international economic order, depends on the health of our own economy.
We were pleased to see some acknowledgement of this relationship in the statement by the Assistant Director-General of the
Food and Agriculture Organisation though his analysis was not
fully applicable to a country such as New Zealand.

That does not mean, of course, that we disagree with his
basic premise that developed countries have both the responsibility and the means to bring about changes which will permit
developing countries to participate more equally in the inter-

national economy. For its part, New Zealand remains committed
to the target of 0.7 percent of GNP and ODA transfers, although
the serious balance of payments deficits we have experienced
since 1973 impose limits on our ability to sustain an expanding
development assistance programme. We have endeavoured, in accordance with our support for the Manila Communique and Mexico
Declaration, to implement to the fullest extent possible the
recommendations of the World Food Council and the resolutions
of the World Food Conference. But we are obliged to record
that our capacity to help in solving world food problems has
been diminished by our current economic difficulties. In the
past New Zealand provided sizeable amounts of bilateral food
aid. It is not, unfortunately, possible for us to continue to
do that at the present time. We have, however, endeavoured to
maintain the level of our support for the World Food Programme
and other multilateral commodity assistance institutions.

New Zealand has a very real and close interest in the successful outcome of the Committee's work at this session. I do,
however, want to make one final point. While it is natural,
and very proper, for this Committee to focus on the problems
and needs of developing countries, we should not lose sight of
the fact that this is a Committee of the Whole membership of
the United Nations. Its agreed conclusions should accordingly,
encompass the legitimate interests of all its members.

If I may take the liberty of speaking briefly to item 4 of
the Committee's agenda, I should like to conclude by announcing
that my Government has just approved the cancellation of nine
development loans to Fiji, Western Samoa and the Cook Islands.

New Zealand is not a significant creditor of developing
countries. Indeed, for some time now, all of our bilateral aid
has been provided on a purely grant basis. Nevertheless, a few
small development loans were extended in earlier years when
different policies and perceptions governed our bilateral assistance. My Government has concluded that cancellation of
these loans would now be appropriate, in keeping with resolution 165 of the Trade and Development Board adopted at its Ministerial Meeting in March 1978. The total debt outstanding,
before this decision was taken, was NZ$3.465 million. NZ$1.72
million of this amount related to a development loan to Fiji
for highway construction, $1 million to Western Samoa for general
development purposes and $745,000 to the Cook Islands for hous-
ing and communications projects. The present discounted value
of the debt service due on these loans is $2.23 million. I
would invite the Committee to note this decision as a further
manifestation of New Zealand's commitment to the development of
developing countries.

Japan: Mr. Seiya Nishida

As to assistance Japan has rendered in promoting the self-help
efforts of developing countries, I should point out that in addition to aid programmes which it had already implemented in
many developing countries, Japan began a new bilateral assistance programme in 1977 under which it extends grant assistance
in the form of fertilizers, pesticides and farm machinery. In
the first year, 6 billion yen was appropriated for this purpose, and in 1978 this amount jumped to 16 billion yen. My
Government intends, subject to the Diet approval, to increase
this assistance in 1979 by an amount thirty percent over the
figure for 1978. I would also like to refer to the pledge made
by my Government to contribute US $55 million during the period
from 1977 to 1979 to the International Fund for Agricultural
Development. Two-thirds of the sum pledged was already contributed during 1977 and 1978.

Second turning to the issue of Food Security, in line
with the "International Undertaking on World Food Security"
adopted by FAO at the 62nd conference of its Council, my Government is fully aware that all the countries concerned must
continue close collaboration in meeting the imperatives of Food
Security. Furthermore, we are fully conscious of the responsibility that all of us share for achieving a solution to this
problem. It is on the basis of this fundamental recognition
that my Government has positively participated in the negotiations for the New International Wheat Agreement, and it was
regrettable that the negotiation could not reach an agreement.

As regards the International Emergency Reserve, I am happy
to inform you that my Government will, subject to the Diet approval, make a direct contribution of US $800,000 to IER in
1979. This comes on the heels of a series of measures taken in
1978 to earmark US $500,000 for IER in the budget appropriated
to the Food Aid Convention.

Third, as to Food Aid, I should like to point out that
in spite of the difficulties that Japan's own position as a
major importer of foods imposes upon our efforts to provide
food aid in kind, my country has found a variety of ways to
extend considerable food assistance on both bilateral and multilateral bases. For instance, based on the Food Aid Convention
Japan extends food aid of US $14.3 million a year in the form
of rice purchased from rice-producing developing countries and
agricultural equipments and materials. Furthermore, in view of
the important role being played by the World Food Programme, my
Government has increased its contribution to the Programme in
each of the past several years and has pledged to contribute US
$10 million in 1979-1980.

Fourth and last turning to the issue of Food Trade, my
delegation would like to state that under the Tokyo Round of
Negotiations Japan has, with regard to tropical products, in-

troduced such measures as the addition of 11 products as new
items to the GSP. My delegation would like also to state that
Japan has already actively participated in the negotiations on
a Common Fund under the integrated Programme for Commodities
and will continue to do so in the hopes of reaching a successful conclusion.

The European Community: Mr. Jacques Leprette

Starting from the idea that the growth of food production cannot be separated from rural stimulus, the European Economic
Community is concentrating a substantial part of its effort on
rural development. Within the context of the current Lome Convention, it is devoting $1,115 million to rural development at
an annual rate of $223 million.

EED wishes to confirm its adherence to the principles set
out in the Declaration of Mexico. In particular, it approves
the major thrust of that Declaration towards intensified efforts on the part of the international community in the area
which is of concern to us and towards the fullest possible implementation of national plans for nutritional development. In
that connection, it fully subscribes to the opinion expressed
by the World Food Council to the effect that "the growth of
production in the developing countries is fundamental to any
solution to the world food problem". It shares the view of the
Executive Director of WFC that food production does not enjoy
sufficient priority and that a reversal of present policies is
essential. It is up to the developing countries to give the
necessary priority to rural development within the framework of
their general development policies. In our view, there can be
no real development without sustained growth in the agricultural
sector and without better income-sharing. In this connection,
the European Economic Community regards the forthcoming World
Conference on Agrarian Reform and rural Development as an important step.

EEC's financial and technical aid is not, however, limited
to its partners in this Convention: since 1976 it has also
benefited other developing countries, especially in connection
with their food production. Such aid rose from $24 million in
1976 to $84 million in 1978. Finally, the agreements reached
with the countries of the Maghreb and Machrek also allow for
the provision of financial and technical aid, part of which
will be allocated to agricultural development.

The Community's total aid to the agriculture of the developing countries quadrupled from $143 million in 1974 to more
than $596 million in 1978. Allotments by member States to ag-
riculture reached $683 million in 1976 and $942 million in 1977.
When the obligations undertaken both by EEC and by its member
States are totalled, it becomes clear that agriculture's share

of total public aid to development has been rising steadily for
some years, from 8.5% in 1973 to 16.7% in 1977.

India: Mr. Romesh Bhandari

I hope you will now permit me to make some observations regarding efforts made by India in the agricultural front, the policies we are adopting and the results we have achieved. As in
other forms of development, in the area of food and agriculture
as well, the primary responsibility must be of the concerned
governments. We are fully conscious of this fact. The highest
priority is now being attached by our government to agriculture
and rural development. 40% of our resources have been ear-
marked for this sector. Several measures have been taken to
make agricultural inputs available to the farmers at reasonable
prices. We have implemented institutional reforms through
which credits are made available to farmers on easy terms.
Special programmes have been launched for the benefit of small
farmers and agricultural labourers. Measures have been initiated to remove unemployment and under-employment. Special operations have been launched in rural areas which would generate
employment. We are paying concentrated attention to integrated
rural development programmes which involve intensive agriculture, mixed farming, minor irrigation, land development, animal
husbandry, dairying, fisheries, forestry and horticulture. As
the vast majority of our population is rural, we are giving
priority to village and cottage-industries and technical and
other training. We have achieved a record output food grains
of 125.6 million tonnes during 1977-78 which was 14.4 million
tonnes higher than the previous year. It is as a result of
efforts in many directions to make agricultural production less
vulnerable to climatic conditions. The following specific factors have contributed to making India's agricultural growth
both strong and stable:
  (a)   the additional capital formation resulting from a
        quantum jump in the irrigation potential of 2.6 mil-
        lion hectares in a single year of 1977-78 from an
        average of 1 million hectares during the first 5
        years of the present decade;
  (b)   the step-up of about 900,000 tonnes in the consump-
        tion of fertiliser nutrients;
  (c)   the enlargement in the flow of co-operative credit by
        about approximately $140 million;
  (d)   a sound research infrastructure which is yielding
        location-specific results and the new modes of ex-
        tension, for an effective transmission of the same to
        the farmers' fields. The breakthrough in an agri-
        culture production brought through by the introduction
        of high yielding varieties may be particularly men-
        tioned.

(e)   a deliberate thrust to bring small and marginal
      farmers within the ambit of production activity; and
(f)   the implementation of a set of interconnected policy
      decisions comprising incentive prices, free internal
      trade, and other production-oriented measures which
      have helped to create a conducive framework for the
      functioning of agricultural and rural development
      programmes.

Yesterday, a reference was made by the distinguished Representative of the World Bank to the present food grain stock
position in India. He said, and I quote "As the current Indian
situation illustrates - where many million remain malnourished
even as the country accumulates a 20 million stockpile of surplus production". In our view our stock policy has not been
presented in its proper perspective. India was one of the
first countries to have subscribed to the International undertaking on World Food Security. After a detailed study, we formulated our national stock policy. The present stock in our
country is the result of three good successive crops. This has
been possible due to concerted national effort and implementation of a number of measures which, I have just now enumerated.
The acquisition and maintenance of stock has to be done at considerable expense. This is, however, inescapable because of
our own earlier experiences of fluctuating production and the
current fragile international food security system. Our
stocks, Mr. Chairman, besides ensuring easy availability of
foodgrains all over the country through the network of public
distribution system, have significantly contributed to a measure of stability in the international market.

We are conscious of the need to link production and consumption. A number of measures have been taken to generate
employment in rural areas. We are utilising a part of our foodgrain stock to create gainful employment for landless labourers
and agricultural workers. During 1977-78, we launched a massive 'food for work' Programme in rural areas with 1 million
tonnes of food grains from our stock intended to generate additional employment to the tune of 400 million man days by way
of payment of wages partly in kind. The programme is intended
to create durable community assets in the rural areas by construction of irrigation works, taking up soil and water conservation measures, afforstation work, construction of roads
and other infrastructure facilities. We propose to further
intensify and expand the programme and the target for 1979-80
has been further stepped up.

In conclusion may I say that there is a fantastic potential
in the agricultural sector. According to studies recently undertaken we are at present only exploiting 3% of our production
potential. The maximum production can be 30 times that of the
present level. To tap this potential calls for greater national
and international efforts, the primary responsibility is cer-

tainly the national one. The responsibility of the international community is however, no less.

Mexico: Mr. Jorge Eduardo Navarrete

The Delegation of Mexico cannot help but congratulate itself on
the fact that the main subject for this second series of meetings by the Plenary Committee is to be agriculture and food.
In your brilliant opening speech yesterday, (Mr. Chairman) you
underscored the crucial importance of this subject in the area
of international economic cooperation; it is also one of the
two basic pillars of the Mexican Government's economic policy.
President Lopez Portillo has repeatedly pointed out that the
present economic strategy of Mexico aims at achieving an accelerated growth rate in the economy and assuring equitable
distribution of its benefits to all the people (the only manner
of achieving real progress) and is based on two priority objectives for development: food and energy.
     Mexico recently drew up and put its National Plan for Ag-
riculture into operation. This consisted of agreements and
concrete contracts setting goals, listing resources, actions
and officials of the Federal, state and municipal governments
and the producers themselves. The purpose of this National
Plan for Agriculture is to achieve, consolidate and maintain
the country's self-sufficiency in food production; the plan
covers questions such as mechanization, organization and equipment of the producers, rehabilitation and levelling of irrigated
lands and increase financial resources under cultivation to
agriculture: between 1,400 and 1,500 million dollars are to be
set aside for it every year. The plan is also expected to reduce gradually the differences in development and productivity
between high-yield, modern agricultural zones and those worked
with traditional methods by communal farms, commoneros and small
landholders; it is in these latter where investments will yield
the greatest benefits in terms of production, productivity and
number of jobs. This earlier fact led the President of Mexico
to state, in his second report from the Government that, "Agriculture and animal husbandry are primary, but not necessarily
primitive activities. In the modern age their extreme technical backwardness will make them lose out. The concept of
good management is not wedded to government ownership. We
foresee economic prosperity for Mexico, based on units of production - public, mixed and private - having sufficient elements
to be productive."

Switzerland: Mr. S. Marcuard

We are trying to concentrate our scientific and technical input
on the regional or local programmes of the country with which
we are co-operating. For us, it is a question of attacking a
number of bottlenecks, of responding to the initiatives of the
authorities and the population in order to improve production
techniques and also access to resources – including credit – as
well as the sale of production. We support such efforts to
improve the economic and social infrastructure of the region.
In addition to our contributions to international research institutes, we are endeavouring to improve possibilities for the
use of such research at the level of particular regions and
even at the level of the individual farmer. In a number of
countries we have provided support for marketing activities as
well as to FAO's programme of nutritional security by financing
the introduction of a warehousing infrastructure. We therefore
have a relatively large programme of nutritional assistance
implemented through the WFP and UNICEF and in programmes of a
humanitarian character.

German Democratic Republic: Mr. S. Zachmann

The GDR gives developing countries upon their request active
support in their development of progressive socio-economic conditions in rural areas. Specialists from my country work as
advisers in fields such as
-      the development of the public and cooperative sector
       in agriculture;
-      planning, management and organization of agricultural pro-
       duction, including processing of food, and veterinary medi-
       cine;
-      the mechanization of agriculture, including maintenance
       and repair;
-      training and advanced training of agrarian personnel from
       developing countries.
       The number of agrarian specialists of the GDR working in
developing countries has increased particularly since the World
Food Conference. Equally important is the training and advanced
training of personnel from developing countries in my country.
So far, several thousand citizens from more than fifty countries
of Asia, Africa and Latin America have received vocational
training or training in production technology. Management
courses, special courses and courses for advanced training as
well as study and information tours in the GDR were organized
upon the request of many developing countries. Apart from
these activities projects, studies, expertise and research sub-
jects are jointly elaborated by the assignment of experts and
scientists. The GDR also attaches great importance to the delivery of efficient machines, devices, equipment and plant,

potash fertilizer and pesticides in the frame of foreign trade.
These forms of assistance will be continued and extended in
compliance with the development plans of the partner countries.

6 Proposals for Action

This chapter contains both the opening statement, by the
Chairman of the Committee, and the Agreed Conclusion of the
Committee. In between are found the representative statements
proposing various kinds of actions by several specialized agencies and Member States and the four "negotiation" documents.
The chapter thus presents a reasonably clear picture of the
varieties of arguments and their resolution in the Agreed Conclusion.

STATEMENTS OF PARTICIPANTS PROPOSING ACTION

The opening statement by the Chairman of the Committee is
reproduced in its entirety because it clearly presents the role
of the COW and the arguments for the necessity for action. Of
the other statements, all of which are excerpts, the ones by
Mr. Aziz of IFAD, Mr. Yudelman of the World Bank, Ms Wells of
the United States and Mr. Greet of Australia, are particularly
noteworthy for the arguments they make for specific action, all
of which, finally find their way, in modified form and work
cases, into the Agreed Conclusions.

The Opening Statement by the Chairman of the Committee:
Mr. Thorvald Stoltenberg

Distinguished delegates,
We now turn to the main item on our agenda: the problems
of food and agriculture. The importance of this item is obvious. In a world where more than 450 million people are
chronically hungry and undernourished, the highest priority

must be given to national and international efforts to increase
food production, improve nutrition and food distribution and
facilitate agricultural development.

I have been asking myself how this Committee could most
constructively address the fundamental problems of food and
agriculture. The increasing specialisation of the UN system is
also apparent in the field of food and agriculture. It seems
to me that we could benefit from a basic framework, a unifying
idea that could provide a common yardstick for the many experts
and committees dealing with different aspects of this complex.
To me the overriding question must be: Can the Committee of the
Whole be of assistance in renewing the goals and objectives for
food and agriculture in the light of the increasing interdependence in the world today?

I have found it useful to reflect on the changing perceptions of food and agriculture in relation to development which
we have witnessed over the last decades.

The First Development Decade was characterized, as we know,
by a fairly narrow economic growth approach, with the expectation that the fruits of economic development would in due time
automatically "trickle down" to all people in society - including the poor. Also in agriculture growth was equated with
development. Any fruit of agricultural development would, it
was thought, reach the poor in the form of food. However, it
soon became apparent that even when the main idea was to increase the production of food, there would be no guarantee that
it would be channelled to the hungry.

Having understood this, experts began to argue that equitable distribution was as important as production. But distribution was generally thought of as a separate process, which,
given the necessary political will, could only take place after
the production goals had been achieved.

Slowly it is being realized that the potentials for equitable distribution may lie in the production process itself,
and in the general distribution of resources among people. In
a paper to be discussed by the FAO Committee on Agriculture
next month it is stated: (quote) "Given adequate purchasing
power and/or access to productive land, people will tend to
feed themselves adequately" (unquote). This is a significant
change in attitude from only five years back, when the World
Food Conference considered increased food production per se as
the major prerequisite to end hunger and malnutrition.

Before the Third Development Decade and the adoption of
the new International Development Strategy, I therefore think
we should seriously reconsider the basic assumptions for food
and agriculture. Our debate in the Committee of the Whole could
be a point of departure for such a process of reconsideration.
First of all, we could discuss whether or not the goals are
of a dual nature. This could perhaps help us to avoid con-
fusing ends and means, and we could get a clearer picture not

only of the complexity of the problems, but also of the different responsibilities involved for nations on the one hand, and for the international community on the other.

In the early history of the FAO, the idea was introduced, by one of the founders of the Organization, of the need to "marry food and agriculture". These words are still used as cosmetics for speeches, yet no nation ever thought of such a marriage - however happy it might have turned out to be - as the only possible basis for the use of land. Nations have used agricultural land, on the one hand, as any other raw material - to respond for instance to a demand for needed foreign exchange, and on the other, to produce food for domestic consumption.

We will have come a long way towards understanding how agriculture - through national and international efforts - can serve the objective of eradicating hunger and malnutrition in addition to achieving other goals for national development, if we could begin to separate the goals for agricultural development in the narrow economic sense from the goals for providing food for domestic needs. We would have to analyze to what extent different objectives could, under certain circumstances, be contradictory.

It seems to me that there has always been and will always be a double objective for agriculture. The balance between the two can only be decided by governments. What I want to point out is that neither they nor international organizations should confuse the two objectives. There is a reason for each of them, each requires different approaches by governments, and each requires different responses by the international system. The latter can in any case only act as a support for governments once they have decided upon their policy priorities. In addition, international fora provide opportunities for governments to exchange experiences about what measures actually lead to the desired results in the view of set objectives.

In this connection it might be useful if the Committee could attempt to identify a "division of labour" between governments and international organizations, by sorting out those policy issues that will remain the prime responsibility of governments, and those which must be settled through international negotiations and agreements.

These general ideas could perhaps be a point of departure in the Committee and constitute a framework for consideration of specific issues as they are presented to us in documents submitted by the FAO and the World Food Council. One important issue is the question of food security.

Basically, the problem of hunger and malnutrition must be understood at the level of the human being. It is the right of every man, woman and child to have enough and the right kind of food. Therefore, food security must be established for each and everyone. This is and must be the goal of national and international efforts.

In order to reach this goal it is necessary that Governments accord higher priority to food, agriculture and nutrition
in their development plans. There is, however, increasing evidence of a growing commitment by a number of developing countries in this field. It is clearly understood by all countries
that in order to secure the implementation of such plans in
developing countries an important element of external assistance
is needed. The FAO document submitted to the Committee, refers
to an estimate that about 1/3 of the necessary agricultural
investment would have to come from external sources. The establishment of national plans for food and agriculture is, however,
a fundamental prerequisite for a concerted national and international attack on the problems of hunger and malnutrition.
    As far as the need for external resources is concerned,
international aid agencies have on the whole responded well to
the call for increased assistance in the field of food and agricultural development. I think it would be appropriate for
the Committee to take note of this positive response and encourage the multilateral agencies to further efforts. With
some exceptions the record of bilateral donors is in general
not satisfactory and should be improved. This is obviously in
a large measure due to the fact that the performance of most
donor countries lag seriously behind the target for official
development assistance.
    The result of these two closely interlinked factors – the
lack of adequate national planning and the lack of sufficient
resources – is obvious: Not only have we failed to reach the
average growth rate of 4 % for agricultural production in developing countries, but we have so far also failed to contribute to the efforts to establish a more equitable international
economic order and to achieve the social objectives for the
large groups of people who today are deprived of the fundamental necessities of life. I am convinced that food, agriculture
and nutrition are key factors in the overall economic picture
and that an increased emphasis on working out solutions to the
problems we face in this area, will release energies within
nations which wll greatly benefit their general economic development.
    In this connection I would like to mention that although
there is a growing awareness that the economies of the developed and developing world are becoming more and more integrated, this perception has yet to make its full impact on planners
and policy-makers. The mutual benefits to be reaped from development cooperation must be clearly understood. It must be
realized that the growth and progress of the poor countries
will have a positive impact on economic growth and employment
levels in the industrialized world as well. I believe that, as
stated by the Secretary-General during the ECOSOC summer session
last year (quote): "The world economy is increasingly becoming
a coherent system in which the policies of each country affect

other countries and in which all sectors of activity are inter-
related. This new awareness is, I believe, a promising phenom-
enon because it can lead to the planning of collective action
which will be in the common interest of all the parties concerned." (unquote).

I would at this point like to say a few words about the
situation with regard to the negotiations for a new grains arrangement. The breakdown of these negotiations last February
was a great disappointment. A viable grains arrangement is an
important international instrument for the creation of food
security. The International Wheat Council is now meeting in
London to discuss inter alia the possibilities for a further
expansion of The International Wheat Agreement, 1971, and a resumption of the negotiations for a new agreement. I believe it
would be appropriate for this Committee to emphasize that it is
indeed essential that the negotiations are reopened as soon as
possible. The excellent opportunity for agreement afforded by
the present situation with regard to recent production trends
and stocks, must not be wasted. If this Committee could make a
positive contribution to the efforts to find agreement on a new
grains arrangement and/or a food aid convention, this would
indeed be an achievement.

The World Conference on Agrarian Reform and Rural Development (WCARRD) will meet in Rome in July. The successful outcome of this conference will be of major importance, both on
its own merits and as an element in the preparation of the next
International Development Strategy. I think it is essential
for us to bear this perspective in mind in view of the fact
that this Committee is linked to the 1980 Special Session of
the General Assembly which is to adopt the IDS. I therefore
think that we in an appropriate manner should express to the
World Conference the importance we attribute to its work.
Furthermore, I would like to inform you that I have been
invited to present a report to the Conference in my capacity
as Chairman of this Committee.

The meeting of the World Food Council in Ottawa in September is another important event. The General Assembly has
recommended that the Council at this meeting should inter alia,
consider the impact of trade on the solution of food problems.
In our deliberations we should bear in mind that it obviously
is one of our responsibilities to assist and support the Council with a view to securing a successful outcome of the Ottawa
meeting.

Before concluding it would be appropriate for me to say a
few words about the non-paper I prepared some weeks ago. I intended this document to serve as a basis for my consultations
with developing and developed countries as well as with international organizations. My aim was to make a contribution to
the psychological and factual preparations for this meeting. I
now feel that the document has served its purpose.

In conclusion I would like to thank the Director General
of the FAO and the Executive Director of the World Food Council
as well as the Secretariat for the excellent documentation they
have prepared for this session of the Committee. I would also
like to remind you that as general background information we
have before us the Declaration and resolutions adopted by the
1974 World Food Conference, the Manila Communique and Mexico
Declaration of the World Food Council of 1977 and 1978 respec-
tively and, of course, the basic documents concerning the establishment of a New International Economic Order.

This documentation gives, indeed, ample proof that the
issues of food and agriculture have been extensively discussed
in various international fora over the last years. I would
also venture to say that as a result of these discussions there
exists today general agreement on the need for a number of measures in this field. The problem is, as always, to transform
this general consensus of opinion into concrete action. As
stated in the FAO document: "In most cases the action required
is mainly the implementation of measures or targets that have
already been agreed in various intergovernmental conferences".
The FAO document expresses the hope – and I agree wholehearted-
ly – that the Committee will provide new impetus in this direction. The fact that the Committee of the Whole has decided to
make food and agriculture the priority item on the agenda of
this session emphasizes the concern we all feel in this respect.
It has been gratifying to note that there is considerable interest and willingness on all sides to contribute to action
oriented conclusions of our work.

Mr. S. Aziz of the IFAD

In looking towards the future, it is clear that the momentum and the concern generated by the World Food Conference has
already been lost and in the face of the complex reality of the
world food problem, there is no prospect of reaching the goal
of eradicating hunger and malnutrition by 1985. There is an
urgent need to reaffirm the commitment of the international
community to eradicate hunger and malnutrition and to work
out more detailed targets and programmes for moving towards
this goal with provision for high level intergovernmental review
and monitoring to ensure effective implementation. It is also
important to take into account the difficulties of implementing
the resolutions of the World Food Conference. Some concrete
ideas are outlined below to illustrate the degree of specificity
that is required.

   (a)   The investment requirements for achieving a sustained
         increase of 4 percent per annum in the agricultural
         production of developing countries between 1980 and
         1990 must be recalculated to reflect more recent ex-
         perience of various financing institutions. The

present estimates and targets are based essentially
on FAO's Indicative Plan for World Agriculture formulated about 15 years ago.

(b)   The projected requirements must be supported by sub-
targets for major financial institutions and bilateral
donors. To meet these targets all donors and institutions should earmark a certain minimum percentage
of their total assistance for agriculture. For countries which have not yet reached the target of 0.70
percent of GNP for total development assistance, this
earmarking must be based on additional commitments.

(c)   Within the sub-targets for different financial institutions, the replenishment of IFAD on a substantial
scale should receive special priority because funds
channelled to IFAD do not compete with demands from
other sectors, they are focussed on the target group
and the administrative expenses involved for a given
volume of lending are the lowest.

(d)   Efforts by the institutions and agencies concerned
must be intensified to improve the quality of projects
for the benefit of the target group, with greater
flexibility in lending terms and greater reliance on
local institutions and expertise as an important feature of technical cooperation among developing countries (TCDC).

(e)   In improving financial and technical assistance, higher priority should be given to developing countries
which are committed to helping the poorest segments
of their population through policies of agrarian reforms and rural development in line with the recommendations of the forthcoming Conference on Agrarian
Reform and Rural Development.

Mr. Maurice Yudelman of the World Bank

Looking ahead

All the analysis indicates that there will be growing pressure
on supplies of grain. It will be important to diversify the
source of world supply as well as to increase output. There
will have to be substantial increases in domestic production
especially in the poorer countries of Asia, Africa and Latin
America which cannot afford to use scarce foreign exchange to
import food. All the indications are that the marginal cost of
expanding agricultural production is rising in real terms and
that substantial investments will be required to increase production. For example, rehabilitating existing irrigation works
to manage water resources more efficiently and increase yields
costs around $800/ha (with yields increasing perhaps a ton per

ha). To construct totally new works may cost eight times as
much without including the social and infrastructure costs required to assist farmers to take full advantage of their new
assets. These costs are escalating quickly; far faster than
general inflation rates; and will continue to do so as we move
into new and progressively more undercapitalized regions. Based
on our experience and given the needs, there would appear to be
a strong case for a level of investment in agriculture which is
well above present levels.

The future volume of our lending for agriculture will depend
in large measure on the resources available to the Bank. This
is presently being discussed in other fora, in the context of a
general capital increase for IBRD and IDA VI. If we assume
that enough resources will be forthcoming for lending to expand
by 5% a year in real terms then, taking inflation into account,
this would be more than a doubling of current Bank annual investment in 1985 in nominal terms. If agriculture's share of
total Bank investment remains at around one-third of all lending, then total annual commitments in 1983 to agriculture could
be as much as $6 billion per annum; a cumulative total of $20 to
$25 billion between 1978 and 1983 or a total of $50 billion
including locally financed elements in Bank projects.

The total investment requirements of the developing world
are difficult to calculate, however estimates based on partial
data indicate that total investment in agriculture in the developing world was around $12-13 billion in 1975. The great
bulk of this was used to maintain and expand rural infrastructure. We would estimate that if food production in the lower
income countries is to meet future demand - even while allowing
for increased imports by middle and upper income countries who
will be expanding and shifting their own agricultural sectors
- then something like $40 billion of investment in all develop-
ing countries will be needed in 1985. The Bank's projects may
well continue to provide 15-20% of this, with other external
sources meeting 10% of the need. However, the greatest increases must come from the developing countries themselves.

The poor countries must raise their investment rates in
agriculture - which are now running at about 50% of the investment rates for their economies as a whole. Judging from the
successful experiences of Taiwan, the Republic of Korea, Ivory
Coast, and others, this should prove possible. Overall, investment as a percentage of total agricultural product must
rise from the current 7-8% to 11-12% in 1985. Studies have
shown that marginal savings rates in rural areas exceed those
of urban areas with small farmer marginal saving rates equal to
that of larger operations. This implies that, given the correct
mix of domestic policy incentives and investment opportunities,
the estimated $28 billion to be provided by farmers - large and
small can be realized. If it is, then projected annual increases in food production could rise by perhaps a third, from

2.3% to 3.3%. While this would have a marginal impact on trade
(particularly because it would primarily affect rice production
consumed directly by malnourished inhabitants in relatively
isolated rural areas) the nutritional and income effects would
be substantial.

Confining my remarks to five aspects of a vastly increased
investment program for agriculture, I would like to say:

First: We and governments have learned that it is possible to devise projects that can help make small-scale producers
more productive. There can be no doubt about this. However,
such projects usually involve higher administrative costs and
are more manpower intensive than are projects intended to benefit large-scale producers. Thus it has been easier for those
governments with a plentiful supply of skilled manpower and
relatively strong administrative services to undertake these
projects on a large scale than for governments with weak services and low levels of trained manpower. Some countries have
shown how to build up an effective institutional and infrastructural framework to assist the small farmers who account
for the bulk of total production and population. Continuing
this task will become increasingly expensive as we expand our
reach but returns will more than justify costs. Bank projects
which directly assist low income farmers in the poorer developing countries demonstrate this trend. Although per capita
benefits seem small in absolute terms, they represent substantial proportions of the poor's income - often projects bring
about a 100% increase in living standards. It has taken roughly $3 of investment to increase small farmer output by $1. Our
analysis indicate that this investment ratio may well rise by
1980 for reasons indicated above. Even if costs do rise though
this will still be lower than the incremental costs for increasing production in Western Europe and Japan.

Second: Looking ahead, there is a need to devise a strategy which can meet future needs of rural areas. It is clear
now that the "food problem" is not only a production problem
- even where there are adequate supplies of grain there are substantial numbers who are not adequately fed. There is thus a
need to think of strategies that link production and consumption. As the current Indian situation illustrates - where many
million remain malnourished even as the country accumulates a
20 million ton stockpile of "surplus production" - much must be
done to raise incomes and minimal diets of those actually living
in food producing areas. This is why the Bank is moving into
new areas such as non-farm employment and development of small
scale rural industries. Today perhaps a third of all rural inhabitants are engaged in non-farm activities and in many countries the problem of landless agricultural workers have proven
most difficult to alleviate. New ways to increase the productivity of these groups, enabling them to support needed services and food consumption, will have to be found in the future.

The projections of the Bank and others indicate that the problem of absolute poverty in rural areas is far from marginal.
Its resolution will call for a new approach to distribution
systems of food and increasing the incomes of particular groups
in society.

Third: There is a need for a continued and sustained effort to develop the basis for technological change at the farm
level. Most research intended for these purposes is financed
by the public sector and despite the efforts of the Bank and
other external donors there has been a lag in domestic investment in this important area. There will have to be substantial
increases in expenditure on research if there are going to be
the yield increases necessary to produce the foods needed in
the future. For example there will have to be much more crop-
ping on a year round basis in the future - this will take considerable effort by researchers in many parts of the world. In
addition there is a need for much more work to be done in the
rainfed areas of the world if these large areas are to be more
productive. Post harvest technology must be made more efficient
to reduce waste that is reported to account for as much as 25%
of total production in some countries.

Fourth: Most important of all is the requirement for sound
domestic policies. Increasing investment and the supply of
external capital to agriculture are important but in our view
making better use of existing investments, with comparatively
modest incremental outlays to improve efficiency, can be much
more important than a program of major new investments. Furthermore, the World Bank has found that there is no substitute
for sound domestic policies to ensure agricultural production.
National policies on pricing, land reform, taxation and so forth
are at least as important in influencing production as the total
flow of resources to a particular country.

Increased investment in itself is seldom, if ever, a substitute for suitable price policies. Elaborate infrastructure
and equipment will not substitute for price incentives. Determining effective producer incentives is often difficult considering the matrix of subsidized inputs, private credit and
land tenure systems, but we have found that very often a first
requirement for increasing production by small farmers is a
change in prices - without which little will be gained from
costly investments. In the Ivory Coast, for example, production increased over 50% in the two year period after prices, in
real terms, went up approximately 45%. Similar experiments in
Argentina, Taiwan, The Republic of Korea, Kenya and the Peoples'
Republic of China show the efficacy of price incentives. We
have estimated that, in the aggregate, a 10% increase in producer food prices in the developing world could well lead to a
5-8% increase in production. The International Rice Research
Institute has shown that pricing policies for fertilizers, improved seeds and farmgate produce are directly related to yields
on even the smallest Asian farms.

The limited capabilities of operating agencies within developing countries is often a bottleneck which most governments
are trying to overcome. A concerted effort to improve agricultural training is urgently needed to overcome the specific manpower and institutional limitations affecting services designed
to benefit farmers and the capacity to prepare and implement
projects. The current quality and size of the project pipeline
for food and agriculture needs to be increased. More needs to
be done to lay the groundwork for large scale investments which
will have to come on stream in the middle and late 80s, to sustain and increase production. The decline in technical assistance effort, has exacerbated problems of absorptive capacity
and project preparation. Possible solutions to this set of
problems are: new approaches to large scale lending, especially
sector lending and a greater reliance on domestic authorities;
better sector work; coordination of technical assistance and
training efforts; flexible small scale projects to build up
institutions capable of implementing large projects and which
test technical packages. Overall, we at the Bank believe that
agencies and governments must begin planning on the basis of
sector needs, as opposed to rationalizing present budget allocations.

In conclusion I would like to emphasize four items which
may be of special interest to you.

The first relates to the need for an increase in external
resources for food production. We remain confident that substantially larger investments are needed and can be effectively
utilized; we would be very hesitant to endorse a precise estimate of requirements without much further analysis.

The second relates to the importance of both external
donors and domestic authorities focusing a larger effort on
establishing appropriate conditions and institutions for the
effective use of external capital flows. This means a much
greater effort to expand the institutional capacity to utilize
these resources.

The third relates to the importance of ensuring that more
be done about the linkage between available supplies and actual
consumption levels among low income groups. We in the Bank are
considering how security schemes based on decentralized storage
systems, perhaps in the context of an international grains
agreement, could benefit the malnourished. Overall, the World
Bank will consider how it can expand and support for more efficient food distribution that must be the centerpiece of any international effort at reaching the malnourished.

Finally, we would like to emphasize the Bank's support for
government efforts to develop specific strategies for overcoming their food problems. We stand ready to assist governments wishing to plan programs aimed at turning the Declarations
of the World Food Conference into realities. It is clear that
there is no task more important than meeting the most basic

human need for an adequate diet. We believe that if others
follow the World Bank and devote increased resources to solving
this problem, the critical food situation could well be alleviated by the end of the century.

Mr. Nurul Islam of FAO
FAO's Five Point Plan of Action*

While calling on the entire international community to implement
the Undertaking, the proposed action concentrates on measures
to protect people in the most vulnerable developing countries.
The five points are as follows: (i) the adoption by all countries of national reserve stock policies and targets in accordance with the provisions of the Undertaking; (ii) the establishment by FAO's Committee on World Food Security of criteria for the release of such reserves; (iii) the adoption of
special measures to assist low-income food deficit countries to
meet their current food import requirements and emergency needs;
(iv) new arrangements to intensify and coordinate assistance to
developing countries in strengthening their food security, including the establishment of food reserves; and (v) measures
to promote the collective self-reliance of developing countries
through regional and other mutual aid schemes.

This Plan of Action will be discussed at the Fourth Session of the Committee on World Food Security, which is to be
held from 5 to 11 April, with a view to its submission to the
FAO Council for approval in June and to the full FAO Conference
for adoption in November. It would also be transmitted to the
World Food Council for endorsement. In the meantime, Mr. Chairman, your Committee is meeting at a most opportune moment to
get the Plan of Action under way with the strong political support that it will undoubtedly require if it is to become a
reality.

The United States: Ms. Melissa Wells

I now would like to turn to some specific points, while increasing global agricultural production is certainly desirable,
this alone will not reduce the incidence of hunger and malnutrition in a given country or worldwide. Increases in food
production must be complemented by measures to ensure that the
benefits of increased production are made available to those
groups which are most vulnerable to hunger and malnutrition.
This effort requires a complex of national and international

---

*A comprehensive discussion by Mr. Islam of the Five-Point Plan
of Action may be found in Chapter 9, Section 2.

actions, involving both the private and public sectors. Difficult political decisions may be involved, since a redistribution of resources or the establishment of a different set of
priorities, whether on a national or international basis, is
always difficult. Our governments must find the courage to make
those decisions.

Some of the areas which involve international efforts are:

- Increased resource flows - in many instances developing
countries require external assistance to complement domestic
efforts to promote the development of the food and agriculture
sectors. Attracting such external resources in the magnitudes
needed will be possible over the long term only if they contribute to economic and social development and complement sound
domestic investment.

- Using food aid increasingly as a developmental tool to
support agricultural production.

- Focusing agricultural research and transfer to technology increasingly for use in developing countries, particularly those countries where the problems of hunger and malnutrition
are most severe.

- Concentrating international assistance efforts, or
programs to help meet the basic nutritional and health needs of
the poorest people.

- Taking action to halt and reverse the growing degradation
of the production capacity of the world's agricultural and
grazing lands due to excessive use, neglect and the absence of
sound management programs.

- Bringing under cultivation land in areas such as Middle
Africa where the presence of endemic debilitating diseases prevent the utilization of potentially productive lands.

- Liberalizing agricultural trade to support greater efficiency in global agricultural production and distribution.

- Establishment of food reserves to promote price stability and to meet emergency food needs.

- Reaching agricultural commodity agreements, when appropriate, as a means of stabilizing prices.

Other areas for action to achieve the objectives I have
cited are primarily domestic in scope and thus require decisions
by individual governments. Among those are:

- Developing national food and agricultural plans; such
plans would manifest the political willingness of governments to
place a high priority on and commit significant resources to
increasing agricultural production and reducing the incidence
of hunger and malnutrition.

- Promoting an economic climate which encourages increased
investments, both from external and internal sources, in agriculture and related infrastructure.

- Eliminating disincentives, such as artificially low
prices to producers, export taxes, and marketing restrictions,
which undermine increased indigenous agricultural production.

-- Improving distribution channels to insure that the
available food can reach all segments of the population efficiently and at fair prices.

-- Improving land and water management techniques.

-- Reducing of high population growth rates so that increases in agricultural production are not offset by population
increases.

Thus it is clear to us that all countries must contribute
to the struggle to increase food production and improve nutrition in developing countries.

The above listing of national and international actions is
illustrative. Other areas will be identified during this week.
Achieving success in some of these areas doubtlessly will require compromises within individual countries, between and among
developed and developing countries. Often, difficult political
decisions will be involved. Given the goal involved, namely
demonstrating the humanity and resolve of mankind by eliminating
hunger and malnutrition from our world, these decisions must be
taken.

We have demonstrated the seriousness with which we regard
these issues by submitting a detailed paper at this session of
the Committee. It expresses our views on all the points raised
by our colleague in the Group of 77, and adds language reflecting some of the concerns I have raised today. We believe the
Committee of the Whole can make a major contribution to the
solution of problems confronting us in the realm of food and
agriculture -- by giving new impetus and urgency to existing
commitments, and pointing the way to solutions to problems we
have yet to solve. Our negotiations on these issues have begun
this morning. My delegation is fully prepared to make a maximum
effort to bring them to a positive conclusion.

Turkey: Mr. Tashin Tarlan

The characteristics of demand in the developed countries and
the dwindling of the aggregate demand of the developing countries leads us to believe that special importance attaches to
increased agricultural demand in the latter as a means of helping recovery in the industrialized countries and the growth of
the developing countries.

In this context, we consider that it is essential to increase the volume of assistance provided to the developing
countries by international organizations and donor countries in
the field of agriculture and food production. Such assistance
should be designed in particular to reduce unemployment in the
rural sector, to increase production and enhance productivity
in the agricultural and rural sector. It should also seek to
minimize harvest losses, to modernize the warehousing infrastructure and to stimulate the agro-industrial capacity of the
developing countries in order to ensure speedy self-sufficiency.

We also consider that it is equally urgent that global
agricultural and food production should be restructured in
favour of the developing countries and that trade policies
should be implemented with a view to increasing the export receipts of such countries.

However, we regret to note the increasing tendency of the
industrialized countries to impose protectionist measures on the
finished and semi-finished agricultural products of the developing countries. At the cost of depriving the developing countries of free access to the markets of the industrialized economies and of reducing the export receipts of these countries,
the protectionist trend favours certain relatively burdensome
economic sectors and stimulates inflation in the industrialized
countries.

In contrast to protectionist measures incompatible with
the concept of a free market, we are convinced that the long-
term interests of all countries would be better served by policies of sectoral readjustment based on the principles of comparative costs and the strivings for a worldwide dynamic. Such
policies would help to eliminate the inequalities of the existing order and would facilitate the establishment of the NIEO.

Australia: Mr. R.J. Greet

As others have said before me, the dimensions of the food problem are known. The needs are known. Agricultural development
is acknowledged to be a vital and integral part of overall development.

We know that if per capita food production can be increased, and if the range and quality of foodstuffs available
to the world's hungry could be improved, it would be realistic
to expect results in terms of:

a.   improvements in health, nutrition and life expectancy
      of the populations of the developing countries;
b.   an easing of the problem of unemployment in rural
      communities;
c.   a surplus of financial resources for funding further
      agricultural and industrial development.

Agricultural development is not itself self-contained, of
course, nor self-sustaining, but should be linked to other development projects and activities - transport systems, establishment of storage and marketing facilities, and rural education programs. We note the very commendable work which is being
done by ESCAP and FAO in developing ideas regarding integrated
agricultural development and strongly support its continuance.

The importance of increased agricultural development and
food production is given further emphasis when we review the
conclusion of recent work undertaken by the Asian Development
Bank on the supply/demand situation for major cereals up to

1985. According to the Bank's assessment, the Asian region is
unlikely to be in a position to meet its requirements of cereals
in 1985 from its own production. The net deficit is not expected to be lower than 11.3 million tons per year and may prove
to be as high as 34.9 million tons, depending on the assumptions
regarding likely trends in supply and demand. Among the developing countries of the region, only two are likely to have an
exportable cereal surplus by 1985, and even that surplus is by
no means assured.
     More important, the study indentifies certain common con-
straints in the agricultural sector which raise doubts whether
even the moderate trends in production increases recorded in
the early 1970s can be realistically expected to continue in a
sustained manner in the mid-1980s. These concern dificulties
in adding to the cultivable area, limitations from an ecological point of view concerning those areas where the technology
of improved seeds and chemical fertilizer could be successfully
applied. There are also difficulties and likely delays in
devising an array of adapted technologies tailored to varying
ecological and institutional requirements, and water management
problems.
     According to the Asian Development Bank, as far as most
countries of the ESCAP region are concerned, a basic conclusion
would appear to be that priority in development efforts should
be given to raising the rate of growth of agricultural output
in order to minimise nutritional problems, avoid excessive food
imports and provide a growth of rural output consistent with
the expansion of domestic manufacturing. This conclusion holds
a fortiori in the case of the low-income countries of the region.
This assessment must be a matter of serious concern to governments in the region. It would seem that a similar serious
situation will apply to the African region. It emphasises the
need to re-double efforts to meet the problems we will face in
the next decade.
     A point that has been made by a number of speakers in this
debate, and with which the Australian delegation fully concurs,
is that the primary responsibility for agricultural development
lies with national governments. At the same time, we also re-
cognise that substantial external inputs will continue to be
needed by many developing countries. The prospects for obtaining such inputs, whether in the form of official development
assistance, commercial loans or capital investment, will be
enhanced by developing countries making a clear commitment to a
high priority for agricultural development, backed by a coherent
national strategy. Agricultural development plans, to be effective, must closely involve the rural population in the planning and execution of projects. In other words, the rural peoples
must be both motivated and mobilised to throw their full weight
behind development efforts. Beyond this there is no universal
prescription: countries differ in their natural endowments and

in the degree to which various skills are developed. Hence, in
practical terms, their options will differ. Some will aim at
self-sufficiency in basic foods, others will seek to finance
substantial purchases from the proceeds of exports of goods and
services in whose production they have a natural advantage. We
expect that the coming World Conference on Agrarian Reform and
rural development will provide a valuable forum for the exchange
of information on the ways in which such options are chosen and
the methods adopted for putting them into effect.

Australia has consistently sought to support and strengthen
the international bodies dealing with food and agriculture. We
have encouraged, and will continue to encourage, the World Food
Council to concentrate its attention on the practical measures
required to fulfill the basic food needs of the many millions
of undernourished peoples in the developing countries. We feel
that the Council should concentrate above all on the practical
and fundamental issue of increasing production and consumption
of staple foodstuffs, and not devote too much time to general
issues. We would not wish to see the Council's energies ex-
pended, as has occasionally been the case in the past, on inter-
minable wrangling over the wording of declarations and resolutions.

Just as the needs are known, so in many cases are the measures required to meet them. As the representative of FAO said
yesterday what is now required is very largely a question of
implementing measures that are already the subject of long-
standing accord. But we would not wish to underestimate the
difficulties that surround negotiations on these critical
issues.

The Union of Soviet Socialist Republics:
Mr. Evgeny Nikolaevich Makayev

Among the international means directed at solving the food problem, special attention should be paid, in the opinion of the
Soviet delegation, to the working out of a means for stabilizing the prices of agricultural products exported and imported by
the developing countries. Such stabilization, together with
other measures for the improvement of trade, is necessary to
increase the exchange resources of the developing countries. It
might be possible to utilize these resources as a supplementary
source for improving the agriculture of the developing countries
as well as to ensure the import of food where necessary. We are
prepared to contribute constructively to the solution of concrete questions of international collaboration in the area of
stimulating agricultural production and regulating prices in
the world market of food products.

And in connection with the discussion of the food problem,
the delegation from the USSR would like once again to emphasize

that it is in complete agreement with the position of the Charter of Economic Rights and Duties of Governments and the Declaration with regard to the Establishment of a New International Economic Order in that the fundamental responsibility for
economic, social, and cultural progress of their peoples resides
in the governments themselves.

The historical experience of various nations shows that
the solution of the food problem is possible only on the basis
of the general raising of the economy, of the comprehensive
development of both agricultural products and of industry. As
experience has demonstrated, the nations that achieve the
greatest results in economic and social development are those
that implement progressive changes in the socioeconomic structure and especially transfer the center of gravity to developing their industry in the government sector, employing the
principles of the common approach to socio-economic development,
implementing long-term economy planning and forecasting, carrying out a policy of nationalization of foreign enterprises,
establishing sovereignty over their own national resources, and
actively preparing their own cadres.

The solution of the food problem is connected in the first
place to the measures undertaken by the developing nations in
the area of developing means of production in agriculture and a
self-sufficient food supply. The fundamental raising of agricultural production may be ensured only when there is democratic agrarian reform, the liquidation of the supremacy of foreign
capital, the instillation of progressive forms of land ownership and land exploitation, of broad cooperative peasant economies, the application of novel methods of agrotechnology, the
discovery and diffusion of high-yield growing methods, and the
mechanization and chemicalization of agriculture.

Speaking of means for the radical solution of the food
problem, we are guided most of all by our own experience. In
spite of the exceptionally complicated historical situation in
which the Soviet Union developed, we were successful finally in
releasing the people from the perils of hunger and malnutrition.
Only in the last 28 years did the consumption of meat per person
in the Soviet Union increase more than twice, that of milk and
dairy products almost 2.5 times, and of eggs almost 5 times.
During this time the proportion of the rural population in the
USSR steadily decreased. Of course, we still have complex
problems and difficulties. But we still intend to do everything necessary to solve them.

We understood the significance for the developing countries of economic, including food supply, aid from outside.
Nevertheless, attracting outside resources may bring positive
results only when the necessary progressive socio-economic reforms have been carried out. In the opposite case, the outside
capital investments will only aggravate foreign dominance,
promote the accumulation of riches in the hands of the few and

the misery of the broad masses of the workers, and aggravate
social inequality.

These resources act most of all in the interests of those
imperialistic powers and their monopolies, which continue to
exploit the natural and human resources of various countries.
Therefore, the Soviet delegation believes it just for the developed countries, that bear the responsibility for the calam-
itous economic situation in the majority of the developing
nations to procede, to implement the demands formulated in the
Group 77 document. At the same time, we once again affirm our
main position relative to the groundlessness for well known
reasons of the accusation against the socialist nations with
regard to these demands, which the developing nations advance
about the developed capitalist nations. Our position as to the
whole complex of the food problem was stated in the Declaration
of the Soviet Government on the Restructuring of International
Economic Relations, 1976, and also in the Declaration to the
World Food Conference, Rome, the 3rd and 4th sessions of the
World Food Council, and other agencies, and it remains in
force.

For its part, the Soviet Union, in the framework of economic and scientific technological collaboration with the developing nations, takes into account the importance of the problems that confront these nations in the area of agricultural
development and the provision of food to their populations.
Therefore, along with assistance in the areas of industry, advanced technology, the training of national cadres, and other
fields of economics, a large part consists of aid in developing
their agriculture and increasing their food supply. The Soviet
Union has for many years rendered a great deal of comprehensive
assistance to the developing countries in connection with numerous modern and effective agricultural objectives, including
national economies in the development of agriculture, cattle
farms, veterinary stations, irrigation and land-reclamation
units, rolling machinery installation, agricultural laborator-
ies, etc. With the help of the USSR an industrial base for
chemicalization, mechanization, and electrification of agriculture has been created in many of the developing countries.
Units for the preservation, processing, and transportation of
food-stuffs have been created. With the aid of the USSR 280
separate production units for use in agriculture have been
built or are under construction in the countries of Asia,
Africa, and Latin America. With our cooperation interested
countries have irrigated and drained more than 132 thousand
hectares of land. Aid from the Soviet Union has made it possible for the developing countries to increase their yearly
growth in the production of grain by 10 to 12 million tons.
The training of locally qualified workers in the various
branches of agriculture has been an important part of this co-
operation. These workers, either directly or indirectly, play

a role in the solution of the food problem of the developing
countries. The Soviet Union, in the spirit of traditional
internationalism has rendered and is rendering through its
state capital and social organizations, and will continue to
render further aid in an even greater degree in food and other
emergency help to other countries and peoples, especially to
those who have suffered damage as a result of the aggressive
actions of reactionary or imperialistic forces.

The collaboration of the Soviet Union with the developing
countries in the field of furthering agriculture and other
areas connected with food production is absolutely equitable.
It is based on long-standing governmental agreements, and the
countries involved completely respect each others' sovereignty.
Such an arrangement enables the developing countries to
strengthen their political and economic independence. It as-
sists them in their struggle with the remnants of the colonial
yoke, apartheid, racism, and neocolonialism within the framework of restructuring international economic relations of a
just, equal, and democratic basis. The Soviet Union expresses
its willingness to cooperate in economic and technical fields
with interested developing countries. Thus, and with multi-
faceted aid, we can relieve them of their burden of food production and help them in the struggle against famine and malnutrition, employing those forms and methods of cooperation that are
applicable to local socio-economic conditions. These methods
have been proven effective in actual practice and receive wide
acceptance from all the developing countries.

Bulgaria, Byelorussia, Czechoslovakia,
German Democratic Republic, Mongolia
Poland, Ukraine, USSR:
Mr. Dimiter Kostov

The socialist countries would like to emphasize once again that
they are in complete accord with the position stated in the
Declaration to Establish a New Economic Order. It states that
Nations themselves bear the basic responsibility for the economic, social and cultural progress of their peoples. Experience
shows that countries acquire the best results in economic and
social development: (a) when they transfer the center for
industrial development to the state sector; (b) when they
change to the principle of a united approach to social and economic development; (c) when they implement long range national
economic planning and forecasting; (d) when they introduce the
policy of nationalization of foreign businesses; (e) when they
establish sovereignty over their natural resources; (f) and
when they actively prepare their own work force.

The solution of the problem of food is connected, first of
all, with methods to develop the work force in agriculture and

self-sufficiency in food production by the developing countries
themselves. The basic upgrading of agricultural production can
be assured only when: democratic agrarian reform is introduced,
when the predominance of foreign capital is eliminated, the
introduction of progressive forms of ownership of land and use
of the land, with widespread use of cooperative farms, the adoption of the newest methods of technology, the introduction and
widespread use of high-yield crops and the mechanization and
use of chemicals in the field of agriculture.

     Among the international methods put forth as a solution to
the food problem, the delegations of the socialist countries
feel that the establishment of a means for developing international trade in foodstuffs must be considered. By this, we
mean a normalization of the conditions for such trade. The
Western countries must reject the policies of protectionism and
the prices of agricultural products must be stabilized. This
stabilization in conjunction with other methods for improving
the conditions of trade are necessary to increase the curren-
cy resources of the developing countries. These resources
could be used as a supplementary source in order to raise the
level of agriculture in the developing countries, and to ensure
the import of food wherever the need arises. The socialist
countries are ready to make constructive contributions to the
solution of the concrete problems of international cooperation
in order to stimulate agricultural production and the regula-
tion of food prices on the world market.

Mexico: Mr. Jorge Eduardo Navarrete

My delegation believes that the basic double priority of
Mexico's economic strategy of giving food and energy could be
applied on an international scale. In recent years, a great
number of developing countries have had to cover two growing
accounts at the same time: import of food and import of energy.
This double pressure on the very limited foreign exchange resources available to these countries threatens to wipe out their
economic growth and social progress. The international community must find a satisfactory answer to this pressing problem.

     As you, Mr. President, pointed out, when we look into the
questions of agricultural development and food production, it
is worthwhile to distinguish between questions of policy which
fall under the responsibility of individual governments and
those others which must be resolved by negotiation and international agreements. The document concerning these latter questions presented by the Group of 77 to the second series of meetings of the Plenary Committee is, in the opinion of my delegation, a balanced and coherent presentation of the propositions
for action.

The document covers the questions which must be dealt with
in the area of international economic cooperation if a significant contribution is to be made toward solving the agricultural
and food problems of the developing countries. Outside assistance to increase agricultural and food production in the developing countries, food safety and aid, trade in agricultural
products, industrial activity related to agriculture and nutritional problems, are all priority matters for the developing
countries, according to yesterday's speech by the distinguished
President of the Group of 77, His Excellency Ambassador Mestiri.

Switzerland: Mr. S. Marcuard

It is in the interest of every country to plan the development
of the agriculture and the improvement of its food situation.
In that regard, external aid is of a complementary or subsid-
iary character. In particular, it should help to improve economic and social programmes for the benefit of the rural masses
so that farmers can obtain seed, fertilizer and pesticides on
conditions they can afford, as well as credit without risk of
being ruined, and can sell their production at sufficiently
remunerative prices. In some cases, the farmer must be helped
to irrigate by means of techniques suited to his needs and means.
Within the framework of his rural community, he should also
have available a minimum level of social infrastructure - health,
education - and a regular supply of essential consumer items.
Such a set of conditions - which is to be considered during the
forthcoming conference on agricultural reform to be held in
Rome next July - assumes that each Government will have not
only an agricultural policy but also an economic and social
policy clearly tilted in favour of the rural masses. This calls
for organization, the introduction of specific programmes at
the regional and local levels, with qualified specialists using
appropriate techniques. It also implies the participation of
the populations involved. We consider that a greater effort -
both national and international - must be made in the field of
rural development if the purpose is not only to produce more
but, in particular, to produce for those whom it is desired to
feed.

THE CHAIRMAN'S NON-PAPER
AND OTHER NEGOTIATION DOCUMENTS

The documents included are the Chairman's non-paper, the
first Group of 77 text, the paper submitted by the United States
of America, and the revised text of the Group of 77, which to a
large extent formed the framework of the agreed conclusions.

The intention behind the Chairman's non-paper was that it
should serve as a basis for the Chairman's advance consultations with developing and developed countries as well as with
international organizations and thus contribute to the psychological and factual preparations for the March meeting. The
main purpose was to instigate Member Countries and groups to
start their preparations for the meeting at an early stage, a
purpose which, no doubt, was accomplished.

The Chairman's non-paper was never presented as an official document or meant to be used as a basis for the actual
negotiations. The point of departure of these negotiations was
the first paper presented by the Group of 77.

The Chairman's Non-Paper

1. The solution of world food problems lies primarily in rapidly increasing the food production in developing countries. An
accelerated development of their food and agricultural sectors
is also essential for their overall development. In this connection the interdependence between agricultural development
and industrialization should be emphasized. In spite of the
general recognition by governments and international organizations of the major importance of food and agriculture, progress
in these fields has been far too slow.

2. In order to achieve the goals established inter alia by the
World Food Conference it is essential that governments and relevant international organizations deal with such crucial issues
as
-   food production and external assistance;
-   world food security and food aid;
-   food trade.
Furthermore, urgent attention should be given inter alia
to agrarian reform, investment in agriculture, agricultural
credit, the transfer and application of relevant technology and
research, the development of extension services and improved
food distribution.

Food production and external assistance

3. Developing countries, particularly food priority countries,
should as a matter of urgency formulate basic food and nutrition plans within the context of national development strategies and seek, as appropriate, the cooperation and assistance
of developed countries and international agencies in the elaboration and implementation of such plans. In their efforts to
increase food production and improve nutrition, the countries
should continue to consider practical ways and means to achieve
a more equitable distribution of income and economic resources
so as to ensure that increases in food production result in a

more equitable pattern of food consumption. In this connection
it is noted that income and employment opportunities of the
rural poor lag seriously behind population growth and the rate
of growth in agricultural production.

4. At its resumed first session the Committee agreed that
there is urgent need for all developed countries which have not
reached the 0.7 percent target for ODA to exert all their efforts to increase effectively and substantially their assistance toward this target. Against this background developed
countries and international organizations are urged to increase
effectively and substantially their assistance to the developing countries for food production and agricultural development,
particularly to food priority countries, in order to enable
them to achieve the growth target of at least 4 percent per
annum for their agricultural sectors.

5. To reach this growth target the estimated external assistance need (i.e. US dollars 8.3 billion at 1975 prices with US
dollars 6.5 billion on concessional terms on an annual basis)
which has been established by the World Food Council, should be
reached as soon as possible.

6. The International Fund for Agricultural Development was
established to channel increased resources to agricultural development for the benefit of the rural poor in developing countries. In order to secure and further extend these activities
the resources of the Fund should be substantially increased
through replenishment in 1979-80.

7. Furthermore, developed countries and international organizations should consider

-    extending and increasing their financial and technical
     assistance to developing countries, in order to enable
     them to establish and expand fertilizer and pesticide pro-
     duction and storage facilities;

-    increasing substantially their contribution to the inter-
     national fertilizer supply scheme and/or coordinate their
     bilateral contributions with the FAO in order to reach the
     agreed target of 1 million tons of plant nutrients per
     annum.

Food security and food aid

8. Deep regret is expressed at the suspension - once more -
of the negotiations on an international arrangement to replace
the International Wheat Agreement 1971, as extended, and the
governments participating in these negotiations are requested
to reach as a matter of urgency a definitive agreement and to
reaffirm their commitment to world food security. It should be
considered, with a view to an early resumption of the negotiations, to extend the Wheat Agreement 1971 for only one more
year. An early resumption of negotiations is imperative in

order to take full advantage of the recent trends in world grain
production and the present stock situation.

9.   It is through these negotiations and the international
undertaking on world food security that a sound system of world
food security must be created, including an adequate international grain reserve and a new food aid convention aiming at
at least 10 million tons.

10. The new international grain arrangement should ensure inter
alia, that:

a)   –   The overall size of the grain reserve is large enough
         to ensure a high degree of world food security as
         well as being able to offset production fluctuations,
         especially in times of widespread crop failures in
         developing countries.

b)   –   The reserves are released at prices which will allow
         developing countries to satisfy their essential import
         requirements.

c)   –   Special international assistance is available to de-
         veloping countries for the establishment of storage
         facilities for national reserves, the acquisition of
         stocks and the payment of carrying charges.

11. A new food aid convention is an important element in the
negotiations for a new international grains arrangement. During these negotiations new contributions have been pledged by
the donor countries. The countries concerned are urged to consider these higher contributions as replacing their minimum
contributions under the Food Aid Convention 1971, as extended.
At the same time new donor countries are urged to accede to
that convention until a new Food Aid Convention has been concluded.

12. All countries should reconsider their provisional pledges
to the UN/FAO World Food Programme so as to reach the target of
US dollars 950 million for 1979/80 in order to enable the programme to continue to enter into new commitments at the current
rate of US dollars 300 million per year. Countries should make
multi-annual pledges when announcing food aid to the World Food
Programme.

13. Food aid should essentially be on a grant basis, donor
countries should channel a more significant proportion of food
aid through the World Food Programme.

14. Governments are urged to implement fully the recommendations to establish the international emergency reserve of 500,000
tons of cereals as a continuing reserve with yearly replenishment determined by the Committee on Food Aid Policies and Programmes and placed at the disposal of the World Food Programme.

Food trade

15. The prime objective of the agricultural policies of the
developing countries as a whole should be to increase food pro-

duction in order to eradicate hunger and malnutrition. In the
context of this overall objective, trade in food products has
an important role to play, both in relation to the development
plans of net exporters of food products and for developing countries who are dependant on purchases in the world markets.
16. It is important to improve the contribution of trade to
the solution of fundamental food problems. In this context it
is noted with concern that the export prospects of the developing countries are impaired by the high levels of protection in
force in most developed countries for agricultural commodities
and some products especially suited to production and export by
several developing countries. These products have suffered
further from the adverse effects of increased protection during
recent years.
17. Attention is drawn to the recommendation adopted by the
General Assembly at its 33 session that the World Food Council
at its fifth session, give consideration to the impact of trade,
including the protectionist measures harming the exports of the
developing countries and put forward specific recommendations
thereon.
18. In this connection developed countries should consider
drawing up programmes for phased adjustment in agriculture in
order to effectively facilitate access to their markets for
food and agricultural products of export interest to developing
countries, both in raw and processed form.
19. Developed countries should also endeavour to:
a)   Extend the GSP to a wider range of agricultural commod-
     ities including processed products of direct export in-
     terest to developing countries;
b)   Provide increased technical assistance (including assis-
     tance in the field of research, development and marketing)
     to enable developing countries to take full advantage of
     such concessions.
20. In providing food grains and food grain financing on soft
terms to developing countries, developed countries and the World
Food Programme should ensure that such assistance includes,
wherever possible, purchases of food from the food-exporting
developing countries.
21. It is of vital importance that the multilateral trade negotiations and the follow-up actions of these negotiations should
take fully into account the interests of developing countries
and their requirements on issues related to trade in agricultural products.
     The World Food Council should at its fifth session revise
and evaluate the results of the multilateral trade negotiations
in the field of agriculture.

The Proposals of the Group of 77

Introduction

The Committee, after reviewing the world food and agricultural
situation, expressed its deep concern at the deteriorating situation in the developing countries in this field. The target of
4 percent rate of growth in food and agricultural production
has not been reached. In fact, between 1961-1970 and 1970-1977
agricultural growth rate in developing countries as a whole has
decreased from 2.9 percent to 2.5 percent and per capita growth
in food production has dropped from 0.6 percent to 0.5 percent.
Furthermore, despite the decisions of the World Food Council at
its Manila and Mexico sessions, as well as of the General
Assembly, no improvement has taken place in food and agricultural production, food security, local processing of food and
agricultural products, food trade of the developing countries
and improvement of nutritional standards. The world stocks of
grains are still concentrated in the hands of a few industrialized countries. There was no progress towards the establishment of an international system of reserves as the International
Wheat Conference could not reach any agreement and the negotiations for a new Food Aid Convention remained to be concluded.
The target of 10 million tons of food aid was not reached during
1977-78 as only 9.5 million tons of food aid was provided to
the developing countries. The contributions to the International
Emergency Food Reserve of 500,000 tons were not increased during
1978 over the figure of 348,000 tons. There was a sharp decline
in the terms of trade of the agricultural exports of developing
countries aggravated by the persistence and increase of protectionist measures harming these exports.

External assistance to increase food and agricultural production
in developing countries

The committee considers that a rapid increase in food and
agricultural production in developing countries is essential
for their over-all development.
    The Committee recognizes that there is an increasing evi-
dence of a growing commitment by developing countries to the
accelerated development of their food and agricultural sectors.
However the shortfall in external assistance to developing countries for agricultural development is a matter of grave concern
to the international community as a whole. External resource
flows for food production remain at less than half of the minimum requirement estimated at 1975 prices at the level of $US
8.3 billion, with the element of concessionality gradually deteriorating.
    The Committee, therefore, agrees that:

(i) The targets for external assistance (i.e. $US 8.3 billion with 6.5 billion on concessional terms at 1975 prices) which were established by the World Food Council should be reached not later than the end of 1980;

(ii) International development institutions and developed countries should increase substantially their assistance to the developing countries for agricultural development, with a higher degree of concessionality; in this context special attention must be given to the food priority countries and other developing countries with large food deficits and whose food production situation is still deteriorating;

(iii) The resources of the International Fund for Agricultural Development should be substantially increased through regular replenishments, the first replenishment to take place in 1979-80;

(iv) There is need to ensure, at the request of participating developing countries, continued support of donor countries and international organizations through financial and technical assistance to specific programmes and projects for agricultural and food co-operation among developing countries at subregional, regional and interregional levels;

(v) International organizations and donor countries should increase substantially their contributions to the International Fertilizer Supply Scheme in order to reach, by the end of 1979, the agreed target of assistance of 1 million tons of plant nutrients per annum. It is important that the operations of this scheme should be continued through the replenishment of its resources to a higher level. Furthermore, developing countries should have access to imports of fertilizers and pesticides at competitive prices and not at prices higher than domestic prices in the developed exporting countries. International organizations and donor countries should provide financial assistance to developing countries for the acquisition of fertilizers and pesticides;

(vi) International organizations and donor countries should increase their financial and technical assistance to developing countries in order to enable them to expand substantially fertilizer and pesticide production facilities as well as storage, with the aim of doubling fertilizer and pesticide utilization and reaching self-sufficiency for developing countries by 1985;

(vii) Donor countries should increase their contributions to the Special Account for the Prevention of Food Losses and to the Seed Improvement and Development Programme of the FAO, to reach the agreed funding level of $20 million for each to be replenished on an annual basis.

The Committee endorses the understanding of the World Food Council about the necessity of allocating a share of resources, which would be freed as a result of the reduction of military expenditures, to finance the measures directed to advancing the development of developing countries, including their food situation.

Food security

The Committee considers that while increased food production is the basis for enhanced food security, the latter requires implementation of the principles and objectives of the International Undertaking on World Food Security. In this connexion the Committee agrees that an internationally coordinated system of national food reserves at adequate levels must be established urgently.

The Committee expresses its deep regret at the failure of the "United Nations Conference to negotiate an international agreement to replace the International Wheat Agreement 1971, as extended" to come to an agreement up to now and urges that unresolved issues be reviewed in a positive manner so that the Conference may be resumed as soon as possible with a view to conclude the agreement with specific provisions in favour of the developing countries, so as to contribute to solving the world food problem.

To this end the Committee agrees that the new international arrangement should ensure, inter alia, that:

(a) The over-all size of the grain reserve is large enough to ensure the necessary degree of world food security; the reserve should be sufficiently large to offset production fluctuations, in times of widespread crop failures or natural disasters in developing countries;

(b) The reserves are released at prices which will allow developing countries to satisfy their import requirements, especially in periods of global shortage without adversely affecting their economic development;

(c) Special international assistance is available to developing countries for the acquisition of stocks, the payment of carrying charges and the establishment of storage facilities for national reserves.

The Committee further agrees that donor countries should ensure that the agreed target of 500,000 tons of cereals of the International Emergency Food Reserve, which has not hitherto been achieved, should be attained in 1979. The Committee also emphasizes the decision of the General Assembly to establish this reserve as a continuing reserve with yearly replenishment determined by the Committee on Food Aid Policies and Programmes and placed at the disposal of the World Food Programme.

The Committee urges international organizations and donor countries to substantially increase their support to food security schemes in developing countries including food aid; such schemes should provide, as appropriate, support for stocks, storage and transport.

Food aid

In view of increasing food deficits anticipated for the 1980s,
the Committee considers that it is imperative that food aid
be substantially enlarged and made more flexible.
    To this end, the Committee agrees that:
    (i)   All food aid should be provided on a grant basis;
    (ii) An increasing proportion of food aid should be chan-
nelled through the World Food Programme;
    (iii) All countries should exert their efforts to enable
the World Food Programme to reach the target set for 1979/80 of
$950 million. Countries should make multiannual pledges in
physical terms when announcing food aid;
    (iv) The negotiations for the new Food Aid Convention should
be resumed in order to ensure continued availability of grains
for food aid at levels commensurate with the increased needs of
developing countries. The new FAC should initially ensure the
continued availability of at least 10 million tons of grain.
In view of the projected increase in food deficits in the 1980s,
the target for 1985 should be of the order of 15-16 million
tons of cereals. The conclusion of the new Convention should
no longer be held up by the state of the negotiations on the
new international arrangement;
    (v)   In providing food and other assistance, including
financing on soft terms to developing countries, developed
countries and international organizations concerned should take
due account of the interests of food - exporting developing
countries and should ensure that such assistance includes, whenever possible, purchases of food from such countries.

Agricultural trade

The Committee notes with deep concern that no significant
progress has been made towards solving the long standing problems of international trade in agricultural products of export
interest to developing countries.
    The Committee notes, in this context, that the high levels
of protection in the markets of the developed countries against
agricultural imports from developing countries continue to increase and are compounded by internal measures within the developed countries supporting uneconomic domestic production to
the detriment of the interests both of the exporting developing
countries and of their own consumers. Such protectionist
policies of developed countries have a serious adverse impact
on food and agricultural production, food security and the export earnings of developing countries, with negative consequences for the over-all development of these countries.
    In view of this, the Committee agrees that:
    (i)   Developed countries should take urgent action in the
different negotiating fora to approve and implement long-

standing proposals which will bring about the removal of distortive patterns of production, maintained through a system of subsidies and protectionism;
  (ii) Developed countries should in particular:
    (a) draw up concrete programmes for adjustment of their agricultural and other related sectors in order to facilitate the access of developing countries to their markets of food and agricultural products, both in raw and processed form, thus promoting the agricultural development of developing countries;
    (b) expand the Generalized System of Preferences to a wider range of agricultural commodities, including processed and semi-processed agricultural products of direct export interest to developing countries. In this connexion the system of information on using the G.S.P. should be enlarged and improved and technical assistance, including assistance in the field of research, development and marketing should be made available to developing countries at their request so as to enable them to take full advantage of the preference granted.

Agro related industries

The Committee recalls that the Lima Declaration and Plan of Action for Industrial Development and Co-operation stresses, inter alia, that the integration of different sectors of the economy can be furthered through the encouragement and support of rural industries, allowing increased local processing of agricultural products and raw materials as an important part of integrated rural development policies.
  The Committee recognizes that the rapid improvement of agricultural production in developing countries entails long-term investment in land improvement, agricultural research and development and the provision of agricultural inputs such as fertilizers, pesticides and agricultural and farm equipment.
  In this connexion, the Committee agrees that:
  (i) It is important to continue, making it more effective and action-oriented, the consultation system in UNIDO in the sphere of agro-industries;
  (ii) Increased financial and technical assistance from developed countries and international development institutions should be channelled to the expansion and modernization of agro-industries in developing countries;
  (iii) The subregional, regional and interregional co-operation mechanisms of developing countries in the field of production and commercialization of technical agricultural inputs should receive adequate financial support and technical assistance of developed countries and international organizations.

Nutrition

The Committee notes that there has not been a significant
flow of resources and technical help for nutrition programmes
from the donor countries, in spite of avowed commitments to the
eradication of malnutrition by 1985 as agreed at the World Food
Conference.

In this connexion, the Committee agrees that developed
countries and international organizations concerned should assist developing countries, at their request, through increased
financial and technical assistance, to meet their goals for
eradication of malnutrition, especially among children.

The United Nations system should improve its capacity to
respond to requests by Governments of developing countries in
nutrition planning and programme execution.

The Paper Submitted by the United States of America

Introduction

The Committee, after reviewing the world food and agricultural
situation, concluded that no serious short-term crisis, such as
existed in 1972-1974, now exists. It also recognized that individual Governments and the international community in recent
years have directed greater attention to food and agricultural
issues of particular concern to developing countries. Despite
significant progress, serious problems persist. In certain instances they have become more acute. These problems relate not
only to the global dimensions of hunger and malnutrition but
also to the inadequacy of governmental actions, including economic and social reforms, necessary to achieve greater agricultural production and to lessen hunger and malnutrition.

The Committee notes that agricultural production of developing countries increased at an average rate of 2.5 percent a
year in the period 1970-1977, a rate well below the IDS target
of 4 percent. Of even greater concern is that agricultural
production in the 45 most seriously affected countries rose by
only 1.9 percent annually during the same period. Rapid population growth in many of these countries resulted in negative
growth in per capita agricultural production. Clearly, increased
per capita agricultural production in developing countries,
most particularly in the poorest countries, must remain an over-
riding priority for national and international action.

The Committee recognizes that increased agricultural production will not resolve all global food and agricultural problems. In certain countries which enjoy substantial total agricultural production, the internal distribution of food supplies
is badly flawed. Thus, despite the availability of food, the
incidence of hunger and malnutrition in some regions or among

particular groups may be high. The responsibility for correcting internal anomalies of this nature rests primarily with the
Governments of those countries themselves. The Committee calls
upon these Governments as a matter of high priority to implement
measures necessary to permit and encourage: (1) increased food
production throughout their countries, most particularly in
regions where the incidence of hunger and malnutrition is greatest; (2) more equitable food distribution to all segments of
the population; and (3) national economic policies to permit
their low-income rural citizens, who often have the greatest
degree of hunger and malnutrition, opportunities to participate
more fully in their country's economic well-being.
    The Committee is also concerned that Governments are not
actively taking steps to implement in full the recommendations
of the World Food Conference. Specifically, the Committee believes that resource flows from both external and internal
sources must be increased if the 4 percent rate of growth in
agricultural production in developing countries called for at
the World Food Council is to be achieved. The Committee calls
upon Governments to introduce reforms which are prerequisite to
achieving increased production and better nutrition for all.

Investment in agriculture

The Committee notes that the World Food Conference and
subsequently the World Food Council estimated that to achieve 4
percent annual increases in agricultural production in developing countries, annual investments in agriculture, both from
external and internal sources, would have to be considerably
augmented. The World Food Council estimated that the annual
level of resource flows needed to do this should be about $25
billion (1975 prices), two thirds of which would come from internal financing by the concerned countries and one third from
external financing. Investments in food and agriculture have
increased substantially. For instance, total commitments of
external assistance for agricultural development in developing
countries doubled from 1973 to 1976 - from $2.6 billion to $5
billion. Nevertheless, domestic and external investments are
well below the needed levels.
    The Committee finds that increasing the rate of such invest-
ments requires:
        (1) recipient countries to undertake economic and social
    reforms to ensure that increased investments from both
    external and domestic sources, will be attracted to the
    food and agricultural sectors; and (2) greater willingness
    on the part of donor countries and institutions to direct
    resources to the food and agriculture sectors.

The Committee therefore recommends that:
    (1) increased resource flows, from both external and in-
    ternal sources, be directed to the agricultural sector of
    developing countries.

(2) special multilateral efforts be directed to food
priority countries, where hunger and malnutrition is most
acute.

(3) actions be taken to halt and reverse the growing degradation of the production capacity of the world's agricultural and grazing lands due to excessive use, neglect
and the absence of sound management programmes.

(4) developing countries undertake the requisite economic/
social reforms to provide incentives for increased investments in the food and agriculture sectors.

(5) donor countries and institutions provide financial
and technical assistance to facilitate co-operation in
food and agriculture among developing countries at the
subregional, regional and interregional levels.

(6) technological co-operation among developing countries
in food and agriculture be given special priority.

(7) developing countries formulate national food strategy
plans, thereby ensuring a governmental commitment to specific goals and measures to achieve increased agricultural
production and more equitable distribution of food within
countries to promote greater per capita nutrition. This
should be accompanied by measures which would support the
development of institutions capable of ensuring the most
efficient use of agricultural investment to promote agricultural development and eliminate incidence of hunger and
malnutrition.

(8) efforts be made to strengthen agricultural research
capacity in developing countries so that the unique problems of these countries can be met on an urgent basis.
Emphasis should be placed on the development and adaptation
of technology for use by small and medium-sized farmers.

(9) the United Nations Conference on Science and Technology for Development relate food and agriculture to the
body of global problems it will be addressing.

(10) donor countries ensure that their bilateral fertilizer
assistance or their contributions to the International Fertilizer Supply Scheme reach the agreed target of 1 million
tons of plant nutrients per year.

(11) that donor countries increase the contributions to
FAO's Post-Harvest Losses Scheme to reach the agreed funding level of $20 million. They also should substantially
increase resources available to the FAO's Seed Improvement
and Development Scheme.

Food security

The Committee urges that:
an international, co-ordinated system of national food reserves at adequate level be established.

The Committee regrets that the 22 January–14 February
UNCTAD Grains Negotiations failed to achieve a new International
Wheat Agreement and a new Food Aid Convention. The Committee
urges all participants in the adjourned UNCTAD Conference to
review the unresolved issues in a positive manner so as to create
the conditions which would permit resumption of these negotiations as soon as possible.

To this end, the Committee agrees that the new Agreement
should ensure, inter alia, that:
(1) the over-all size of the wheat reserve is sufficiently large to ensure adequate world food security,
(2) the price band within which wheat price stabilization
would take place is such as to encourage maximum world-wide
wheat production by efficient producers and to encourage
maximum imports of cereals.
(3) special attention is devoted to the needs of the developing countries to enable them to participate effectively in an agreement.

The Committee further agrees that donor countries should
ensure that the International Emergency Food Reserve of 500,000
tons of cereal should be attained in 1979 and that replenishments should occur at periodic intervals.

The Committee welcomes the Five-Point Plan of Action proposed by the FAO and urges that these measures be given positive
consideration by Governments at the fourth session of the Committee on World Food Security.

Food aid

The Committee agrees that:
(1) minimum food aid contributions (by donor countries)
should be expanded;
(2) food aid should, when possible, be used as a tool for
agricultural development;
(3) all donor countries should review their pledges to
the World Food Programme with a view to achieving maximum
food aid flows in 1979/80;
(4) agreement should be attained on the text of a new
Food Aid Convention to ensure continued availability of
cereals food aid commensurate with the increased requirements of developing countries. The 10 million metric ton
target level should be reached by contributions from new
donors as well as current donors.

Agricultural trade

The Committee finds that existing trade policies in many
countries impair the access of agricultural exports, including
those of developing countries, to their markets. These policies
have serious adverse impacts on production of food and other

agricultural commodities, food security and export earnings.
They also have negative consequences for the over-all economic
development of exporting countries. The Committee urges that a
liberalized international agricultural trading order be achieved.
Specifically, the Committee agrees that:
(1) the international trading community should seek to
eliminate to the maximum extent possible the distortions
in agricultural production patterns caused by agricultural
protectionism;
(2) all countries should institute domestic adjustment
programmes designed to assist those sectors adversely affected as a consequence of increased agricultural imports;
(3) the Generalized System of Preferences (GSP) should be
extended to a wider range of agricultural products, including processed and semi-processed agricultural products
exported by developing countries.

Rural participation in development

The Committee stressed the importance of the participation
in national development of the entire rural population, especially the small farmer and landless labourers who constitute
the vast majority of the rural poor. The Committee emphasized
the importance of agrarian reforms and the development of rural
co-operatives as well as appropriate institutions. More emphasis should be placed on the development of co-operatives in
national policies, especially when they can be implemented so
as to involve the lowest income groups, through their own organizations.
The Committee therefore agrees, _inter alia_, that a policy
of active encouragement to small farmers and rural workers organizations should be pursued to enable them to participate
effectively in the implementation of:
(a) programmes of agrarian reforms, distribution of surplus lands and land settlement;
(b) programmes for developing ancillary services such as
credit, supply of inputs and marketing;
(c) programmes concerning other employment generation
schemes, such as public works, agro-industries and rural crafts.
The Committee also agreed that systematic surveys and analyses of the developing countries' experiences in carrying out
agrarian reforms and organizing co-operatives should be reported
to the Economic and Social Council.
Within the context of the foregoing conclusions, the Committee urges all member States to participate fully in the World
Conference for Agrarian Reform and Rural Development.

Agro-industries

The Committee believes efforts to promote increased agricultural production and to reduce hunger and malnutrition must
be reinforced, when appropriate, through the integration of
activities in different sectors of the economy. In many countries where the incidence of hunger and malnutrition is greatest,
the majority of the population is located in low income rural
areas. Addressing this problem requires integrated efforts to
increase on-farm and off-farm employment opportunities. Thus,
increased local processing of agricultural products and raw
materials often will be an important element of integrated rural
development policies. Such measures would generate additional
income, thus increasing demand for indigenous agricultural production, and helping to achieve balanced economic growth. Donor
countries should, whenever appropriate, support integrated rural
development policies through financial support and technical
assistance.

Food consumption/distribution/nutrition

The Committee noted that programmes to improve food consumption, distribution and nutrition receive insufficient attention by Governments in spite of the World Food Conference goal
by eradicating hunger with a decade. It agreed that concerned
donor countries and international organizations, as well as
developing countries, should take actions to meet the goal of
reducing the incidence of malnutrition, especially among vulnerable groups such as young children, pregnant women and nursing
mothers.
     National food and agricultural programmes as well as de-
velopment programmes should, as far as possible, introduce nutritional considerations. These should include operational goals
and targets capable of being monitored to reduce hunger and
malnutrition.

                 The Revised Proposals of the Group of 77

Introduction

1.   The Committee, after reviewing the world food and agricultural situation, expressed its deep concern at the deteriorating
situation in the developing countries in this field. The target
of 4 percent rate of growth in food and agricultural production
has not been reached. In fact, between 1961-1970 and 1970-1977
agricultural growth rate in developing countries as a whole has
decreased from 2.9 percent to 2.5 percent and per capita growth
in food production has dropped from 0.6 percent to 0.5 percent.
Furthermore, despite the decisions of the World Food Council at
its Manila and Mexico sessions, as well as of the General

Assembly, no improvement has taken place in food and agricultural production, food security, local processing of food and
agricultural products, food trade of the developing countries
and improvement of nutritional standards. The world stocks of
grains are still concentrated in the hands of a few industrialized countries. There was no progress towards the establishment
of an international system of reserves as the International
Wheat Conference could not reach any agreement and the negotiations for a new Food Aid Convention remained to be concluded.
The target of 10 million tons of food aid was not reached during
1977-78 as only 9.5 million tons of food aid was provided to
the developing countries. The contributions to the International Emergency Food Reserve of 500,000 tons were not increased during 1978 over the figure of 348,000 tons. There was
a sharp decline in the terms of trade of the agricultural
exports of developing countries aggravated by the persistence
and increase of protectionist measures harming these exports.

Food and agricultural production in developing countries and flow of external resources

2.   The Committee considers that a rapid increase in food and
agricultural production in developing countries is essential
for their over-all development.
3.   The Committee notes that the World Food Conference and
subsequently the World Food Council estimated that to achieve 4
percent annual increases in agricultural production in developing countries, annual investments in agriculture, both from
external and internal sources, would have to be considerably
augmented. The World Food Council estimated that the annual
level of resource flows needed to do this should be about $25
billion (1975 prices), two thirds of which would come from internal financing by the concerned countries and one third from
external financing. The Committee recognizes that the responsibility of the development of the food and agricultural production lies primarily in the developing countries themselves; and
that there is an increasing effort and growing commitment by
developing countries to the accelerated development of their
food and agricultural sectors. Although the external assistance
had increased from $US 3.5 billion in 1974 to $US 4.3 billion
in 1977 at 1975 prices, the shortfall from the requirements
estimated at 1975 prices at the level of $US 8.3 billion and in
the degree of concessionality is a matter of grave concern to
the international community as a whole.
4.   The Committee agrees that
      (i) Urgent measures should be taken to reach the target
           of 4 percent annual growth rate in agricultural pro-
           duction in developing countries for which an estimated
           requirement of external assistance of $US 8.3 billion,
           with 6.5 billion on concessional terms, at 1975 prices,

as agreed in the Manila communique of the World Food
Council should be reached not later than by the end
of 1980;

(ii)   International development institutions and developed
countries should increase substantially their assistance to the developing countries for agricultural
development, with a higher degree of concessionality;
in this context special attention must be given to
the food priority countries and other developing countries with large food deficits and whose food production situation is still deteriorating;

(iii)   The resources of the International Fund for Agricultural Development should be substantially increased
through regular replenishments, the first replenishment to be agreed upon before the end of 1980;

(iv)   There is need to ensure, at the request of participating developing countries, continued support of donor
countries and international organizations through
financial and technical assistance to specific programmes and projects for agricultural and food co-
operation among developing countries at subregional,
regional and interregional levels;

(v)   In accordance with resolution 3362 (S-VII), developed
countries should provide through bilateral and multilateral channels the fertilizer assistance to MSA
countries of one million tons of plant nutrients per
annum by the end of 1980;

(vi)   International organizations and donor countries should
further increase substantially their contributions to
the International Fertilizer Supply scheme. Furthermore, developing countries should have access to imports of fertilizers and pesticides at competitive
prices and as a general rule not higher than domestic
prices in the developed exporting countries; international organizations and developed countries should
further provide financial assistance to developing
countries for acquisition of fertilizer and pesticides;

(vii)   International organizations and donor countries should
increase their financial and technical assistance to
developing countries in order to enable them to expand
substantially fertilizer and pesticide production
facilities as well as storage, with the aim of doubling fertilizer and increasing pesticide utilization
as well as reducing import dependency of developing
countries in these areas;

(viii) Donor countries should increase their contributions
to the Special Account for the Prevention of Food
Losses and to the Seed Improvement and Development
Programme of the FAO, to reach the agreed funding
level of $20 million for each and to replenish them
on an annual basis;

Furthermore, the Committee invites donor countries to support the FAO medium-term programme, endorsed by the FAO Council in November 1978, to assist developing coastal States, at their request, in developing their fisheries;

(ix) Economic, technical and technological co-operation among developing countries in food and agriculture should be strengthened and assisted;

(x) Efforts should be made nationally and internationally to strengthen agricultural research capacity in developing countries so that their specific problems can be met on an urgent basis;

(xi) The United Nations Conference on Science and Technology for Development should take into account the requirements of the food and agricultural production in developing countries.

5. The Committee supports the understanding of the World Food Council about the necessity of allocating a share of resources, which would be freed as a result of the reduction of military expenditures, to finance the measures directed to advancing the development of developing countries, including their food situation.

Food security

6. The Committee considers that while increased food production is the basis for enhanced food security, the latter requires implementation of the principles and objectives of the International Undertaking on World Food Security. In this connexion the Committee agrees that an internationally co-ordinated system of national food reserves at adequate levels must be established urgently.

7. The Committee expresses its deep regret at the failure of the "United Nations Conference to negotiate an international arrangement to replace the International Wheat Agreement 1971, as extended" to come to an agreement up to now and urges that unresolved issues be reviewed in a positive manner so that the Conference may be resumed as soon as possible with a view to concluding the agreement with specific provisions in favour of the developing countries, so as to contribute to solving the world food problem.

8. To this end the Committee agrees that the new international arrangement should ensure, inter alia, that:

(a) The over-all size of the grain reserve is large enough to ensure both the necessary degree of world food security and reasonable markets and prices stability; the reserve should be sufficiently large to offset production fluctuations, in times of widespread crop failures or natural disasters in developing countries;

(b)   In determining the price range, to ensure that the
developing countries would be in a position to satisfy their
import requirements without adversely affecting their economic
development and to ensure an adequate return to producers;
(c)   Special international assistance is available to developing countries for the acquisition of stocks, the payment
of carrying charges and the establishment of storage facilities
for national reserves.
9.   The Committee further agrees that donor countries should
ensure that the agreed target of 500,000 tons of cereals of the
International Emergency Food Reserve, which has not hitherto
been achieved, should be attained in 1979. The Committee also
emphasizes the decision of the General Assembly to establish
this reserve as a continuing reserve with yearly replenishment
determined by the Committee on Food Aid Policies and Programmes
and placed at the disposal of the World Food Programme.
10.   The Committee urges international organizations and donor
countries to substantially increase their support to food security schemes in developing countries including food aid; such
schemes should provide, as appropriate, support for stocks,
storage and transport.
11.   The Committee welcomes the Five-Point Plan of Action by
FAO and urges that these interim measures be given positive
consideration by Governments at the fourth session of the Committee on World Food Security and other appropriate bodies pending the conclusion of the new international grains agreement.

THE AGREED CONCLUSIONS OF THE COMMITTEE ON SOME
ASPECTS CONCERNING FOOD AND AGRICULTURE

1.   The Committee, after reviewing the world food and agricultural situation, agreed on the following:

Food and agricultural production in developing countries and
flow of external resources

2.   The Committee considers that a rapid increase in food and
agricultural production in developing countries is an essential
element for their over-all development.
3.   The Committee notes that the World Food Conference and
subsequently the World Food Council estimated that to achieve 4
percent annual increases in agricultural production in developing countries, annual investments in agriculture, both from external and internal sources, would have to be considerably
augmented. In order to achieve this target, it has been estimated
that the annual level of resource flows needed are about $US 25
billion, at 1975 prices, two thirds of which would come from
internal financing by the concerned countries and one third from
external financing. Despite the recent increase in external

assistance for food and agricultural production in developing
countries, there is a shortfall from the estimated need of
$US 8.3 billion, at 1975 prices, and in the degree of con-
cessionality,* which is a matter of great concern to the
international community as a whole.

4.   The Committee recognizes that the responsibility of the
development of food and agricultural production lies primarily
in the developing countries themselves and that there is an
increasing effort and growing commitment by developing countries to the accelerated development of their food and agricultural sectors. The Committee considers that developing countries which have not done so thus far, should formulate and
implement food and agricultural development plans envisaging,
if necessary, reforms and other comprehensive internal measures
within the context of their national development strategies,
and should pursue efforts for allocating to this end adequate
domestic resources, supplemented with additional external resource transfers of significant proportions, with the aim of
achieving self-reliance.

5.   The Committee agrees that:

(a) Urgent measures should be taken to reach the target of 4
percent annual growth rate in agricultural production in developing countries for which an estimated necessary element of
external assistance of $US 8.3 billion, with 6.5 billion on
concessional terms, at 1975 prices,** as mentioned in the Manila
Communique of the World Food Council, should be reached if possible by the end of 1980.

(b) International development institutions and developed countries should increase substantially their assistance to the
developing countries for agricultural development, with a high
degree of concessionality; in this context, special attention
must be given to food-priority countries and other developing
countries with large food deficits and whose food production
situation is still deteriorating.

(c) The resources of the International Fund for Agricultural
Development (IFAD) should be replenished on a continuing basis,

---

*See foot-note to para. 5 (a) below.

** $US 8.3 billion is a WFC secretariat re-evaluation in 1975
prices of the $US 5 billion for which there was broad support
at the World Food Conference. $US 6.5 billion is a secretariat
estimate produced at the request of the World Food Council at
its second session (for the report of the World Food Council on
the work of its third session, held at Manila, see Official
Records of the General Assembly, Thirty-second Session,
Supplement No. 19 (A/32/19).

with the first replenishment to be decided upon by the Governing Council before the end of 1980. The Governing Council should in this regard consider the need for an increase in real terms of the resources of the Fund.

(d) There is need to ensure at the request of participating developing countries, continued support of donor countries and international organizations through financial and technical assistance to specific programmes and projects for agricultural and food co-operation among developing countries at subregional, regional and interregional levels.

(e) In accordance with General Assembly resolution 3362 (S-VII), donor countries should provide through bilateral and multilateral channels the fertilizer assistance to the most seriously affected countries to enable them to meet their plant-nutrient requirements of 1 million tons on an annual basis. The appropriate international organization and donor countries should substantially increase their aid in fertilizers and pesticides through the most appropriate bilateral and/or multilateral channels.

(f) International organizations and donor countries should further increase substantially their contributions to the International Fertilizer Supply Scheme. Furthermore, developing countries should have access to imports of fertilizers and pesticides at competitive prices and preferably not higher than domestic prices in the developed exporting countries; international organizations and developed countries should further provide financial assistance to developing countries for the acquisition of fertilizer and pesticides.

(g) International organizations and donor countries should increase, when appropriate, their financial and technical assistance to developing countries, in order to enable them to expand substantially fertilizer and pesticide production facilities as well as storage, with the aim of doubling fertilizer and increasing pesticide utilization as well as reducing import dependency of developing countries in these areas.

(h) Donor countries should increase their contributions to the Special Account for the Action Programme for Prevention of Food Losses of FAO to reach the agreed funding level of $US 20 million. Donor countries and international organizations should increase their contributions to the Seed Improvement and Development Scheme of FAO in order to achieve at least the agreed level of $US 20 million, in accordance with the resolution adopted by the nineteenth Conference of FAO. The aim for these two programmes should be to ensure their successful and continued operation and financing.

(i) Donor countries should support the FAO medium-term programme, endorsed by the FAO Council in November 1978, to assist developing coastal States, at their request, in developing their fisheries in their economic zones.

(j) Economic, technical and technological co-operation among developing countries in food and agriculture should be strengthened and assisted.

(k) Efforts should be made nationally and internationally to strengthen agricultural research capacity in developing countries so that their specific problems can be met on an urgent basis.
(1) The United Nations Conference on Science and Technology for Development should take into account the requirements of the food and agricultural production in developing countries.
(m) Action should be taken to halt and reverse the growing deterioration of the production capacity of the world's agricultural and grazing lands.
6. The Committee agrees with the understanding of the World Food Council on the necessity of allocating a share of resources, which would be freed as a result of the reduction of military expenditures, to finance the measures directed to advancing the development of developing countries, including their food situation.

Food security

7. The Committee considers that, while increased food production is the basis for enhanced food security, the latter requires implementation of the principles and objectives of the International Undertaking on World Food Security, adopted by FAO in 1974, which is a voluntary undertaking. In this connexion, the Committee urges that, in accordance with the Undertaking, all countries should establish food reserves at adequate levels, taking into account the need for an internationally co-ordinated over-all system of national food reserves.
8. The Committee expresses its deep regret at the failure up to now of the "United Nations Conference to negotiate an international arrangement to replace the International Wheat Agreement, 1971, as extended" to come to an agreement and urges that unresolved issues be reviewed in a positive manner so that the Conference may be resumed as soon as possible with a view to concluding the agreement, in order to stabilize the cereal markets and which includes provisions in favour of the developing countries, so as to contribute to solving the world food problem.
9. To this end the Committee recommends that the Negotiating Conference on a New International Grains Arrangement should aim at ensuring, inter alia, that:
(a) The over-all size of the grain reserve is large enough to ensure both the necessary degree of world food security and reasonable market and price stability; the reserve should be sufficiently large to offset production fluctuations in times of widespread crop failures or natural disasters in particular in developing countries;
(b) In determining the price range, the developing countries would be in a position to satisfy their import requirements without adversely affecting their economic development and to ensure an adequate return to producers;

(c) Special consideration is given to adequate provision for
special international assistance to developing countries, which
assume stock-holding obligations in the acquisition of stocks,
carrying charges and building storage facilities for national
reserves so as to assist them in carrying out such obligations.
10.   The Committee recommends that the proposals of the developing countries concerning a reserve stock financing fund be kept
under consideration.
11.   The Committee further agrees that donor countries should
ensure that the agreed target of 500,000 tons of cereals of the
International Emergency Food Reserve, which has not hitherto
been achieved, should be attained in 1979. The Committee also
emphasizes the decision of the General Assembly to establish
this reserve as a continuing reserve with yearly replenishment
determined by the Committee on Food Aid Policies and Programmes
and placed at the disposal of the World Food Programme.
12.   The Committee urges international organizations and donor
countries to increase substantially their support to food security schemes in developing countries, including food aid; such
schemes should provide, as appropriate, support for stocks,
storage and transport.
13.   The Committee welcomes the initiative of the Director-
General of the Food and Agriculture Organization of the United
Nations in proposing the Five-Point Plan of Action and requests
the Committee on World Food Security at its next session, and
other appropriate bodies, to give it careful consideration.

Food aid

14.   In view of increasing food deficits anticipated for the
1980s, the Committee considers that it is imperative that food
aid be substantially enlarged and made more flexible.
15.   To this end, the Committee agrees that:
(a) Food aid should be provided essentially on a grant basis
to developing countries, in particular to the least developed
and most seriously affected among them.
(b) An increasing proportion of food aid should be channelled
through the World Food Programme.
(c) Traditional donor countries and other countries in a position to do so should ensure at least 10 million tons of cereals
as food aid per annum, preferably by forward planning, as appropriate, in physical terms on a multiyear basis.
(d) The United Nations/FAO Committee on Food Aid Policies and
Programmes should give consideration to the use of food aid by
bilateral donors and the World Food Programme in assisting developing countries in establishing national reserve stocks.
(e) The Committee urges that participating countries in the
UNCTAD grains negotiations should make maximum efforts to
create the conditions which would allow for an early resumption
of the negotiations and the rapid conclusion of a new inter-

national wheat agreement and a new food aid convention. Pending the conclusion of a new food aid convention, the donor countries which have made higher food aid pledges should do their
utmost to honour those pledges, taking into account the progress
made during the UNCTAD negotiations. The Negotiating Conference
should enable and encourage the participation of new members in
the Food Aid Convention.
(f) In view of the projected increase in food deficits in developing countries, in the 1980s, the Committee on Food Aid
Policies and Programmes should examine the necessary level of
food aid in coming years, taking into account the FAO secretariat's estimate that it would be in the order of 15 to 16
million tons in 1985.
(g) In providing food and other assistance, including financing on soft terms to developing countries, developed countries
and international organizations concerned should take due account of the interests of food-exporting developing countries
and should ensure that such assistance includes, whenever possible, purchases of food from such countries.

Agricultural trade

16. The Committee notes with deep concern that only limited
progress has been made so far towards solving the long-standing
problems of international trade in agricultural products, particularly those of export interests to developing countries.
17. The Committee also notes with concern the increase in protectionist trade practices that affect the economic development
of the whole international community, and, particularly as they
reduce the export possibilities of developing countries, affect
their economic development potential and reduce their capacity
to import food they need and have negative consequences for
their over-all development.
18. In this context, the Committee notes with particular concern that the access to markets of agricultural products, including many of special interest to developing countries, continues to face obstacles.
19. The Committee stresses that the acceleration of the agricultural production in the developing countries and a consequent
increase in their export earnings through greater access to international markets would not only facilitate the development
of the developing countries, but would also contribute to the
process of sound economic recovery of the entire international
community.
20. In view of this, the Committee agrees that:
(a) With the increase in protectionist trade practices that
affect the economic development of the whole international community and, particularly as they reduce the export possibilities
of developing countries, affect their economic development potential and reduce their capacity to import food they need, it is

essential for the developed countries to make their best efforts
to adjust those sectors of their agriculture and manufacturing
economies which require protection against developing country
exports.
(b)   The general system of preferences should be expanded to a
wider range of processed and semi-processed products and wherever possible agricultural commodities.
(c)   The system of information on using the general system of
preferences, providing technical assistance (including assistance in the field of research, development and marketing),
should be enlarged and improved to enable developing countries
to take full advantage of such preferences.
21.   The Committee expresses its concern with the instability
of the prices of agricultural products exported by developing
countries which have detrimental effects on the export earnings
of those countries and it considers that measures aimed at stabilizing commodity prices should be taken within the Integrated
Programme for Commodities.
22.   The Committee notes the recommendations of the General
Assembly in its resolution 33/90 that the World Food Council,
at its fifth session, should, inter alia, consider the impact
of trade, including the protectionist measures harming the exports of developing countries, on the solution of the food problems of developing countries and put forward specific recommendations thereon.

Agro-related industries

23.   The Committee recalls that the Lima Declaration and Plan
of Action for Industrial Development and Co-operation stresses,
inter alia, that the integration of different sectors of the
economy can be furthered through the encouragement and support
of rural industries, allowing increased local processing of
agricultural products and raw materials as an important part of
integrated rural development policies.
24.   The Committee recognizes that the rapid improvement of
agricultural production in developing countries entails long-
term investment in land improvement, agricultural research and
development and the provision of agricultural inputs, such as
fertilizers, pesticides and agricultural and farm equipment.
25.   In this connexion, the Committee agrees that:
(a)   It is important to continue, making it more effective and
action-oriented, the consultation system in UNIDO in the sphere
of agro-related industries, in co-operation with FAO and other
appropriate bodies;
(b)   Increased financial and technical assistance from developed
countries and international development institutions should be
channelled to the expansion and modernization of agro-related
industries in developing countries;

(c) The subregional, regional and interregional co-operation
mechanisms of developing countries in the field of production
and commercialization of technical agricultural inputs should
receive adequate financial support and technical assistance of
developed countries and international organizations.

Rural development

26. The Committee stresses the importance of the equitable
participation in national development of all segments of the
rural population. In this connexion, it considers that it is
important to integrate women more effectively in training and
development programmes concerning food and agriculture. The
Committee expresses hope that all Governments will participate
actively in the World Conference on Agrarian Reform and Rural
Development.

Nutrition

27. The Committee notes that there has not been a satisfactory
flow of resources and technical help for nutrition programmes
from the donor countries, in spite of avowed commitments to the
eradication of malnutrition by 1985, as agreed at the World
Food Conference.
28. The Committee agrees that countries, in particular developing countries, should continue establishing specific operational
goals for nutritional improvement and elaborate and implement
programmes with a view to attaining further concrete progress.
In this connexion, the Committee agrees that developed countries
and international organizations concerned should assist developing countries, at their request, through increased financial
and technical assistance, to help them to meet their goals for
eradication of malnutrition, especially among vulnerable groups,
such as young children, pregnant women and nursing mothers.
29. The United Nations system therefore should continue to
improve its capacity to respond to requests from Governments of
developing countries for assistance in the formulation of food
and nutrition policies and plans as part of their general development planning. The Committee welcomes the recent efforts
of the newly established Sub-Committee on Nutrition of the Administrative Committee on Co-ordination to strengthen the attention to food and nutritional considerations within the United
Nations as a whole, and recognizes as part of these efforts the
beginning activities of FAO to assess the nutritional impact of
the various programmes as a follow-up of resolution 8/77,
adopted at the nineteenth FAO Conference.

II

The Specific Issues

7 Food and Agricultural Production in the Developing Countries and the Flow of Agricultural Resources

The specific issue of food and agricultural production and the international flow of resources was addressed in all its complex detail by the Specialized Agencies and by a number of Member States. The reader should note the text in the Mexico Declaration of the WFC on the question of increasing food production, and the IFAD reference document which reviews the Fund's work in assisting the rural poor to increase food production.

THE MEXICO DECLARATION OF THE WFC:
INCREASE IN FOOD PRODUCTION

1. All developed countries should take urgent steps to reach the official development assistance target of 0.7 percent of gross national product,* bringing the over-all grant element of the official development assistance to at least 86 percent. Bilateral donors and international and financial institutions should take urgent steps to provide the external resources needed to reach at least the 4 percent annual growth in food production, which had been estimated on an annual basis of $US 8.3 billion at 1975 prices, of which $6.5 billion should be concessional.** Consequently, the World Food Council urges all donor countries to increase effectively and substantially their

---

* As agreed by the General Assembly at its seventh special session and as stated in para. 20 of the Manila Communique.

** As expressed in para. 3 of the Manila Communique.

203

commitments for food production, particularly to food priority
countries, so that noticeable progress can be reviewed at its
fifth ministerial session. Such additional external assistance
should be combined with essential internal efforts in developing countries in order to achieve, as soon as possible, the
growth rate of at least 4 percent in food production in developing countries.
  2. To catalyze political action to remove major obstacles
impeding more rapid increases in food production and gain the
necessary political and financial support to do so, the Council
stresses:

    (a) The importance of ensuring that continued attention
is given at the international and national levels to
    (i)   Encourage a larger flow of external resources for
        food production;
   (ii)   Improve the co-ordination of activities of different
        multilateral and bilateral donors providing financial
        and technical assistance for food production;
  (iii)   Ensure a more effective use of available resources.
    (b) The need to ensure continued support of donor coun-
tries and international organizations, in the context of subparagraph (a), to provide financial and technical assistance to
specific programmes and projects for agricultural and food co-
operation among developing countries on subregional, regional
and interregional levels designed: to increase their agricultural production and fisheries, inputs production and development of technologies, to improve security and conditions of
supply, to promote their nutritional programmes, to expand their
reciprocal trade, to develop technologies and to increase their
joint negotiating capacity in international markets.
and recommends that:
    (c) Developing countries should discuss and review, with-
in their existing regional groupings and bodies as appropriate,
the internal and external constraints they have encountered so
far in increasing their food production and in making more food
available, and should develop specific proposals to overcome
the constraints to raising the priority for food and nutrition
projects and programmes and to accelerating development and
implementation of such projects and programmes, including obstacles to development assistance;
    (d) All existing and potential donor countries should
review, within their existing forums, ways and means by which
they can support more effectively the efforts of developing
countries and should identify the problems and bottle-necks in
the increase of official development assistance within these
groups and seek to overcome them;
    (e) The major international financing institutions, espec-
ially the World Bank, the regional banks, the International
Fund for Agricultural Development and the United Nations Development Programme, together with the Food and Agriculture

Organization of the United Nations, should address these same
issues in an appropriate forum of their choosing; the new international lending institutions could be asked to join in this
effort;

(f) Representatives of these various groups should be
invited to report to the Council secretariat and bureau by the
end of February 1979 so that they can put together proposals to
be presented to the Council at its fifth session with a view to
mobilizing the highest possible political support for overcoming
obstacles and putting these proposals into action.

3. To stimulate more rapid and specific action in developing
countries, the Council invites interested food-priority countries to formulate and implement basic food and nutrition plans,
within the context of national development strategies, and to
seek the co-operation and assistance of donor countries and
international agencies, in particular, the Food and Agriculture
Organization of the United Nations, the World Bank, the United
Nations Development Programme, the International Fund for Agricultural Development and the regional banks, with the Council
facilitating this process when requested by the interested
parties; and when such plans are formulated, the Council will,
if requested by the developing country, seek the co-operation
of donor countries and the above-mentioned agencies in an intensive accelerated programme of specific country action:

(a) To identify, with the proper urgency, the projects
and programmes that form part of this plan that, the participants agree, warrant immediate support;

(b) To identify other projects and programmes which require further technical preparation or policy resolution before
they can be implemented, and determine how and over what time
period this can be done;

(c) To pursue jointly, through existing institutional and
consultative arrangements, the means to support these programmes and projects through adequate financing and technical
assistance.

4. When asked by Governments concerned to further develop
food plans, or to accelerate action on them, the Bureau and
secretariat of the Council will seek to establish suitable
arrangements for these undertakings on an urgent basis and
provide the necessary co-ordination to ensure that adequate
support is provided and that important policy issues are
brought before the Council for solution.

5. The secretariat should identify and approach appropriate
bodies which are willing and able to analyse data on the internal resources that are being devoted to agriculture, food production and the reduction of food losses in developing countries and should report this information as part of this analysis of resource commitments, in particular, to food production
in developing countries. This information should be brought to
the attention of the Council. On that basis the support that

should be given to food production in developing countries could
be reviewed, taking into account the competing claims of development in other fields.

6. The Council reaffirms the recommendations concerning agricultural inputs contained in its Manila Communique. To stimulate progress in this field, the Council instructs its secretariat to prepare, in co-operation with the competent agencies,
especially the Food and Agriculture Organization, a review of
the progress and proposals for further necessary action for
consideration at the fifth session. Meanwhile, donor countries
are urged to increase their assistance for fertilizers, pesticides and other basic inputs to food priority countries through
the most appropriate bilateral and/or multilateral channels,
including the International Fertilizer Programme of the Food
and Agriculture Organization. The Council also calls on all
countries to support actively the FAO Action Programme for Prevention of Food Losses and the FAO Seed Improvement and Development Programme and appeals to donor countries to make substantial contributions to the special arrangements within the Food
and Agriculture Organizations, each of these funds being $US 20
million, and/or through bilateral programmes in order to
achieve the desired progress in these fields.

7. All interested countries, as well as competent international organizations (African Development Bank, Asian Development Bank, Caribbean Development Bank, Food and Agriculture
Organization of the United Nations, Inter-American Development
Bank, Organization of Afican Unity, Organization of American
States, Sistema Economico Latinoamericano, United Nations Development Programme, World Bank and others) should give priority
attention to the formulation and implementation of national and
regional programmes and projects connected with the utilization
of fish resources and the Council instructs its secretariat to
report on the need for funding and exchange of information in
this area to its fifth session.

8. All Governments should participate actively in the World
Conference on Agrarian Reform and Rural Development.

9. Developing countries should take account, in their food
production plans, of the effect of climate on food production
and seek to establish strong agro-meteorological services in
their countries, and donors in a position to provide technical
or financial assistance should do so.

10. The Council further:

   (a) Stresses the importance of ensuring that continued
attention is given at the international levels to:

   (i)   Encouraging a larger flow of external resources for
         food production,

   (ii) Improving the co-ordination of activities of different
         multilateral and bilateral donors providing financial
         and technical assistance for food production,

   (iii) Ensuring a more effective use of available resources;

(b)   Notes the assurance given by the World Bank, the Food
and Agriculture Organization and the United Nations Development
Programme that they are providing and will continue to provide
maximum assistance feasible within their work programmes to
Governments wishing to examine their food and nutrition situation and develop investment strategies to meet these needs, and
will facilitate follow-up investment by other donors through
existing consultative groups and consortia, or other appropriate
means, and that the Food and Agriculture Organization is taking
steps to continue the compilation of data on international resource flows for agriculture;

(c)   Recognizes that the objectives set out in subparagraph
(a) above are an essential element of the Council's responsibility to generate all possible improvements in the world food
situation;

(d)   Instructs its secretariat to co-operate actively with
the three agencies which formerly sponsored the Consultative
Group on Food Production and Investment in Developing Countries
and with the International Fund for Agricultural Development in
order to fill any gaps which might appear in over-all monitoring
or stimulation of flows of financial and technical assistance
for food production, which its secretariat could undertake without additional staff or financial resources, and which the
President and Executive Director consider would represent a
worth-while contribution to the objectives stated in subparagraph (a) above.

FOOD AND AGRICULTURAL ORGANIZATION (A/AC.191/37):
FOOD AND AGRICULTURAL PRODUCTION

The acceleration of the increase in the agricultural production
of the developing countries to an average rate of 4 percent a
year is a basic objective of the International Development
Strategy (IDS) adopted for the Second United Nations Development Decade (DD2).   Yet, during DD2 so far, the rate of increase
in the developing countries as a whole has barely matched that
achieved in the 1960s, and in Africa and in the poorest countries in general it has fallen considerably below it.

This disappointing agricultural production performance has
necessitated a rapid expansion of the food imports of the developing countries, thus thwarting their efforts to achieve
greater self-reliance.   It has impeded the narrowing of the
gaps between rich and poor countries envisaged under a New International Economic Order (NIEO).   It has also contributed
heavily to the failure to achieve the social objectives of the
IDS, since most of the world's poorest people live in the rural
areas of the developing countries, and depend on agriculture
for their meagre livelihood.

A faster increase in the agricultural production of the
developing countries depends in particular on their according
higher priority to agriculture in their national development
plans. Their resources are limited, however, and it is estimated that about a third of the necessary agricultural investment would have to come from external sources. Although commitments of external assistance for agriculture have recently increased substantially, they remain only about half of the target
level agreed by the World Food Council (WFC). Even if the over-
all IDS target for official development assistance on concessional terms were to be realized, the WFC target would imply a
rise in agriculture's share of the total. It is therefore necessary for more bilateral donors to follow the example of the
multilateral agencies in giving much greater priority to agricultural and rural development.

A much more than proportionate increase is needed in external assistance on concessional terms for the agriculture of
the poorest developing countries, where the slow growth of production is linked with the fact that, per head of their populations, they have received less external assistance for agriculture than the other developing countries. Another immediate
concern is the need to ensure the replenishment and expansion
of the initial resources of the International Fund for Agricultural Development (IFAD), especially in view of its unique
status as the only major international financing institution
created exclusively for agriculture.

Side by side with such efforts to expand the agricultural
investment resources available to the developing countries, it
will be necessary to enhance their capacity to make effective
use of these resources. Especially in the poorest countries,
increased assistance (including training) will be needed in the
identification and preparation of viable investment programmes
and projects. External assistance is increasingly being directed
to programmes and projects in favour of small farmers, involving
a high proportion of local financing. This may require changes
in the traditional appraisal and monitoring systems of both
bilateral and multilateral agencies, if new delays are not to
be introduced in the utilization of external finance.

For production to be increased sufficiently rapidly, there
are a number of areas that require special emphasis both by the
developing countries themselves and in external assistance, as
well as in economic and technical co-operation among developing
countries (ECDC and TCDC) in appropriate cases. It is estimated
that land and water development would take about 40 percent of
the total investment requirements. Such investments will have
to be even larger to the extent that greater regard is paid in
the future to environmental dangers such as soil degradation,
the loss of forest cover, and desertification. Particularly
large investments will be required in the extensive areas to be
cleared of disease and opened up for development under the FAO

Programme for the Control of African Animal Trypanosomiasis,
and the Onchocerciasis Control Programme, in which UNDP, the
World Bank, WHO and FAO are associated.

Another crucial area is to ensure that the developing countries can obtain sufficient supplies of the improved seeds,
fertilizers and other inputs essential for raising production.
Investment in fertilizer production capacity in these countries
will contribute not only in this regard but also to the achievement of the target of the Lima Declaration and Plan of Action
on Industrial Development and Co-operation. Greatly increased
fertilizer assistance is required, both bilaterally and through
FAO's International Fertilizer Supply Scheme (IFS). Important
international targets that have still not been met include the
1 million tons a year of fertilizer assistance for the most
seriously affected (MSA) countries recommended by the seventh
special session of the General Assembly, and the $20 million
for the FAO Seed Improvement and Development Programme (SIDP)
called for by the CAO Conference.

A reorientation and expansion of assistance is needed for
the adjustment of fishery programmes to the extended jurisdiction acquired over exclusive economic zones (EEZ), and in order
to avoid a fall in production during the adjustment period.

A major effort has to be made to strengthen national agricultural research systems in the developing countries, in part
so that they can take better advantage of the recent large expansion in research at the international level. Improved technology has to be developed for small farmers, and a better feedback established between them and researchers, so that their
needs are more fully reflected in research programmes.

MR. NURUL ISLAM OF FAO:
REQUIREMENTS FOR ACHIEVING PRODUCTION INCREASES

There is no doubt that the over-riding need is for a substantial
acceleration of the increase in food and agricultural production
in the developing countries. I have already mentioned some of
the reasons why this is so important. FAO's detailed studies
indicate that such an acceleration is indeed feasible. Given
their unexploited potential and their present limited use of
fertilizers and other modern inputs, they should be able to
secure large increases in output without a significant rise in
economic costs and without serious environmental consequences.

A major requirement for achieving the necessary production
increase is a massive expansion of agricultural investment.
There is evidence that the governments of some, but by no means
all of the developing countries have recently given greater
priority to agriculture in their investment programmes. There
is also greater awareness of the need to reconsider macroeco-
nomic policies and incentive structures.

FAO has estimated that the annual investment in the agriculture of the developing countries would have to be approximately doubled during the 1970s in order to achieve the necessary expansion in their production, and that about one third of the total would have to come from external assistance. On the basis of these estimates, the World Food Council agreed on a target, endorsed by the General Assembly, of $8,300 million (in 1975 prices) for external assistance to agriculture by 1980. Yet the latest figures indicate that, in spite of a big increase in real terms, official commitments of external assistance to agriculture are little more than half this target. The shortfall in assistance on concessional terms is even larger.

The main requirement for bridging this gap is of course the speedy attainment of the overall target for development assistance on concessional terms agreed in the International Development Strategy. But even if this basic target were to be met, agriculture would probably still require a larger share of the total. Since this target is very far from having been met, it is all the more imperative that more bilateral donors should follow the recent example of the multilateral agencies in giving much greater priority to agricultural and rural development.

A much more than proportionate increase is needed in external assistance on concessional terms for the agriculture of the poorest developing countries, which per head of their populations, have so far received much less such assistance than the others. Another immediate concern is the need to ensure the replenishment and expansion of the initial resources of the International Fund for Agricultural Development (IFAD), especially in view of its unique status as the only major international financing institution created exclusively for agriculture.

A very large part of the increased investment in agriculture will be required for land and water development, including measures to prevent environmental dangers such as soil degradation, the loss of forest cover, and desertification. Large investments will also soon be required in the extensive areas to be cleared of disease and opened up for development under the FAO Programme for the Control of African Animal Trypanosomiasis, and the interagency Onchocerciasis Control Programme.

Greatly expanded external assistance is needed to ensure that the developing countries can obtain sufficient supplies of the improved seeds, fertilizers, pesticides and other inputs essential for raising production. Fertilizer assistance has never reached the target agreed at the Seventh Special Session of the General Assembly. Contributions to FAO's International Fertilizer Supply Scheme have fallen sharply. Assistance for seed improvement and development is considerably below the target of $20 million agreed by the Conference on International Economic Cooperation as well as the FAO Conference and subsequently endorsed by the General Assembly.

Closely related to increasing production is the prevention of the huge avoidable losses of food. The Seventh Special Session called for the reduction of these losses by at least half by 1985. FAO's Action Programme for the Prevention of Food Losses has so far received only about three quarters of the target of $20 million agreed for its first two years of operation. Project requests already exceed the contributions received and are likely soon to exceed the target itself.

A reorientation and expansion of external assistance is also needed for the readjustment of fishery programmes to the extended jurisdiction that has now been acquired over exclusive economic zones. The FAO Council has recently approved a comprehensive medium-term programme to assist developing coastal states in managing and developing fisheries in these exclusive economic zones.

Along with efforts to expand the agricultural investment resources available to developing countries, it will be necessary to improve their capacity to make effective use of them. FAO is strongly emphasizing assistance of this kind in its own programmes, particularly those in cooperation with the World Bank and other financing institutions. Changes may also be needed in the traditional systems of approving and monitoring projects, especially those oriented towards small farmers, if external finance is to be more effectively utilized.

Increased technical assistance, including training, will be needed for preinvestment activities, as well as for the preparation of investment programmes and projects. FAO is active in a wide range of technical assistance at the country level, covering all aspects of food, agriculture, fisheries, forestry and rural development. The UNDP is our major source of funding for these programmes, and we are happy to be entrusted with the execution of most of its projects in these fields, which amount to about 30% of its total programme. We appreciate this emphasis on the food and agricultural sector. As development efforts accelerate, we expect requests for assistance to increase further, and we thus look forward to still closer cooperation with UNDP in the future.

MR. MONTAGUE YUDELMAN OF THE WORLD BANK
THE BANK'S PROGRAM IN ENCOURAGING FOOD PRODUCTION

The Bank's program in agriculture and rural development is consistent with the changing pattern of grain production, utilization and trade. The Bank recognizes the productive capacity of the grain surplus nations, most notably the US, and takes account of the needs of developing countries. In this context the objectives of Bank lending for agriculture can be divided into three broad categories:

First: The Bank has shifted its efforts to encourage production of staples for domestic consumption rather than emphasizing export crops. Most of the Bank's current lending program
is directed towards increasing cereal production, with about
three-quarters of all project induced output consisting of
staples, most of which is consumed domestically. A classic
illustration of this has been the shift in Bank lending to India where the government and Bank staff jointly concluded that,
despite the substantial increase in wheat production, rice production in the sub-continent's rice areas in the river delta
regions need be increased to raise incomes and to limit imports.
As a result the Bank and the Government have invested $1.8 bil-
lion in rice producing projects in the past five years which
may well lead to an increase of 1-1.5 million tons of milled
rice in output enough to provide basic nutritional needs for
4-6 million people or provide an important 400 calories (usually the difference between nourished and malnourished) for 25-38
million people.

Second: The Bank has continued to emphasize and expand
support for the inputs that contribute most to increase in
cereal production. Specific inputs financed by the Bank include:

a)   Fertilizers - It has been estimated that perhaps 40%
      of recent increases in yields in cereal production in
      developing countries is the result of increased fer-
      tilizer use; the World Bank group has been the most
      important source of technical and financial support
      for fertilizer manufacturing in the developing world.
      It has loaned over $1 billion from 1974-77, for this
      purpose, and expects that Bank financed plants will
      provide almost one-third of all incremental fertilizer
      production in less developed countries in the 1978-85
      period.

b)   Irrigation - The relationship between increasing
      rice output and irrigation has been widely recog-
      nized. When the rice economy countries of Asia are
      divided into groupings according to the percentage of
      total paddy area irrigated, the importance of water
      control becomes obvious. Countries with less than
      35% of irrigated farmland have yields of 2.0 MT/ha;
      countries with 75% farmland irrigated have yields of
      +4.0MMT/ha; while Japan, with 98% of its farmland
      irrigated, realized yields of over 6.0 MT/ha. Per-
      haps 40% of total increases in yields over the past
      decade and well over half of total increase in output
      can be attributed to "irrigation" and this is the
      largest single component of Bank lending in agricul-
      ture. In the past five years the Bank has generated
      approximately $8 billion investment in rehabilitating
      or developing new irrigation systems, which I estimate

to represent about 25% of the total worldwide investment in irrigation in developing countries.

c)   Research - Many Bank projects involve introducing
     higher yielding varieties of grains whose productiv-
     ity lies in their responsiveness to fertilizers or
     irrigation. The Bank serves as chairman of the Con-
     sultative Group for International Agricultural Re-
     search and provides 10% of total funding for the in-
     ternational research system which is in the forefront
     of developing new high yielding varieties of seeds.
     The Bank also provides support for national research
     programs; in recent years we have assisted in the
     development of at least eight national programs -
     last year the Bank invested $100 million for this
     purpose and we expect this to be the fastest growing
     element in Bank lending for agriculture.

d)   Infrastructure - Bank financing has also involved
     large investments in building infrastructure and land
     clearance - in the last five years some $1 billion
     has been loaned for the latter alone. I estimate
     that a fifth of total investment in rural road net-
     works in developing countries is Bank induced, with
     40,000 km of construction annually (in the past three
     years the Bank has helped to finance a rural road
     system larger than the entire interstate highway system
     of the US). The Bank has been equally important in
     other areas, such as rural electrification with 40
     million people benefiting from the last five years of
     projects.

e)   Institution Building - Institution building is the
     least quantifiable but arguably most important aspect
     of the Bank's work. Innovative projects in India,
     Turkey and Thailand have pointed out the impact of
     reforming agricultural extension services and other
     supporting services. Bank projects designed to im-
     prove existing extension services have, at a cost
     equal to $.50 to $1.50 per ha, resulted in substan-
     tial increases in yields - with no additional inputs
     or irrigation. Elsewhere the Bank has had to work,
     sometimes initially on a very small scale, to create
     and then build up institutional capabilities so that
     increased capital can be used effectively.

MR. MAURICE J. WILLIAMS OF THE WFC:
INCREASING FOOD PRODUCTION WHEN IT IS MOST NEEDED

Increasing food production in food deficit countries means
decisions by governments that are primarily political in nature,

and only secondarily related to natural resource and technical
factors.   There are no major physical or technological limits
to the expansion of world food supply to meet the likely growth
of population over the next three to four decades.   Studies by
FAO and others have pointed out that land resources are more
than adequate.   The necessary investments can be found to assure inputs of such essentials as water and fertilizers, and
promote research and extension.

The application of these resources and this technology,
however, is far from simple.   It requires a multitude of decisions at all levels in the governmental process and careful
analysis to identify the appropriate solutions in any particular
case.   While the technological capacity to solve food problems
is available, the precise technologies required for the best
results in many parts of the world have still to be developed,
and then applied.   This is a complex process which will require
strengthening of research institutions, the establishment of
adequate links between those institutions and the farmer
through improved extension service, the organization of the
necessary inputs, and the improvement of marketing and distribution systems.   In many countries it will also require substantial improvements in the infrastructure of roads and communications as well as major irrigation and drainage works; in
some countries land reform also will be necessary.   The capacity to do all this exists – to mobilize the investment and organize the manpower required – and, in fact, to do it with a
fraction of the resources which is currently devoted to armaments.
But to marshall and to organize that capacity will require decisive direction.   Political determination and mutual understanding between developed and developing countries must underpin
this process at every stage if commitment is to be translated
into action.   It is for these reasons that the work of the World
Food Council is seen as being primarily oriented to political
action and coordination within the framework of agreed world
food objectives.

INTERNATIONAL FUND FOR AGRICULTURAL DEVELOPMENT (A/AC/191/38):
   REVIEW OF ACTIVITIES IN 1978 AND PROGRAMME FOR WORK FOR 1979

1.   The establishment of IFAD in 1977 constituted a major mile-
stone in the efforts of the international community to cope
with the problems of food production, malnutrition and rural
poverty in the developing world.   As a concrete expression of a
new and important partnership between developed countries, the
OPEC developing countries and other developing countries for
promoting agricultural development.   IFAD's creation also represents an event of historic significance.

2.   After intensive discussions during 1975 and 1976, an intergovernmental Agreement Establishing the International Fund for
Agricultural Development was adopted at a United Nations Conference of Plenipotentiaries on 13 June 1976. The Agreement
was opened for signatures by the Secretary General of the
United Nations on 20 December 1976 when the target of one billion dollars in total pledges was reached. The Agreement entered into force eleven months later on 30 November 1977, when
it was ratified by countries pledging a total of US$ 750
million.
3.   IFAD began its operations on 13 December 1977, when the
Fund's Governing Council held its first session and the Executive Board and the first President of the Fund were elected.
The Fund's Executive Board consists of eighteen members and
seventeen alternates. The total membership of the Fund has
now reached 126. Of these, 104 states have completed all
necessary formalities and are already members of the Fund.
The remaining states have yet to complete the legal steps
necessary to become members.
4.   The initial resources pledged to the Fund are slightly
more than one billion dollars with 56.5 percent contributed by
developed (OECD) countries, 43.5 percent by developing contributing countries (i.e. the Oil Exporting Countries (OPEC) and an
additional 2 percent by developing recipient countries. The
adequacy of the Fund's resources will be reviewed by the Governing Council periodically. The first such review is to take
place at the next Session of the Governing Council before the
end of 1979.
5.   IFAD is a new kind of institution in the United Nations
system and the governing bodies which will supervise IFAD's
operations are structured along innovative lines to better reflect the interests of both developed and developing countries.
6.   By the end of 1978 the Executive Board is expected to have
approved ten loans totalling US$ 117 million for projects in
Sri Lanka, Tanzania, Guyana, Haiti, Ecuador, Thailand Cape
Verde, Bangladesh, the Philippines and Nepal.
7.   The Fund's loan operations fall in two main groups - namely co-financed projects and projects initiated by the Fund.
All the ten projects approved during 1978 are co-financed with
other cooperating institutions. In the early years of the
Fund's life co-financing operations will continue to play a significant role. The selection of projects for co-financing is
based first and foremost on whether the project conforms to the
Fund's policies and criteria. An intensive screening process
occurs at the first round of discussions with the cooperating
institution concerned, followed by an in-depth review of selected projects coupled with a field visit to the country concerned.
The Fund's staff participates in appraisal missions and negoti-
ates the loan agreement with the government concerned.

8.   The Fund can only fulfil the objectives for which it was
created if it actively pursues the development of those types
of projects which focus on the Fund's target groups, particularly in certain priority countries. Thus, the development of
the Fund's own project pipeline has in its first year, received
special attention. During 1978 project identification missions
were sent to sixteen member countries: Bangladesh, Democratic
Yemen, India, Guinea, Niger, Malawi, Pakistan, Benin, Tunisia,
Senegal, Sudan, Philippines, Honduras, Chad, Cuba and Liberia.
9.   The initial list of countries for possible assistance from
the Fund was formulated on the basis of official requests received and with due attention to population, food and poverty
considerations. The need for regional balance in the Fund's
operations was also kept fully in view.

Lending terms and conditions

10. Under the terms of the Lending Policies and Criteria adopted by the Governing Council in December 1977, the Fund may lend
to member states on highly concessional, intermediate or ordinary terms. Highly concessional loans carry a service charge of
1 percent, a maturity of 50 years and a grace period of 10 years,
while intermediate loans are at 4 percent, 20 years maturity
and a grace period of 5 years. The terms fixed for ordinary
loans are 8 percent, with 15 to 18 years maturity including a
grace period of 3 years.
11. The Fund's diversified lending terms - highly concessional,
intermediate and ordinary - are designed to meet varying needs.
Many recipient countries qualify for the Fund's softest terms.
However, the adverse financial situation and debt servicing
capacity of many economically more advanced countries dictates
the need for some concessional lending. The intermediate loan
terms provide considerable flexibility in coping with such
situations.
12. The Fund's lending policies can only be tested in the
context of particular countries and projects. One of the
attractive aspects of the Fund's policies for some recipient
countries relates to the relative flexibility of the Fund with
respect to local cost financing. The acute lack of local resources in some developing countries is often a major constraint
in implementing development programmes. The Fund has used its
capacity for local cost financing judiciously, depending on
country considerations and the nature of the project. In fact,
the most desirable projects from the Fund and country's standpoint are those which maximize the use of local factors of production, e.g. labour, thus implying a large local cost component.

Some constraints

13. While the first year of operations has been encouraging,
it has also revealed some constraints which will affect the
level of the Fund's operations and the rate at which the Fund
will be able to develop projects of the quality that it seeks.
14. The most serious of these is that, with few exceptions,
most member countries of IFAD have a very limited capacity for
project preparation. The Fund invites the active cooperation
of member governments in seeking a solution to this problem.
While some institutions, e.g. FAO and the Economic Development
Institute of the World Bank, undertake training courses in
project preparation work, a much more concerted effort is
required.
15. The Fund stands ready to join hands with FAO, UNDP and
other development agencies to assist governments to develop
project preparation units in the appropriate ministries of the
countries concerned through the establishment of core groups at
the central or regional or provincial levels, whose task would
be to develop a pipeline of high priority projects. The members of such core groups would be encouraged to visit ongoing
investment projects in countries that can provide the relevant
experience.
16. Governments can also play a significant role in stimulating the development of locally based agricultural consulting
firms. Faced with the mushrooming costs of consultant services
from the developed world, it is time to think in terms of a
partnership between expatriate firms and local expertise, particularly as the latter's knowledge of the human, social and
institutional aspects, would undoubtedly improve the quality of
project preparation and implementation. An analysis of the
experience of rural development in some countries shows, for
example, that after the expatriate technical expertise has left,
a vacuum results in the project management which adversely affects the project's implementation. The development of local
consulting services would be a powerful tool to supplement the
usual government administrative structure during various stages
of project implementation.
17. Another constraint is the length of the project cycle which
on average requires two or two-and-a-half years to bring a
project to fruition. The Fund hopes to explore with its cooperating institutions practical approaches to shortening the
project cycle. If the focus can be shifted away from exhaus-
tive project preparation and loan documentation in favour of a
more flexible approach to permit changes during the project implementation phase, a great deal of time could be saved without
sacrificing project quality in the case of many projects.

Interagency co-operation

18. In December 1977, after the IFAD Agreement entered into
force, the United Nations General Assembly and the Fund's Governing Council approved a key agreement between the United Nations and the Fund which brought IFAD into relationship with
the United Nations as a Specialized Agency. In addition to
conferring specialized agency status on the Fund, the Agreement
sets out of a framework for cooperation between the two organizations in a number of specific areas, including reciprocal
representation at meetings; exchanges of information and documents; and in the budgetary, financial and personnel field.
One of the most important of the provisions of the Agreement
calls for IFAD to cooperate closely with the United Nations in
the latter's effort to coordinate effectively the policies and
activities of the United Nations system and to participate in
the work of the Administrative Committee on Coordination and
other United Nations bodies which seek to enhance such cooperation and coordination.
19. During 1978, the Fund has moved ahead to fulfil its responsibilities under this Agreement by participating actively in
the work of the ACC and its Sub-Committee on Nutrition and Task
Force on Rural Development; through close collaboration with
the International Civil Service Commission, the Consultative
Committee on Administrative Questions, and the Joint Staff Pen-
sion Board; and through representation on a selective basis at
United Nations meetings and conferences such as the Second
Regular Session of the Economic and Social Council and the
United Nations Conference on Technical Cooperation among Developing Countries.
20. In addition to this fundamental Agreement which provides
the basis for IFAD's overall relationship with the United Nations, the Fund has concluded specific agreements with several
other international institutions with which it plans to cooperate particularly closely. Six such agreements were concluded
in 1977 (with FAO, World Bank, UNDP and the Asian, African and
Latin American Regional Development Banks) and two further
agreements (with ILO and the Islamic Development Bank) were concluded in 1978.

Organization and staff

21. As indicated above, in December 1977 the Governing Council
approved the Relationship Agreement between the United Nations
and IFAD, which was followed by the General Assembly's adoption
of Resolution A/RES/32/107 establishing IFAD as a UN specialized
agency. The Executive Board adopted the provisional use of a
Personnel Policies Manual, proposed by the IFAD Preparatory
Commission and approved the adoption of the UN Common System
for determining the initial salary structure of the staff of
the Fund.

22. Furthermore the Executive Board was unanimous in its view that the President should determine the organizational structure of the Fund. The President has organized the secretariat of the Fund in the light of anticipated programme requirements and has established a departmental structure based on major functional responsibilities. He has appointed a Vice-President at the level of Under-Secretary-General, and three Assistant Presidents at the level of Assistant Secretary-General, in line with the organizational structure of the UN Common System.

Future programme of work

23. As already mentioned, the Fund has so far approved 10 loans totalling US$ 117 million during 1978. For 1979, the Executive Board has endorsed a commitment target of US$ 375 million. This will mean a tripling of the 1978 commitment level during 1979.

24. The Fund has already discussed a very significant number of projects for possible co-financing with the World Bank and the three Regional Development Banks. Of these, at least 18 to 20 projects should be ready for submission to the Executive Board during 1979. The size of these co-financed projects varies but the total amount that may be committed in these projects would range between US$ 180 to US$ 200 million.

25. As indicated earlier, 16 project identification missions were organized during 1978 to identify projects for financing by the Fund. During 1979, it is planned to send another 22 to 25 such missions. Since most of the projects identified by these missions will require at least 12 to 18 months to prepare, appraise and approve, only about 10 to 12 of the Fund initiated projects are expected to be ready during 1979 for submission to the Executive Board. These may involve total commitment levels ranging from US$ 160 to US$ 200 million.

26. By the end of 1979, the Fund expects to have a substantial 'pipeline' of projects for financing in 1980 and subsequent years.

27. To handle the larger programme of work proposed for 1979, the Executive Board has recommended an administrative budget of US$ 10,450,000 including contingencies of US$ 950,000. The budget provides for a total staff of 136 in 1979 - 65 professional and 71 support staff. The budget also includes an amount of US$ 3,100,000 for payments to cooperating institutions and consultants.

28. As envisaged in the Agreement Establishing the Fund, the main objective of the Fund is to assist the rural poor. This objective will be carefully pursued in selecting projects identified by various cooperating institutions and in the work of the project identification missions sponsored by the Fund. In addition, a special effort to design projects and programmes fully in line with the Fund's Lending Policies and Criteria,

will be made by sending <u>special programming missions</u> to 7 member countries.

29. These missions will examine possibilities of a rapid increase in food production and at the same time attempt to profile clearly the rural poverty situation in the country. By bringing together the results of these two enquiries it should be possible for the mission to suggest a strategy that can lead to an increase in production while at the same time improving the income and employment of the rural poor. The mission's work would lead directly to the identification of specific projects and programmes that are suitable for the Fund's financing and also to a discussion of the longer-term policy and institutional implications of the proposed programmes. If this approach is successful in identifying the right kind of projects, it can be extended to a few other countries during 1980.

Conclusion

30. This brief review of the Fund's activities during 1978 should help to highlight the substantial progress already made in commencing the Fund's operations and in moving towards the objective of assisting member countries in their agricultural development. During 1979, the Fund will further strengthen its efforts, not only to reach the commitment target of US$ 375 million but also to move still closer to its real goal of reaching the rural poor.

31. The rate of growth of food production in most of the developing countries, according to reliable studies, has continued to be grossly inadequate. Only a few developing countries have been able to achieve the annual growth target of 4 percent set for the decade in the International Development Strategy. In most other countries the annual increase in food production has been about 2 percent or below, and in a few cases food production has actually declined. According to an FAO survey, during the 1960s, 56 out of 128 developing countries had population growth rates higher than food production growth rates, with the result that the per capita food production declined. During the 1970s, the number of developing countries in this condition rose to 69 and now also include the highly populated countries such as India, Pakistan, Mexico and Egypt.

32. Growth rates in the 42 most seriously affected countries have been particularly disappointing. If such trends are not reversed, it is clear that by 1985 the gap between food needs and food availabilities in the developing countries will be even larger than the 85 million tons predicted at the World Food Conference in 1974. When the food gap of developing countries, as measured in actual imports, was 30 million tons in 1971-72, an estimated 480 million people in developing countries were suffering from hunger and malnutrition. With the continued rapid growth of population this number of hungry people in the world has increased.

33. The large harvests in the main grain exporting countries in the past three years and the resultant increase in cereal supply and stocks have not altered the overall food situation in the developing countries, despite recent improvements in food stock levels in some of them. According to various projections the food imports of developing countries would increase from 60 million tons in 1977 to 85 million (or even 100 million) tons by 1985, unless the average rate of agricultural production in these countries could be accelerated from 2.6 percent per annum in 1970-77 to at least 4.0 percent per annum in the next seven years.

34. These figures, despite the recent improvements in food stock levels in some developing countries, lead to the disturbing conclusion that the real problem of hunger, malnutrition and poverty facing millions of poor people in the developing world has not been alleviated during the past few years. For many it may have actually become worse. At least 20 percent of the population in Africa, Asia and Latin America do not have enough to eat and are confronted each day with the problem of survival.

35. One factor which is of particular importance in accelerating the growth of food production is the flow of external resources for agricultural development in the developing countries. In the past few years, the total flow of external resources to agriculture has increased from US$2,700 million in 1973 to US$6,000 million in 1977, although in constant 1972 prices, the flow is estimated to have increased from US$2,300 million to only US$3,400 million. The actual flow of external resources is considerably less than the proposed target of US$8.4 billion per annum, in 1975 prices, to attain the annual average increase of 4 percent in agricultural production.

36. A serious effort is being made by most bilateral and multilateral agencies to pay greater attention to the needs of small farmers. But it is still unclear if there has been a proportionate impact on improving the productive capacity, employment and well-being of both the small farmers and the landless.

37. IFAD is but one part of a larger international development cooperation effort. While clearly not sufficient given the magnitude of the problem, the resources that have been made available to the Fund do represent a significant step in assuring the larger external assistance contributions that are needed.

38. IFAD's other contributions to the resolution of the food problem - through the emphasis it can give to the problems of the rural poor and through the potential catalytic effect it can have in encouraging larger investments in agricultural and rural development - could also be very substantial over the longer term. IFAD's member countries can therefore expect the Fund to play an important role in their common efforts to reduce, and ultimately to eradicate rural poverty.

STATEMENT OF INDIA BY MR. ROMESH BHANDARI

It is estimated that external assistance of the order of US$
8.3 billion would be required by 1980. This is only 1/3rd of
the total investment which would have to be made. As such, it
would imply that there would have to be a total annual investment of US$ 25 billion. This investment would cover several
aspects of development including the requirement of inputs such
as high-yielding varieties of seeds, fertilizers, pesticides,
etc. the development and reclamation of land and taking of pre-
ventive measures against soil erosion, deforestation, etc., the
development of water resources, prevention of food losses, establishment of Agro-industries, development of human resources,
fisheries, livestock, forestry, storage, marketing, research
and development. My delegation would however, wish to make a
submission that along with the objectives sought to be achieved
and the inputs, both financial and others, required to achieve
these objectives, we have not taken into account the other fall
outs and multiplier effects which in turn would make very
significant contributions towards national and international
development.

STATEMENT OF TURKEY BY MR. TASHIN TARLAN

There is no doubt that responsibility in the sphere of agricultural and food development lies primarily with the developing countries themselves. Estimates relating to world food
production in the 1980s indicate growing deficits. In view of
the concerns which exist within the formal and traditional
sectors in the developing countries and the resulting under-
employment and unemployment in rural regions, the developing
countries are obliged to devote additional resources to agriculture and to non-agrarian rural development. That should
certainly ensure that growth is oriented towards the present
and future needs of those countries. In fact, in certain developing countries there are already encouraging signs of this.
    However, the transfer of internal resources to new objec-
tives requires considerable additional aid on concessional terms
from the industrialized countries which are currently advocating
a new approach to development.
    It is true that, for some years now, an increasing pro-
portion of external resources has been allocated to agricultural
development, although that has not increased the total volume
of assistance provided to those countries.
    It is also true that nothing can replace internal measures
designed to implement agrarian reform, to encourage co-operatives,
to improve market structures and to develop public services, to
mention only a few.

Consequently, we consider that the international efforts made to transfer additional resources in the form of aid and to facilitate trade must be supplemented by national efforts to accord a higher priority to food and agriculture and to implement national reforms. The absence of either one of these essential elements, namely national efforts and additional international resources, could ruin this endeavour. That is how a concept, and one of the most promising at that, can be transformed into a euphemism and serve only for polemics.

STATEMENT OF ARGENTINA BY MR. ENRIQUE J. ROS

The main objective of concerted action by the total international community should be to increase substantially agricultural and food production by the developing countries. This substantial increase in production or productivity should be attained by international measures in two complementary but distant fields: a flow of resources and financial assistance on the one hand, and a compatible commercial policy on the other.

Foreign financing in order to overcome problems of food and agricultural development has a particular relevance in the present-day world. Bilateral and multilateral financial assistance should be focused not only where the need for food is most acute but, also at the same time, should be used for improving production in those countries where a combination of production factors assure high levels of efficiency and a significant potential for an increase in agricultural output.

As a point of departure, the plenary committee in its deliberations should begin with the measures already decided upon. They should be fully implemented into practice and new ones created which will assure a continuous flow of large resources. The measures listed in the first part of the document presented by the Group of 77 are a good example of the financial assistance blue-print needed by the developing countries.

STATEMENT BY DR. PIOTR FEYBERG OF POLAND

We agree with those delegations and with the opinion expressed the other day by the distinguished representative of FAO which hold that the only way to fight hunger and malnutrition is to help food deficit countries increase their own production of food. We do appreciate and support the efforts which seek to mobilize a greater volume of external assistance to speed the development of agricultural sectors in the developing countries. However, this activity should be accompanied by growing reliance on domestic resources to meet the needs of agrarian sectors and should entail introduction of social reforms to ensure a more

equitable income distribution. In this context, the forthcoming Conference on Agrarian Reform and Rural Development
should give a fresh impetus in this direction.

We attach great importance to questions to be considered
during this Conference, because we strongly believe that problems of a structural nature are of primary importance for the
developing countries. In our opinion, socio-economic transformations are the only effective way to ensure a dramatic
breakthrough in food production resulting in permanent improvement of the food situation in the developing countries.

STATEMENT OF EC BY MR. JACQUES LEPRETTE

As the last General Assembly approved the recommendations
adopted in Mexico, the latter undeniably constitute the back-
drop for our discussions in this Committee. That does not pre-
clude our directing our consideration with the Plenary Committee
to issues that may not, as yet, have been discussed in sufficient depth in the various specialized international fora.
Having recalled the consequences for most of the developing
countries of inadequate food production, the Community would
like to address its remarks to two of the principal fields in
which the industrialized countries are able to provide effective
support for efforts undertaken by the developing countries themselves: that of the transfer of resources and that of the transfer of technology for the benefit of agriculture.

With regard to transfers of resources, the European Economic Community is prepared to make an active contribution, on
a bilateral or a multilateral basis, to all activities undertaken by the developing countries in the context of policies
they have defined themselves with a view to increasing their
food production and contributing to their rural development.
In this respect, it is pleasing to note that many developing
countries are now becoming aware of the fact that, all too
often, the production of foodstuffs has not been fully accorded
the necessary priority.

The question of the volume of, and conditions governing,
the aid to be provided to agriculture and, more specifically,
to the food sector, if the minimum target of an annual growth
rate of 4% is to be achieved, is one of the points under discussion in international debates on the development of agricultural and food production.

Since the World Food Conference, some estimates have been
put forward, _inter alia_ by the Secretariat of the World Food
Council, which put the developing countries' needs in respect
of external assistance from all sources at $US 8.3 billion (at
1975 prices) of which $6.5 billion should be on concessional
terms. But it is quite clear that these estimates alone will

not suffice to resolve the fundamental problems which concern,
on the one hand, measures of an economic nature and, on the
other, the establishment of concrete, well thought-out assistance
projects.

That is why the Community intends to participate actively
in the work which the present and potential donor countries
must undertake in order to consider the ways and means by which
they can more effectively support the efforts of the developing
countries to increase agricultural production; it is also willing
to provide particular support to countries which have prepared
their own food and nutrition plan and to provide the necessary
assistance to countries which have established such a plan.

With regard to the second point, the transfer of technology, it is clear that the need to develop the introduction of
improved production technology and, for that purpose, to identify appropriate technologies, is increasingly felt to be one
of the most important keys to the food problem.

On the other hand, it is necessary to develop specific
technologies that will take into account local conditions and
that depend, initially, on traditional methods of production.
The aim pursued would then be not only to increase agricultural
production but also to bring about development of the rural world
that will enable the peoples concerned, in the short term, to
meet their own food requirements and, in the long term, to safeguard their human and natural resources.

In this spirit, the European Economic Community is prepared to support initiatives designed to provide a solution to
food problems by the appropriate technologies. Specifically,
this means that it is prepared to help the countries which
commit themselves, or wish to commit themselves, to a policy of
restructuring their system of research-training extension. It
also means that it is willing to promote the examination of
these ideas at the international level and to collaborate in a
better organization of research at the national and international levels. It means, finally, that the Community is ready to
increase the share of its financial assistance which is devoted
to projects that can, by definition, contribute to the success
of this new policy.

STATEMENT OF SWEDEN BY MR. PER JODAHL

Internal resources and national development efforts must continue to bear the main burden in the development process. But
at the same time they must be supplemented by sufficient external resources. In our opinion the main emphasis should be
on the overall increase of external resources available for
development. The question of distribution of resources between
different sectors should largely be left to the priorities of
the recipient countries.

Consequently, we are hesitant about sectoral targets.
Estimates such as the proposed 8.3 billion dollar target for
external assistance to agriculture might be useful for mobilizing external resources. The response should, however, be a
joint effort, where donors increase the overall flow of resources
and recipients accord an increased priority to agriculture and
rural development in their national development strategies.

Over the last years, we have seen how an increased focus
on the problems of rural development has led to sizeable increases in the share of resources directed towards the development of agriculture. This includes increasing shares of multilateral funding for these purposes. We feel that this type of
political action is a more constructive and efficient contribution to improved resource allocation for agriculture.

An increased transfer of resources could lead to mutual
benefits for both developed and developing countries through a
revitilization of the global economy and an expansion of international trade. Increased attention should be given to possible
mechanisms for such transfers, and how they might be designed
in order to contribute towards a more just international economic order.

It is therefore important that the interest in new mechanisms for the transfer of resources should not lead to a reduction or stagnation of official development assistance. Especially, official development assistance to the least developed
countries must be increased substantially, since they may not
be able to profit from other forms of increased transfer of
resources to the same extent as the more advanced countries.

We should not overlook the question of how the terms and
conditions of development assistance should be modified in order
to meet the internal needs of recipient countries. More attention should also be given to the need to overcome internal
social and economic impediments to rural development and food
production, in order to make more efficient use of available
resources.

A strengthening of the national economies of the developing countries would reduce the lack of balance in negotiating
positions and enable the developing countries to draw equitable
benefits from the global interdependence between countries. In
our view, strategies for agrarian reform and rural development
are therefore indispensable parts of the work towards a more
just International Economic Order.

These issues should be taken up for more substantial discussions in specialized fora such as the World Conference on
Agrarian Reform and Rural Development this summer. We should
draw attention to the importance of these issues in our final
document.

8 World Food Security

The issue of food security is addressed by FAO and a number of states: FAO proposes a new Five-Point Plan of Action.

THE HISTORIC PROBLEM OF WORLD FOOD SECURITY
FAO TECHNICAL PAPER A/AC.191/37

Important requirements for world food security are the faster increase in production in the developing countries and the measures in favour of the poorest groups already emphasized. Even if these requirements can be realized, however, it will also remain necessary to protect food supplies from the fluctuations caused by variations in the weather and other disasters.

Carryover stocks of cereals have increased steadily since 1975/76. Although they may be regarded, in global terms, as sufficient for world food security, they are very narrowly concentrated geographically, and are inadequate in most developing countries. The opportunity provided by these stocks has yet to be seized to establish the system of internationally co-ordinated national reserves envisaged in the FAO International Undertaking on World Food Security. Thus the situation is no better than in 1972/73, when stocks were also large but subject to no international co-ordination, and were quickly run down following exceptionally widespread crop failures. This could even occur again today, in spite of the apparently comfortable level of stocks.

For some years now, it has been hoped that the protracted international grains negotiations would finally result in the formal establishment of the system of reserve stocks called for by the International Undertaking. Governments should assess very carefully the far-reaching implications of the recent

breakdown of these crucial negotiations. Every effort should
be made to reconcile the outstanding differences, with a view
to reconvening the negotiations as soon as possible. In the
meantime, however, it is essential that the major producing and
consuming countries should be prepared without further delay to
implement the stock provisions of the International Undertaking
on a voluntary basis, through the consultative machinery provided
by FAO's Committee on World Food Security (CFS), which will be
holding its fourth session in April 1979.

An important component of world food security, provided for
in the International Undertaking, is assistance to developing
countries in implementing national food security schemes, for
the acquisition of stocks and the establishment of related
facilities, including storage, marketing and transport. In
addition to the need for increased financial support for FAO's
Food Security Assistance Scheme (FSAS), it would be useful if
more donors would co-ordinate their bilateral activities in
this field with those of the FSAS.

The need for better arrangements to meet emergencies is
particularly emphasized by the events in 1978, when such situations were unusually numerous, including serious flood damage
in several Asian countries, desert locust invasion in parts of
Africa and Asia, and outbreaks of African swine fever in the
Mediterranean and Latin America. Contributions to the International Emergency Food Reserve (IEFR) in 1978 again fell far
short of the target. The Mexico Declaration of the fourth session of the WFC stressed that it should be established as a
continuing reserve with yearly replenishment, and placed at the
disposal of the United Nations/FAO World Food Programme (WFP).

As regards food aid in general (for development and nutritional purposes as well as for meeting emergencies), the
minimum target of 10 million tons of cereals has still not been
met in the more than four years that have elapsed since it was
set by the World Food Conference. It was hoped that it would
be possible to agree in the international grains negotiations
on a new and enlarged Food Aid Convention (FAC), designed to
guarantee the achievement of this important target. The failure
to agree on this will aggravate the difficulties already faced
by food deficit countries. The existing FAC is to be extended
by protocol "in the light of the negotiations", and it is
essential that the negotiating donor countries who offered to
increase their food aid commitments should still do so, with
the object of reaching the target of 10 million tons. Moreover, food aid needs are increasing, and it is already necessary to consider a higher target of perhaps 15 to 16 million
tons a year by 1985.

The United Nations/FAO Committee on Food Aid Policies and
Programmes (CFA) should conclude its work as quickly as possible
on guidelines for improved food aid policies. One improvement
that was called for by the World Food Conference was increased

multilateral channelling of food aid. An important contribution in this regard would be to meet the WFP's pledging target
of $950 million for 1979-80.

The reduction of the enormous avoidable losses of food
could greatly diminish the rising food import requirements of
the developing countries and contribute substantially to world
food security. The Seventh special session of the General Assembly called for the reduction of these losses by at least
half by 1985 and the FAO Conference established an Action
Programme for the Prevention of Food Losses with a target of
$20 million in voluntary contributions. It is essential that
this modest target should be met, and that bilateral assistance
in this important field should also be substantially increased.

The Five-Point Plan of Action
Statement by Mr. Nurul Islam of FAO

I come now to the fourth of the main issues, which is world
food security. Basic requirements for world food security include the faster increase in production in the developing countries and the measures in favour of the poorest groups that I
have already stressed. Even if these requirements are realized,
however, it will also remain necessary to protect supplies and
prices from the effects of annual fluctuations in production.
The International Undertaking on World Food Security, which was
adopted by the FAO Council in November 1974, and has now been
signed by 75 governments and the EEC envisages the achievement
of this objective through the establishment of a system of internationally coordinated national stocks.

When this was first mooted, the level of stocks was quite
inadequate to set up such a system. Carryover stocks of cereals
have now been increasing steadily since 1975/76, and we estimate
that by the end of the current 1978/79 seasons those outside
China and the U.S.S.R. will be equivalent to 21% of annual consumption. This may be regarded in global terms, as sufficient
for world food security. However, the ideal opportunity provided by the high level of stocks has yet to be seized for the
formal establishment of the agreed system of reserves. The
stocks are very narrowly concentrated geographically, and they
are inadequate in most developing countries. The situation is
really no better than in 1972/73, when stocks were also large
but subject to no international coordination, and were quickly
run down following exceptionally widespread crop failures. The
same could even occur again today, despite the apparently comfortable level of stocks.

For some time it had been hoped that the protracted international grains negotiations would lead finally to an agreement
that would translate the main elements of the voluntary Inter-

national Undertaking into a legally binding instrument with
clearly defined rights and obligations regarding reserves,
prices, special assistance to developing countries, and other
elements essential for world food security. It was also hoped
that a new Food Aid Convention would provide a means of securing
a legal commitment to the minimum target of 10 million tons of
food aid in cereals, which has still not been met in the more
than four years that have lapsed since it was set by the World
Food Conference.

        However, the Negotiating Conference for a New International
Grains Arrangement adjourned on 14 February, because it was
unable to agree on a number of essential elements, including
the size of the reserve stocks, prices, and special assistance
to developing countries. It recommended that the International
Wheat Council extend the Wheat Trade Convention 1971, and that
the Food Aid Committee extend the Food Aid Convention 1971 in
the light of the work accomplished at the Negotiating Conference.
The Wheat Council and Food Aid Committee are in fact meeting
this week for that purpose.

        Now that the negotiations have been adjourned for an in-
definite period, governments must assess the new situation very
carefully, and in particular its implications for the urgent
human issue of world food security. It is necessary to reach
speedy agreement on the immediate steps required to assure
world food security in the light of the new circumstances.
Every effort must continue to be made to reconcile the outstanding differences, so as to reconvene the negotiations as
soon as possible, and arrive at an international grains arrangement that fully meets the requirements of world food security.
Pending the eventual conclusion of a new international grains
arrangement, however, action is urgently required to implement
the International Unertaking on World Food Security on a voluntary basis without further delay.

        A few hours ago in Rome, the Director-General of FAO an-
nounced a Five-Point Plan of Action that he is proposing for
this purpose. While calling on the entire international community to implement the Undertaking, the proposed action concentrates on measures to protect people in the most vulnerable
developing countries. The five points are as follows: (i) the
adoption by all countries of national reserve stock policies
and targets in accordance with the provisions of the Undertaking;
(ii) the establishment by FAO's Committee on World Food Security
of criteria for the release of such reserves; (iii) the adoption
of special measures to assist low-income food deficit countries
to meet their current food import requirements and emergency
needs; (iv) new arrangements to intensify and coordinate assistance to developing countries in strengthening their food
security, including the establishment of food reserves; and (v)
measures to promote the collective self-reliance of developing
countries through regional and other mutual aid schemes.

This Plan of Action will be discussed at the Fourth Session of the Committee on World Food Security, which is to be held from 5 to 11 April, with a view to its submission to the FAO Council for approval in June and to the full FAO Conference for adoption in November. It would also be transmitted to the World Food Council for endorsement. In the meantime, Mr. Chairman, your Committee is meeting at a most opportune moment to get the Plan of Action under way with the strong political support that it will undoubtedly require if it is to become a reality.

Since the proposals are so new, and since I am sure the Committee will want to give them its special attention, I hope you will forgive me if I take a little more of your time to explain some of their main aspects. One general aspect to which I should draw your attention is that they are designed to take account of the need, in the absence of a legally binding instrument with precise rights and obligations, for the further development and refinement of the existing voluntary arrangements for consultations and for the coordination of international action on world food security.

As regards the first point in the Plan of Action, a large number of countries adhering to the International Undertaking have already adopted national reserve stock policies and targets for cereals. Several countries, however, including some of the major exporters and importers, have not yet done so, some of them because they were awaiting the outcome of the international grains negotiations. It is recommended that all governments which have subscribed to the Undertaking should forthwith adopt such policies and targets, bearing particularly in mind that the special difficulties of developing countries in maintaining adequate stocks place an added responsibility on the rest of the international community. Governments, particularly of developed countries, should take full advantage of the present ample supply of cereals to meet their national stock objectives by the end of 1979.

Coming to the second point, it is recommended that national reserve stocks held in pursuance of the Undertaking should be released in the event of crop failure or natural or manmade disasters, in order to avoid the emergence of acute food shortages, to enable developing countries to satisfy their import requirements on reasonable terms and without adversely affecting their economic development, and to maintain a regular flow of food supplies to consumers both in domestic and, where appropriate, in international markets. In exceptional circumstances, the Director-General of FAO may alert governments to the need for additional releases of stocks to meet the urgent consumption requirements of developing countries.

The third point concerns the important objective of special measures (mainly food aid) to enable low-income food deficit countries to meet their current import requirements and emergency needs. It is recommended that all donor countries should

increase their food aid commitments to the levels they pledged
during the Negotiating Conference, and announce them as amendments to the 1971 Food Aid Convention. The minimum target of
10 million tons of cereals should be progressively raised to 13
million tons by 1982 and 16 million tons by 1985. The IMF
should be invited to consider the feasibility of providing additional balance of payments support to meet the rising food
import bills of low-income countries. All countries in a position to do so should contribute in 1979 to the International
Emergency Food Reserve, so as to achieve the target of 500,000
tons of cereals agreed by the Seventh Special Session. Contributions for 1978 reached only about 70% of this target. The
reserve should be established on a continuing basis with yearly
replenishment, and placed at the disposal of the United
Nations/FAO World Food Programme (the WFP), as was recommended
by the Fourth Session of the World Food Council and endorsed by
the General Assembly. All food aid donors should consider establishing food aid reserves, in order to maintain the continuity of food aid in times of short supplies and high prices, and
earmarking part of them for meeting international emergency
requirements.

        While discussing food aid, I should mention some other
aspects that are not specifically referred to in the new Plan
of Action. It is necessary to expedite the work of the United
Nations/FAO Committee on Food Aid Policies and Programmes on
guidelines for improved food aid policies. One aspect is the
greater multilateral channelling of food aid. In this respect
it is of the utmost importance that the pledges to the WFP for
1979-80 should speedily be raised from the current level of
$695 million to the agreed target of $950 million.

        Returning to the Five-Point Plan of Action, its fourth
point concerns special arrangements for food security assistance to developing countries to establish and maintain the
necessary food reserves. FAO has established the Food Security
Assistance Scheme for this purpose. The Plan of Action recommends additional bilateral and multilateral assistance in this
field, so as to make it possible for developing countries to be
in a position to participate effectively in achieving the objectives of the International Undertaking. It also proposes
certain institutional arrangements under the auspices of the
FAO Committee on World Food Security, to review such assistance, identify gaps and suggest ways of meeting them, and to
facilitate the coordination of the bilateral and multilateral
effort.

        The fifth point in the Plan of Action is closely related.
Some groups of developing countries are already exploring
various collective initiatives to improve their food security,
for example in respect of joint action on reserve stocks, mutual
assistance at times of crop shortfalls, special trading arrangements and joint ventures in food production. It is now all the

more urgent for such efforts to promote the collective self-
reliance of developing countries to be intensified, and to be
fully supported by the international community.

THE INTERNATIONAL WHEAT AGREEMENT AND FOOD SECURITY
STATEMENT OF THE EC BY MR. JACQUES LEPRETTE

With regard to food security, the European Community reiterates
its desire to see the negotiations to replace the 1971 Wheat
Agreement reach their conclusion as soon as possible. After so
much time and effort has been invested in these negotiations,
it profoundly regrets the fact that it has not been possible to
bring them to a conclusion. Having concerns as both an importer and an exporter and, in addition, having close links with a
number of developing countries, it has been able to adopt a
middle-of-the road position. It is still willing to try again,
if all the parties concerned agree to adopt a realistic approach
and show evidence of the willingness to compromise which is essential, in particular with regard to the important question of
prices.

WORLD FOOD SECURITY AND LEVELS OF SUPPORT
STATEMENT OF THE GROUP OF 77 BY
MR. MAHMOUD MESTIRI REPRESENTING

Until current efforts, and those for which we are appealing,
produce the anticipated results on agricultural and food production in the developing countries, our countries will need
increasing food aid to make up our deficits. Furthermore, the
food security system provided for in the International Undertaking on Food Security remains indispensable.
    In both respects, the situation is far from satisfactory.
    The food aid target of 10 million tons, established by the
Rome Conference, has never been reached. Now that forecasts
indicate that the volume of pledges may possibly reach the desired level for the period 1978/1979, it is clear that larger
quantities should be planned for the coming years. We, for
our part, propose that the target for 1985 should be in the
order of 15 to 16 million tons of cereals and that the modalities for food aid should be made more flexible.
    However, we cannot but regret that the conclusion of the
new food aid convention continues to be blocked by delays in the
Conference to Negotiate an International Arrangement to Replace
the International Wheat Agreement.
    This Conference has, in any case, and to our great regret,
reached a deadlock. In our paper, we propose that the Committee

should urgently request that the questions pending be considered
in a positive spirit so that the Conference can resume as soon
as possible and conclude the Arrangement, ensuring that express
provisions in favour of developing countries are included therein, and thus contribute to the solution of the world food problem. The criteria we are proposing are designed to attain this
objective.

We can only regret that contributions to the international
emergency reserve have not yet reached the agreed level of
500,000 tons. We hope that the necessary measures will be taken
to remedy this. We also hope that there will be a rapid follow-
up to the decision adopted by the General Assembly to establish
the emergency reserve as a continuing reserve. It is necessary,
above all, to take full advantage of the current relative abun-
dance of stocks in order to launch the food security system on
solid foundations. Since the stocks are still essentially concentrated in certain industrialized countries, it is the duty
of those countries, and it is also in their interests, to make
every effort to attain this objective so as to spare the world
the disastrous effects of any new food crisis.

THE FINNISH DOMESTIC GRAIN RESERVE STOCK AND THE FAO
PLAN OF ACTION FOR WORLD FOOD SECURITY
STATEMENT OF FINLAND BY MR. JUKKA VALTASAARI

In the field of food security I would like to point out that
Finland has accepted and continues to support the FAO International Undertaking on World Food Security. Accordingly, Finland has already adopted a national reserve stock target for
food grains called for in the FAO Plan of Action for World Food
Security. This food grain target corresponds approximately to
7 months domestic consumption and the Government is in a process of considering to increase considerably the food grain
target and to adopt also a target for coarse grains.

THE ARGENTINE POSITION: MR. EDUARDO J. ROS

One of the chief methods of establishing markets for food is to
accumulate reserves of grain. In this connection, the Argentine
Republic deeply regrets the state in which the negotiations has
fallen concerning the drawing up of a new international agreement on cereals and calls on the governments of the countries
which took part in these negotiations to make a great effort to
achieve concrete results leading to the adoption of a new agreement. In this connection, we need to stress that one of the
aspects which merits particular consideration is that of

financing the establishment of reserves and the necessary infrastructures for the storage of grains.

The Argentine Republic, accepting the challenge presented
to the world economic community by the present food situation,
has responded to it with a systematic increase of its agricultural production during the last three years. Grains, in particular, have been harvested in record quantities in the history of the Argentine economy. Also, significant advances have
been achieved in improving in infrastructure in Argentina, with
assistance from international credits, such as those from the
Interamerican Development Bank and the World Bank and from government agencies and the private sector. We are substantially
enlarging our storage capacity and our system of moving harvests. In the area of commercialization, we have succeeded in
erecting a far more efficient system by reducing red tape and
by coordinating and synchronizing the distribution of the harvests.

But, Mr. President, we reiterate that the international
community should be very clear about the fact that the effort
and achievements of our country as well as of other developing
countries will not contribute to the improvement of the world's
food situation if there is to be no stable and fair international system of production and commercialization.

It should be pointed out that this type of national action
by developing countries introduces an interesting field for
applying agricultural and food cooperation under the Buenos
Aires plan on technical cooperation among developing countries.
Within the Latin American scope, the areas covered by the plan,
through action committees dealing with matters such as grains,
seeds, fruits and oil, fertilizer and food supplements, are a
sufficient proof of this willingness to cooperate among developing countries.

The establishment of an efficient world-wide food assurance
system has been shown to be a difficult task, but the international community has recognized repeatedly that this is an in-
evitable mandatory objective to defeat, once and for all, the
scourge of hunger from the world. Today, once more, the international community faces another opportunity to reach that objective. We hope that out of this exercise in which we are all
involved will come the measures and recommendations laying a
firm, effective groundwork for establishing such a system. We
sincerely believe that the elements for it are within our reach.
It is therefore necessary that we exercise true political will
power so that these elements be harmoniously linked to form a
set of measures for action in the immediate future.

THE NEED TO STRENGTHEN DOMESTIC FOOD PRODUCTION CAPACITY
STATEMENT OF POLAND BY MR. PIOTR FEYBERG

One closely related problem which is in the focus of our attention, is the issue of food security. We approve of the objectives of world food security, and we recognize the importance of establishing international grain reserves.   The establishment of such reserves by the grain exporting countries
would, no doubt, make it easier to provide for grain needs at
times of poor harvests. There remains, however the crucial
issue of financing imports by the grain deficit developing
countries. This again leads us to the conclusion that
strengthening the food production capacity by the food deficit
countries is the only effective means of satisfying food requirements in those countries.

9 Food Aid

The issue of Food Aid is addressed by the World Food Council, Australia, the European Community and Finland. The relevant sections of the Mexico Declaration is included for comparative purposes.

INCREASE AND IMPROVEMENT OF FOOD AID
THE MEXICO DECLARATION OF THE WFC

25. Traditional donor countries and other countries in a position to do so should ensure at least 10 million tons of cereals as food aid per annum, preferably by forward planning, as appropriate, in physical terms on a multiyear basis.
26. A new food-aid convention, aimed at securing at least 10 million tons of cereals per annum, should be negotiated as a matter of urgency during 1978; countries which are signatories to the present Food Aid Convention should make every effort to substantially raise their contribution to a new convention; other countries in a position to do so should contribute substantial additional financial resources or grains for food aid in a new convention; and the Conference negotiating a new agreement should make special provision to enable new donors to join the convention.
27. Food aid to least developed countries should be essentially on a grant basis; donor countries should channel a more significant proportion of food aid through the World Food Programme.
28. Having considered the report of the Committee on Food Aid Policies and Programmes, the Council recommends that the Committee should intensify and complete as early as possible the work it has initiated to develop an improved policy framework

for food aid, including guidelines and criteria, needed to improve the structure and operations of food aid, both bilateral
and multilateral, and to encourage most effective and systematic
use of food aid to promote development and food security, improve nutrition and provide relief in emergency situations.
29.   The Council instructs its Bureau to consult with countries
engaged in the current negotiations to establish a new food aid
convention and requests other countries which might join the
convention to achieve these objectives.

INTERNATIONAL EMERGENCY RESERVE
THE MEXICO DECLARATION OF THE WFC

30.   The General Assembly should establish the international
emergency reserve of 500,000 tons of cereals as a continuing
reserve with yearly replenishment determined by the Committee
on Food Aid Policies and Programmes and placed at the disposal
of the World Food Programme. Reserves not called upon in one
year will be carried over into the next year.
31.   Governments should indicate the amounts of cereals or cash
they are prepared to place at the disposal of the World Food
Programme up to the level of 500,000 tons; such amounts should
preferably be indicated for more than one year in advance.
32.   The Committee on Food Aid Policies and Programmes should
examine the procedures and modalities governing the international emergency reserve of 500,000 tons of cereals to improve
the effectiveness of its operations, including securing its
continuity and its ready availability.
33.   All countries able to contribute to the international
emergency reserve and who have not yet contributed should do so
in order to ensure that the target of 500,000 tons of cereals
is achieved in 1978 and maintained thereafter.

THE CRITICAL NEED TO IMPROVE INTERNATIONAL SECURITY
THROUGH FOOD AID
STATEMENT BY MR. MAURICE J. WILLIAMS OF THE WFC

In the four years since the World Food Conference far too little
progress has been made on the vital promise to improve international food security. Today, in 1979, the world still operates
under the international foodgrain system of 1971 - a system
which was found to be seriously deficient in periods of adverse
weather and food crop failures. What this means is that:

-       food aid is still largely conducted according
        to the rules of surplus disposal available in

fairly large quantities when food production is
high and prices are low, and with no assurance
of sustained supply when there are crop shortfalls and the need for food aid is greatest.
This is what happened in the food crisis of
1972-1974, and under the present Food Aid Convention of 1971 it could happen again;

- there is still no international agreement that
in another world food crisis the low income
countries and the poor of the world would have
access to essential food supplies from developed country exporters at prices they could
afford. Again, as things now stand, the foodgrain market will be left to adjust to shortages by deprivation of food for those most in
need;

- in contrast, the people of the developed countries are protected by pricing and marketing
arrangements, including subsidies and export
controls, which means that they - and even their
animals - can eat well, even when hundreds of
millions of the world's people are priced out
of the international market for food.

The world food system was seen to be inequitable in 1974
when the nations of the world agreed to introduce an element of
supply management into the international grain market. Recent
years of bountiful harvests may have led to complacency, but
they cannot hide the record that governments have so far failed
to meet their responsibilities in the area of world food security. Nor is it possible to gloss over the fact that the member
governments of the International Wheat Council, meeting in
London today, will be backing away from their responsibilities
for building a better system of world food security if they
agree to a prolonged extension of mere voluntary consultation
procedures among themselves, which is what a two-year extension
of the 1971 Wheat Trade Agreement will mean.

History, at the time of the next world food crisis, will
see such dilatory action - or rather inaction - as an irrespon-
sible postponement of the problem.

In the spirit of the World Food Conference, and the responsibilities entrusted to the World Food Council, I call on
governments to return to the negotiating table no later than
September of this year and to come to agreement on at least the
minimum essential elements of world food security which was
promised to the world's people five years ago.

What then are the minimum essential elements of world food
security? We can identify at least three:

First, more adequate levels of food aid than the some 4
million tons pledged under the 1971 Food Aid Convention must be

placed on an assured and sustainable basis. Food aid programmes are now running over 9 million tons. The need will not
lessen in time of world food crisis and food shortage. It is
time for governments to place this programme on a more socially
responsive and humanitarian basis, with an assured level of 10
million tons - as recommended by the World Food Conference -
under an extension of the 1971 Food Aid Convention. This will
mean more equitable and higher contributions by the European
Economic Community, Japan and Switzerland. It also will require acceptance of food aid reserves by the U.S and other
major contributors to the programme.

I reaffirm the World Food Council request to the OPEC
countries to associate themselves with a new Food Aid Convention. In regard to new members, the announcements that Austria
and Norway will join the Food Aid Convention are most welcome.

Second, the world must establish means which are responsive
to international needs, according to rules firmly agreed, when
foodgrain stocks are high. Foodgrain stocks are now high; and
now is the time for governments to agree on a reserve management
plan which protects the essential food needs of the poor, as
well as those of the rich, in time of urgent need.

Third, I fully endorse FAO's five point action plan for
food security with its emphasis on strengthening national production and reserve stock policies, collective self-reliance
among nations, special measures to meet food import requirements
and emergency needs, as well as assistance to strengthen national food distribution and storage facilities. As FAO
Director-General Saouma has said, it is now time to implement
FAO's International Undertaking on World Food Security, which
was endorsed by the World Food Conference in 1974, and formally
adopted by 75 governments and the European Economic Community.

THE FOOD AID CONVENTION AND THE INTERNATIONAL WHEAT AGREEMENT
STATEMENT OF AUSTRALIA BY MR. R.J. GREET

The failure of governments to agree to a new international wheat
agreement last February is an example of the problems that can
emerge.

Australia was disappointed that these negotiations failed.
This Committee can hardly fail to take note of the situation
reached, but clearly this Committee cannot realistically tackle
the complex and inter-related issues involved in this negotiation.
The United Nations has already established a conference for
that purpose and in that context we stand ready to continue the
further negotiations needed to resolve the outstanding issues.
Meanwhile, I should indicate that Australia's food grain aid in
1979/80 will not only meet its commitment under the 1971 Food
Aid Convention but will in fact substantially exceed it.

The Food Aid Convention, in our view, moreover, is an integral part of any new agreement and of the negotiations on that agreement. As delegations will be aware, however, the recent U.N. Conference recommended that the International Wheat Council and Food Aid Committee under the current agreement discuss the future form of the Food Aid Convention and its relationship with the Wheat Trade Convention at their meeting in London which is taking place in London this week. The results of these meetings will be of particular significance to us here.

THE NEW FOOD AID CONVENTION AND THE INTERNATIONAL EMERGENCY RESERVE
STATEMENT OF THE EC BY MR. JACQUES LEPRETTE

The new food aid Convention must be incorporated in the new grains agreement. The Community has acted in accordance with the Manila Conference in providing, at the Geneva Conference, for an increase in the contribution made under the new food aid Convention in the context of an effort on the part of all the traditional and potential donor countries, with a view to attaining the international target of 10 million tons.

The Community has announced its support for establishing the international emergency reserve of 500,000 tons on a continuing basis. Independently of the contributions of its member States, it will continue to participate in that reserve on the same terms as it has in the past.

10 Agricultural Trade

The issue of international trade in agricultural products was addressed by several states and the FAO. The relevant section of the Mexico Declaration is included for reference.

IMPROVEMENT OF THE CONTRIBUTION OF TRADE TO THE SOLUTION OF FOOD PROBLEMS THE MEXICO DECLARATION OF THE WFC

34. The Council notes with concern the increase in protectionist trade practices that affect the economic development of the whole international community and, particularly as they reduce the export possibilities of developing countries, affect their economic development potential and reduce their capacity to import food they need, and urges the developed countries to make their best efforts to adjust those sectors of their agriculture and manufacturing economies which require protection against developing country exports.
35. With the objectives of directing greater world attention to needed trade reforms, market and price stability and economic adjustment and in order to improve the Council's capacity to influence positive actions in both of these areas, the Council recommends that developed countries engaged in the Multilateral Trade Negotiations should act in full compliance with their commitments to the developing countries, as accepted in the Tokyo Declaration, all countries should reaffirm their commitments undertaken at the sixth and seventh special sessions of the General Assembly and in resolution XIX of the World Food Conference* and all countries should take action so that the

---

*See Report of the World Food Conference, Rome, 5-16 November 1974 (United Nations Publication, Sales No. 75.II.A.3), part one, chap. II.

Multilateral Trade Negotiations arrive at a satisfactory conclusion in 1978, taking into account developing country interests in all aspects of the negotiations, including the Codes
of Conduct and, particularly, in those that affect food trade.
36. Developing countries should also review their trade policies, including those that affect this mutual trade with a view
towards contributing to the solution of their own food problems.
37. The Negotiating Conference on a Common Fund should be resumed as soon as possible in 1978; such a Fund should be created,
and all countries, in particular developed countries, should make
all efforts to support and participate in the individual commodity
agreements so that all the objectives set forth in resolution
93 (IV) of the United Nations Conference on Trade and Development will be fully reached.
38. Developed countries should include processed agricultural
commodities in their respective General Scheme of Preferences
systems and, while considering the imposition of limits under
these systems, should take into consideration the special trade
problems of developing countries.
39. The General Agreement on Tariffs and Trade and the United
Nations Conference on Trade and Development, in light of the
completion of the Multinational Trade Negotiations and the experience since the fourth session of the Conference, should
submit for the consideration of the Council at its fifth session an analysis of the impact of these and other negotiations
since the World Food Conference on the trade prospects of the
developing countries.
40. The Council notes the measures on the issue of trade included in the Programme of Economic Co-operation among Developing Countries adopted by the United Nations Conference on
Trade and Development on the subject, which took place in
Mexico, as well as the activities in this matter that are being
undertaken by the Division of Economic Co-operation among Developing Countries of the Conference that require that support
of all countries members of the United Nations system be given
to the Programme.
41. The Committee established under General Assembly resolution 32/174, at its next session, to be held in September 1978,
should give due attention to problems of food and malnutrition
in the developing countries, as expressed in the Manila Communique and in the Mexico Declaration.

THE CONTEXT OF TRADE
FAO TECHNICAL DOCUMENT A/AC.191/37

Recent improvements in the share of the developing coutries
in world agricultural exports and in the terms of trade of
their agricultural exports appear to have been only temporary
reversals of the longer-term declining trend. Their over-all

export earnings (including those from non-agricultural products) also affect the agricultural sector, because of the need to pay for imports of food and of the capital goods and inputs required to increase agricultural production. Improved conditions of international trade are a key aspect of NIEO and it is essential to make faster progress in the many international trade negotiations now under way. Increased export opportunities for processed agricultural products are particularly important for the industrialization of the developing countries.

Although some progress has been made in the UNCTAD negotiations on a Common Fund to finance an Integrated Programme for Commodities, their final outcome is still uncertain. This is also the case with the GATT Multilateral Trade Negotiations (MTN). Among the individual agricultural commodities covered by the Integrated Programme, there has recently been significant progress towards an international agreement only in respect of rubber.

It is essential that the breakdown of the international grains negotiations should not prejudice the Common Fund negotiations and the MTN. Further extension of the Generalized System of Preferences (GSP) is required in order to mitigate the growth of protectionist measures, particularly for processed products, in the developed countries. It is also necessary to expedite the conclusion of liberalized general compensatory financing schemes and of stabilization arrangements for those individual commodities on which early agreement appears likely, and to stimulate research and development measures to enhance the competitiveness of the agricultural exports of the developing countries.

While the developed countries are understandably inhibited in making concessions by their own employment and other problems, they could give more recognition to the fact that adjustments in their domestic agricultural economies and policies would bring long-term benefits to them, as well as to the developing countries, in an increasingly interdependent world economy.

THE IMPORTANCE OF TRADE TO THE DEVELOPMENT OF AGRICULTURE
STATEMENT BY MR. NURUL ISLAM OF FAO

I come now to the question of international trade....International trade in agricultural products has important implications for the growth and stability of the agricultural sector. Many developing countries still derive a large proportion of their export earnings from such products. It is therefore a serious matter that, in spite of some apparently temporary improvement in 1976 and 1977, their share in world agricultural export earnings has declined steadily over the longer term.

Their agricultural export earnings, especially from processed
products, continue to be limited by tariff and non-tariff barriers in developed countries, and to suffer from a damaging
degree of instability. Increased export opportunities for processed agricultural products are particularly important for
their industrialization.

Although some progress has been made in the UNCTAD negotiations on a Common Fund to finance an Integrated Programme for
Commodities, their final outcome is still uncertain. The same
is true of the current round of the GATT Multilateral Trade
Negotiations. Among the individual agricultural commodities
covered by the Integrated Programme, there has recently been
little significant progress towards new international agreements except in the case of rubber. Although the international
grains negotiations, to which I shall be referring in some detail later, lie outside the Integrated Programme, it is essential, not only that they should be resumed as soon as possible, but also that their failure to agree should not be allowed to prejudice the many other important negotiations that
are under way.

Further extension of the Generalized System of Preferences
is required, in order to mitigate the resurgence of protectionism, particularly for processed products, in some developed
countries. It is also necessary to expedite the conclusion of
liberalized general compensatory financing schemes, and of
stabilization arrangements for those individual commodities on
which early agreement appears likely, as well as to stimulate
research and development measures to enhance the competitiveness of the agricultural exports of the developing countries.

At the present time many developed countries are inhibited,
by their problems of unemployment and inflation, in making trade
concessions, expanding development assistance, and facing up to
adjustments in their domestic agricultural economies and policies.
They could, however, give more recognition to the fact that in
the long run such measures, by contributing to the prosperity
of the developing countries and thus their potential as export
markets, would bring benefits to developed as well as developing countries in an increasingly interdependent world economy.

THE COMMON FUND
STATEMENT BY MR. M.A. MCINTYRE OF UNCTAD*

The Common Fund had always been considered a vital element in
promoting greater stability in commodity markets. The third
session of the Negotiating Conference had reached agreement on

---

*Reprinted from the Summary Record (A/AC.191/SR24).

certain fundamental elements, which would permit the drafting
of articles for an agreement which the Conference would be able
to adopt at a future meeting before the end of 1979.

The financial structure of the Common Fund provided for
$400 million for the first window in order to finance buffer
stocks pursuant to international commodity agreements. It was
also envisaged that each member State would make a contribution
of $1 million under a proposal formulated by the Group of 77 as
part of the collective self-reliance programme and the framework
for negotiations adopted at Arusha. Collective self-reliance
had from the outset been an important aspect of the Common Fund,
as was reflected in the provisions governing its financial
structure. It had also been agreed to allocate part of the
contribution of $1 million to the second window, which would be
devoted to the financing of measures other than the buffer
stocks. Accordingly, $70 million would go to the second window
and the balance of $80 million to the first. Of the $320 million remaining from the first window, 10 per cent would be for
countries of the Group of 77, 68 percent for the countries of
Group B (market-economy developed countries), 17 per cent for
the socialist countries of Group D, and 5 per cent for China.
An objective of $280 million in additional contributions had
been proposed for the second window, which would bring the total
to $350 million. In short, the agreement on the financial
element of the Fund provided for total resources of $750 million.

On the basis of the principle of joint financing of reserve
stocks for all participants in the international commodity agreements, it had been decided that the respective entities would
be required to make a cash deposit in the Fund equivalent to
one third of their maximum financial needs, which would give
them credit rights representing two thirds of those needs.

Naturally, it had been necessary in the negotiations on
the Common Fund to take into account the positions of the different groups. Although all the countries had finally reached
a consensus regarding the fundamental elements of the Fund, a
number of explanatory statements had been made after its
adoption. At the present stage of the process, it was to be
hoped that the auspicious results achieved with respect to the
Common Fund would lead to further progress in the Integrated
Programme for Commodities and in co-operation between developed
and developing countries in the establishment of a new international economic order.

THE PROBLEM OF PROTECTIONISM
STATEMENT OF AUSTRALIA BY MR. R.J. GREET

I come finally to the question of international trade. A major
impediment to the achievement of greater stability in food and

agricultural production and trade is without doubt the widespread use of protectionist measures applied in the agricultural area. These measures not only distort production patterns but also inhibit restructuring and therefore reduce efficiency and increase the cost of agricultural commodities.
Moreover, efficient producers, including many developing countries, have the stability of their export trade threatened by
predatory subsidy practices and unfair competition in their
traditional markets. If these practices continue unfettered,
it will be impossible to achieve the objectives of improved
global productive efficiency and capacity. World food security
will not be enhanced and our efforts to promote stable trading
regime to the benefit of both importers and exporters of agricultural products will be further set back.

THE POLITICS OF PROTECTIONISM
STATEMENT OF ARGENTINA BY MR. ENRIQUE J. ROS

In the matter of commercial policy, one ought to bear in mind
that each country's productive structure confronts growing integration and interdependence across international channels of
routing and distribution of food and farm products. A more
efficient use of resources and investments used for the production of food requires the need of a dynamic stabilization of
world prices and assurance of access to markets for food produced by developing countries.
    In this regard the protectionist tendencies which devel-
oped countries are bringing to bear constitute one of the obstacles to the creation of a world-wide, stable system of trade
in agricultural products which would also meet the alimentary
needs of the developing countries.
    These protectionist policies include the granting of heavy
subsidies to domestic production and exports, as well as the
building of strong customs and non-customs barriers which impede and atrophy agricultural production and exports by the
developing countries. Thus, there is sheltering of subsidized
prices and the distribution of agricultural surplus under conditions with which domestic producers in the developing countries cannot compete. The developed countries place the agricultural production of the developing countries into a disad-
vantaged position on the international markets as well as within their own regions.

PREFERENTIAL TARIFFS
STATEMENT BY DR. PIOTR FEYBERG OF POLAND

The question of international trade in agricultural products
cannot be excluded from our discussion. We welcome the fact
that this important issue has found its place in a document
prepared by the developing countries and we do hope that this
crucial subject will be properly reflected in the final document of the current session of our Committee.

Poland has frequently expressed on various international
fora its attitude towards abolishing the barriers which limit
the expansion of international trade and stressing the need for
its full liberalization. As both importer and exporter of agricultural products, we understand very well the problem facing
the developing countries in this respect. That is why we have
always advocated the free development of trade based on the
principles of mutual benefits and rational division of labour
among countries and regions. In this context, we recognize the
needs of the developing countries to achieve better conditions
of access to the markets of the developed countries. Basing on
this premise, Poland has introduced a preferential tariff system
for imports of all products from the developing countries. The
system, which applies to more than a hundred countries and ter-
ritories, has had its far-reaching effects both in terms of the
scope and extent of the preferential treatment it bestows.

Finally, while discussing the question of international
trade, I would like to express our concern over the fact that
protectionist measures are being introduced at a rapidly growing
rate by many developed countries. In our opinion, the diminish-
ing share of the developing countries in world trade is one
result of the protectionist policies being pursued by the developed countries.

We do hope that the question of protectionism will be discussed in depth during the forthcoming UNCTAD-V.

THE EEC'S TARIFF EXEMPTION
STATEMENT OF THE EC BY MR. JACQUES LEPRETTE

In the field of trade, the Community's appearance on the international scene is that of a large importer of agricultural
products. Specifically, while its exports to developing countries reached only $US 6.2 billion in 1977, its imports from
those countries represented $21.2 billion, i.e. approximately
half its total imports.

The Community has eliminated all quantitative restrictions
as a means of frontier protection.

On the other hand, under the generalized system of pre-
ference, it has continued to increase the number of products on
which import duties are reduced or suspended. Further, as from
1 January 1979, the Community introduced a special scheme under
which all agricultural products on the GSP list from the least
developed of the developing countries can be imported completely free of duty.

FINNISH TRADE WITH THE DEVELOPING COUNTRIES
STATEMENT OF FINLAND BY MR. JUKKA VALTASAARI

Many of the previous speakers have discussed the subject of
food trade. Instead of repeating some of those views which
coincide with those of my Government, I would like to illustrate
the case of Finland by stating that agricultural imports from
developing countries to Finland have increased by 75% during
the period 1974-78. Finland has tried to take into account the
agricultural export interests of developing countries within
his GSP-system. Also within the MTN in GATT Finland has made
concessions concerning tropical products which have already
been implemented. We have also consistently supported the conclusion of international commodity agreements designed to bring
more stability in the export earnings of developing countries,
as well as the establishment of the Common Fund, in regard to
which recent progress has been recorded in the Geneva negotiations. We shall continue to carry out these and similar policies in the future, but it must be recognized that a country in
Finland's position cannot sustain this line of action without
regard to her national economic, social and security objectives.

THE NEED FOR TECHNOLOGICAL AND MANAGERIAL SUPPORT
IN AGRICULTURAL TRADE
STATEMENT OF ISRAEL BY MR. BENJAMIN ORON

My delegation wishes to present to this Committee some suggestions in order to encourage the appropriate bodies within the
U.N. system to promote and sponsor technological and managerial
cooperation between developing countries in strengthening the
agricultural supporting system. This initiative, typical of
TCDC, would require great support to lever arrangements between
countries, mainly between those developing countries whose economies rely strongly on the export of agricultural commodities.
The spheres of possible cooperation could be:

a) Joint sales promotion arrangements in foreign
markets in order to use advertising facilities and

infrastructure which one country has developed for
the use of other countries.
b)   Joint handling, packaging and storage arrangements where one country would make available to another country its facilities during the export off
season.
c)   Multi - bi-lateral cooperation and assistance to
help countries to invest in Research and Development
to improve supporting services related to the export
trade of agricultural products.
d)   Multi - bi-lateral cooperation in management
consultancy agreements for turnkey projects related
to post-harvest transport, shipping and wholesaling
agricultural commodities.
e)   Multi - bi-lateral arrangements whereby countries would cooperate in developing quality farm
inputs tailor-made to the specific needs of developing countries such as genetical material for plant
and livestock, compound fertilizers, pesticides,
farm equipment and irrigation equipment.

Although these suggestions cover only one of the aspects
of international agricultural trade, they could improve greatly
the competitiveness of developing countries, if simultaneous
progress is made in other areas impeding the access of their
agricultural product to the markets of developed countries.

11 Agriculture and Industry

THE RELATIONSHIP BETWEEN AGRICULTURE AND INDUSTRY

The Secretariat issued a technical paper (A/AC.191/39), which gives a most comprehensive overview of these issues of agricultural and industrial linkages, patterns of sectoral development, the role of policies and institutions in providing infrastructural facilities, the problems of finance and the problems of barriers to trade. The document is reproduced in its entirety.

Issues of Agricultural and Industrial Linkages

Demand and input linkages

The pace of growth in agricultural incomes is important in determining the size of the internal market for manufactures. This is evident in least developed and many other special-problem countries; and it is often critical in many countries which have already approached the limit of industrial expansion through import-substitution.

On the input side, production, employment and profitability in many industries are directly linked to the level of production of food and agricultural raw materials. Equally, the long-run success of agriculture depends on the creation of industries processing agricultural products, producing capital equipment for agriculture and providing such current inputs as fertilizers and insecticides.

Trade linkages

Lagging agricultural production for export limits the ability of countries to finance imports required for industrialization.

The need to finance substantial and growing food deficits hampers industrial expansion through restricting import capacity for capital and intermediate goods (for instance, in least developed countries). Exports of manufactures can also be the means to finance greater imports or imports of capital equipment and intermediate inputs for agriculture.

Over-all balance

Progress in agriculture and industry is linked, and sustained over-all economic progress requires a balanced expansion of the two sectors. But balanced expansion does not imply any unique relationship between industrial and agricultural growth rates or production patterns. The appropriate relationships vary widely among countries, and within countries at different stages in their development.

Desirable Patterns of Sectoral Expansion

Individual country concerns

A country's pattern of expansion will depend on its own particular circumstances, such as the size of its market, level of industrialization reached and pattern of resource endowments. In least developed countries, for instance, strategies emphasizing agro-based industries may be optimal; in many smaller countries, production for export is likely to be a key concern.

Common features

Whatever the particular circumstances, a few general features are of common interest to developing countries. One such is a process of adjustment of productive structures at the world level, affecting agriculture and industry, and manifested in the case of developing countries by their aspirations for a greater stake in world industrial production. Another is the desire for greater self-sufficiency in basic foods within the context of a more balanced system of international trade in foodstuffs.

Specific factors conditioning choices in agriculture and industry

(i) Possibilities for subregional and wide co-operation among developing countries: These will have an important bearing on the nature and sequence of industrialization, especially in smaller countries, and on whether food self-sufficiency is pursued in a national or subregional context.

(ii) Access to markets in developed countries: This affects decisions on the patterns of industrial production, including the promotion of processing industries, and the emphasis to be given to certain agricultural products.

(iii) Access to technology: This has wide ramifications relating both to productive structures and to national policies concerning technological research and development.

The Role of Key Policies and Institutions

Provision of infrastructural and related facilities

(i) In many countries, a crucial constraint to agricultural development is the lack of adequate and regular supply of irrigation water. Development of water resources involves large investment, requiring substantial external assistance. In other countries, land conservation measures are needed.

(ii) Control of certain diseases assumes particular importance for agriculture in some African countries, as a precondition of development.

(iii) For countries at the early stages of industrialization, a crucial bottleneck is the lack of infrastructure (supply of electricity and gas, roads and transport facilities, etc.), the development of which deserves a high priority and requires large amounts of resources.

(iv) A social infrastructure to promote the spread of literacy, formal and informal education, and technical training is a condition of technological innovation and of improving organizational capacity in both urban and rural areas.

Supply of inputs

Development of agriculture requires a concomitant increase in the supply of inputs like fertilizer and pesticides, necessitating increased domestic production and external procurement.

Institutional arrangements and reforms

(i) Land reform stands out as one of the most important aspects of institutional reforms which are basic to sustained agricultural development.

(ii) Extension services and local organizations for handling credit, marketing, supply of inputs, etc. need to be
strengthened.

Research and technology

(i) Greater efforts are needed in the field of agricultural research, especially in evolving high-yielding varieties
that are suited to particular environments. (Co-operation at
subregional and international levels can make a major contribution.)
(ii) The technological capacities of the developing countries are to be strengthened. Efforts are to be intensified to
secure transfer of industrial technology from the developed to
the developing countries on equitable terms. Collection and
dissemination of information on existing technologies need to
be strengthened.

External Financing of Agriculture and Industry

Present flows and future needs

Investment in both agriculture and industry in developing
countries rarely exceeds one-third of total investment. Roughly the same proportion of external resources goes to these two
sectors, with industry taking the somewhat larger share.
The expansion of both sectors requires increased capital.
FAO estimates that the needs of food production alone call for
a doubling of investment in that activity. The additional investment needs of industry will also be sizable.
A considerable share of finance required will have to come
from external sources, particularly in the case of least developed and other low-income countries. To this end a number of
institutional changes and policy initiatives can be introduced
by developing and developed countries as well as by international financing organizations.

Absorptive capacity in agriculture and industry

Developing countries can increase absorptive capacity in
several ways:

(i)   Specify their requirements in agriculture and elabor-
      ate, where necessary, a strategy and priorities;
(ii) Devise institutions for improved subregional co-
      operation, especially concerning machinery for attract-
      ing finance for multi-country projects;
(iii) Strengthen institutions for identifying, preparing
      and implementing projects, especially in agriculture
      and rural industries;

(iv)   Make precise and known on what terms and under what
conditions they would welcome private investment in
the development of their industries. (International
codes of conduct are relevant.);

(v)   Improve capacity to assess technologies.

Possible steps by providers of finance

(i)   Because much of agricultural development has a high
local cost component and recurrent cost burden, providers can
finance a greater proportion of such cost, especially in least
developed and other low-income countries.

(ii)   Since much worth while development in both agriculture
and rural industries take place in small and scattered activities, they can experiment more with, and support, institutions
that can promote the large scale multiplication of such activities. Where large scale projects are needed, they can assist
with their elaboration, implementation and finance.

(iii) They can co-operate to reduce the administrative burden on countries which deal with many financing agencies.

(iv)   They can provide food aid so that countries can finance their food deficits without curtailing the imports that
supply their industries; or they can provide food aid to back
up far-reaching agrarian reform or efforts to introduce export
crops or large scale experimentation with new agricultural techniques.

(v)   They can supply fertilizer or promote fertilizer industries in developing countries and make resources available in
support of enhanced world food security, especially for the
maintenance of adequate world grain reserves.

(vi)   They can increase substantially resources channelled
through national agricultural and industrial development corpora-
tions or banks, and make more concessional aid available in the
form of programme assistance, especially to countries in which
acute foreign exchange problems restrain capacity use and industrial expansion.

(vii) They can explore ways whereby the cost of private
loans for industrial development could be reduced, maturities
lengthened, greater security of access to established borrowers
guaranteed and access to new borrowers facilitated.

(viii) They can remove any obstacles in their own countries
to private investment in countries which wish to attract such
investment.

Access to Markets and Adjustment of Productive
Structures in Developed Countries

Barriers to trade

(i) Exports of agricultural commodities from the developing countries have been virtually stagnating. This is partly
due to policies in developed countries protecting domestic agriculture through tariff barriers, quantitative restrictions and
support for farm prices and incomes.

(ii) Exports of manufacturers from the developing countries
have been expanding fast till recently, providing an important
source of growth of manufactured output in these countries.
However, the recent upsurge of protectionism in developed market
economies is now seriously threatening this expansion.

Structural adjustment

Increased exports from the developing to the developed
market economies require adjustment in the structure of production in the latter group of countries through speedy transfer
of resources from uneconomic activities to more competitive
ones. Imports of manufactures from developing countries have
contributed very little to the problem of unemployment in the
developed economies. The solution to the problem of unemployment in particular industries lies not in protectionism but in
structural adjustment.

Redeployment of industries

The Lima Declaration calls for redeployment of industries
in favour of the developing countries as one of the elements of
policy to accelerate the process of their industrialization.
The UNIDO system of consultation has been a useful forum for
discussion of the global aspects of development of some of the
industries.

THE IMPORTANCE OF INDUSTRY FOR AGRICULTURAL DEVELOPMENT
STATEMENT OF MEXICO BY MR. JORGE EDUARDO NAVARRETE

The development of agricultural-related industries is an important part of the general process of industrial development in
numerous countries. In Mexico's case, these industries constitute an important element in policies which seek to decentralize
our industrial development and increase occupations for the
population in rural areas, so as to impede the exaggerated
growth of population in the cities. In the system of consultation meetings of the UN Organization for Industrial Development,

the international community has a potentially efficient instrument for promoting such agro-industrial development in the fullest sense of the term. Meetings and consultations have already
been held concerning the fertilizer and vegetable oils industries; the conclusions reached there must be put into practice.
Briefly, consultations will shortly be held on agricultural
machinery in Italy in October, and on food processing later on.
We should not allow the opportunity presented by these meetings
to pass by, in order to further the development of these sectors
and significantly increase participation by the developing countries in them. Latin American regional cooperation using the
Latin American Economic System (SELA), has accorded special
importance to cooperation in the agricultural/agro-industrial
sectors. Five of the action committees set up by SELA cover
the agriculture sector or industrial activity related to it.
That is why my Delegation attributes importance to the proposed
cooperation among developing countries to receive adequate financial support and technical assistance from the advanced countries and international organizations.

AGRICULTURAL AND INDUSTRIAL DEVELOPMENT ARE LINKED
STATEMENT OF YUGOSLAVIA BY MR. MILJAN KOMATINA

It is more or less known that the increase in food production
in the developing countries depends on many factors. As has
always been the case, food can be produced in various ways and
the results depend on us. The basic difficulties that the developing countries are faced with in their efforts to increase
food production reside in their material possibilities, in their
levels of development and the possibility to import the required
inputs, etc. With economic development, every country, has in
most cases, found a solution to its food problems. For many
developing countries it has been very often said that increased
investments in agriculture and rural development are of the
greatest importance for the growth of food production. However,
one very often loses sight of the fact that investments in agriculture alone, irrespective of their size, cannot solve the
problem. Agricultural production is linked with or dependent
on many factors. Investments in agriculture call for parallel
investments in industrial development. Because, if there is no
corresponding industrial base capable of supplying agriculture
with appropriate input, in the form of fertilizers, pesticides
and technical equipment, then it is very difficult to expect
from the developing countries to reach the necessary rate of
growth in food production. We have here particularly in mind
the experience gained in Yugoslavia. Our agricultural production began to develop at an accelerated rate only after a determined period of very intensive economic development of the coun-

try, wherein particular emphasis was put on industrialization
and the establishment of a technical capability through the
training of experts needed for applying in practice the technical
achievements realized in our country and adjusted to its conditions and requirements. As a result of the inter-play of all
these factors, Yugoslav agricultural production in some aspects,
especially with the regard to the yield of grain, has achieved
remarkable successes and has joined the ranks of countries with
a highly developed agriculture.

At any rate, the development of agriculture – not excluding,
of course, the impact of climatic and other factors – depends,
among other things, on the degree of industrial development of
a country. Actually, the reason why the long-awaited "green
revolution" has not yielded satisfactory results are due to
inadequate material and technical conditions in many countries
which have not enabled them to introduce intensive agriculture.

12 Rural Development

The issue of rural poverty as the primary cause of hunger is addressed by the FAO technical document A/AC.191/37. IFAD discusses the problems of tackling the issue of rural poverty, specifically the question of tied-aid foreign experts.

India explains the relationship of poverty, rural development and agricultural production. The United States emphasizes the necessity of equitable distribution of agricultural output in solving the problem of hunger.

MALNUTRITION AND RURAL POVERTY

FAO Technical Document A/AC.191/37

FAO's Fourth World Food Survey estimated that the number of severely undernourished people in the developing market economies rose from about 400 million in 1969-71 to about 450 million in 1972-74, or a quarter of their total population. Virtually all of the increase was in the poorest countries. Partial data for more recent years indicate little, if any, improvement in this disquieting situation.

Essential as it is to accelerate the increase in food and agricultural production in the developing countries, it will not by itself be sufficient for the eradication of hunger and malnutrition. This depends primarily on the reduction of poverty.

A key element in the reduction of poverty is that most of the production increase should come from the small farmers and landless labourers who constitute the vast majority of the rural poor. They thus need improved access to land and other productive resources, as well as suitable institutions not only

for the effective delivery to them of the necessary technology
and physical inputs, and of the price incentives and credit
they need to apply them, but also for their full participation
(including women) in development. Education and training, particularly at the grass-roots level, are essential features in
such a concept of rural development and represent a particularly
fruitful field for increased international assistance. It is
also necessary to promote non-agricultural employment opportunities, including those provided by agro-industries, in rural
areas.

Such problems will be discussed by the World Conference on
Agrarian Reform and Rural Development (WCARRD) in July 1979.
Its conclusions should provide particularly important inputs
for the preparation of the new IDS.

Apart from a direct assault on poverty, of which nutrition
is a principal indicator, special nutritional measures will
continue to be necessary, especially for vulnerable groups such
as women and children. This is an area where increased national
emphasis and international assistance are especially desirable.

A very serious problem in the rural areas of many developing countries, and one that is closely connected with nutrition,
is the growing shortage of fuelwood. It is essential that this
should be fully considered at the United Nations Conference on
New and Renewable Sources of Energy to be held in 1981.

THE PROBLEM OF TIED TECHNICAL AID

Statement by Mr. A. Aziz of IFAD

In determining the likely impact of an increasing flow of external assistance on the production and distribution of food, it
is necessary to go beyond aggregate numbers, to the direction
of this flow. Even more important is the question of the
"quality" of external assistance in improving the nutrition of
the poorest segments of the population.

It will be fair to conclude, on the basis of available
information, that a significant proportion of the increased
investment in the agriculture or related sectors has not so far
led to a corresponding increase in production and has not made
any major impact on the nutrition of the poor. In fact, efforts
to expand external assistance for agriculture are not yet fully
matched by a capacity to design projects for the benefit of the
rural poor. Most donors prefer to tie their contributions to
identifiable projects which encourages recipient countries to
large construction projects with relatively little attention to
essential expenditures for institutional and social development
involving programme assistance and local cost financing. The
cost per hectare or per beneficiary in these large irrigation

or construction projects is often quite high and the project is
not therefore replicable, either for the country or for the
region as a whole. Similarly, the lack of trained manpower and
expertise has prompted the use of foreign consultants for project preparation and project implementation which bring in the
required technical expertise but cannot successfully tackle the
real social and cultural factors essential for grass-root development. Even where training activities are included in the
projects, they cannot make much impact because of inadequate
attention to the evolution of local institutions for attracting
and retaining local expertise. Projects implemented with a
large number of foreign experts or local civil servants, lead to
a large increase in recurrent costs which few developing countries can afford on a continuing basis. Rural institutions
managed by the local population, assisted by a few civil servants, will not only keep recurrent costs down, but will give a
greater sense of participation to the people themselves.

These few examples, based on IFAD's own limited experience,
only help to emphasize that the whole range of problems involved
in designing projects for the benefit of the rural poor must be
carefully analysed if the projected increase in the flow of
external assistance is to lead to the desired increase in food
production _and_ in improving the nutrition of the poor. IFAD,
with the basic mandate to help improve the nutrition of the
poorest segments, has adopted the concept of target groups and
is trying to link food production programmes to the twin aspects
of nutrition and poverty. It is also organizing Special Programming Missions to seven selected countries during 1979 to test
the operational feasibility of this approach.

POVERTY, RURAL DEVELOPMENT AND AGRICULTURAL PRODUCTION

Statement of India by Mr. Romesh Bhandari

In increasing food and agricultural production we not only
tackle the problem of poverty and under-nourishment. The majority of the hungry and undernourished live in the rural sector
and are dependent upon agricultural production for their existence and meagre earnings. The implementation of the programmes
envisaged and the fulfilment of the targets of the flow and
resources, would first of all have a major impact on reducing
the levels of unemployment and under-employment. Furthermore,
it would make a qualitative contribution to the entire psychol-
ogy of those who are under-nourished. It would mean the injection of a new confidence – a confidence that they are no longer
a liability on their fellow human-beings but have become productive members of society. For the donors, it would mean that
the flow of resources is not just to fill empty stomachs but to

convert a large sector of mankind into a group which produces
more food than it consumes. Flowing from this, when larger
sectors of mankind are able to earn their livelihood and the
numbers of unemployed decrease, this higher earning capacity
would in itself lead to greater consumption, and the need for
increased production of a large variety of goods.

Side by side, an investment of the tune of US$ 25 billion
per year, in addition to increased food and agriculture production, the creation of greater employment opportunities and aug-
mentation of consumption, would also stimulate the requirements
of various products, equipment and machinery, the creation of
increased production capacity the impartation of technical
studies etc. Irrigation systems would have to be developed,
road facilities would have to be created, communications improved, storage capacities increased, new units established for
production of fertilisers pesticides and the like. Even projections that we may have of the requirements of inputs would need
to be revised. The main limitation to the greater consumption
of fertilisers, pesticides, improved varieties of seeds etc. is
that of finance. If earnings increase and greater credit and
other financing facilities are made available, the pattern of
consumption and inputs would be a spiralling one.

ROLE OF AGRICULTURAL COOPERATIVES IN AGRICULTURAL DEVELOPMENT
STATEMENT OF MONGOLIA BY MR. BADAMOCHIRYN DOLJINTSEREN

My delegation submits...that the best ways and means to overcome
difficulties and obstacles in the solution of the above problems
lies first and foremost in full and effective mobilization of
internal resources of developing countries themselves and in
securing full participation of all the strata of their populations in the agricultural development as well as in carrying
out far-reaching, progressive socio-economic transformations,
including the agrarian reforms, and in the equitable and just
distribution of land and other means of labour. Particularly,
the experience of the socialist countries, including that of my
own, shows that the introduction of progressive measures such
as the promotion of cooperative movement and the collective
farming have proven to be truly effective in introduction of
modern machinery, planning and other effective measures into
agriculture and rural development.

In this regard, I would like to say just a few words about
the achievements, attained by my country in the agricultural
field. Indeed, the extensive development of agriculture and
full satisfaction of the population demands for meat and milk
production as well as for flour, bread, and bakery in my country
are a logical result of the constructive policy, pursued by my
Government in tackling problems of food and agriculture. From

the very first days of the People's Revolution Victory, the
Mongolian People's Revolutionary Party and the Government of
the Mongolian People's Republic have initiated many important
measures, aimed at the development of modern agriculture and
animal husbandry in Mongolia.

As a result, agriculture in my country has undergone fundamental socio-economic changes since the Revolution. One of
the fundamental changes was the cooperative movement in agriculture, which began in 1930-1940s. At the end of 1950s virtually
all the herdsmen had joined agricultural cooperatives and state
farms on the voluntary basis, which played a most important
role in the modernization of the countryside. There are today
more than 250 agricultural cooperatives and also tens of state
farms as well as of state stock farms and state veterinary stations in our agriculture. Every agricultural cooperative and
state farm in the MPR has been supplied with modern agricultural
machinery, including dozens of tractors and harvesting combines.
It is due to the promotion of the successful cooperative movement and establishment of state farms that made it possible and
useful for my country to extensively introduce modern machinery
into agriculture and intensively utilize therein modern farming
methods.

Apart from the cooperative movement, there was also initiated a complex development of virgin lands, another important
measure designed to meet all the home needs of the population
of the Republic for wheat and other grains. Development of
virgin land and establishment of modern farms of new type are
essential factors for further growth of well-being and cultural
level of the rural population. Many modern settlements with
all conveniences have been set up in the countryside.

This year, my country and people are celebrating the 20th
anniversary of the successful completion of cooperative movement
in our agriculture, which has been most instrumental in the
modernization of the countryside of the Republic. Today all
the people and population of the Mongolian People's Republic
are fully self-supplied with home-produced flour, meat and other
agricultural products. We are firmly convinced that these
achievements have been attained thanks to the fundamental socio-
economic changes occured in the Republic as well as due to our
fruitful cooperation with the fraternal socialist countries in
the family of the Council for Mutual Economic Assistance.

THE NEED FOR EQUITABLE DISTRIBUTION OF PRODUCTION

Statement of the United States by Ms. Melissa Wells

I want to emphasize my government's view that increasing agricultural production per capita is only part of the answer in solv-

ing the problem of hunger and malnutrition. The equitable distribution of that output is equally necessary. Agricultural
development in many countries is inextricably linked to
overall economic development in the rural sector, where the
majority of those afflicted by hunger and malnourishment live.
In many developing countries insufficient employment opportunities exist in these sectors to permit people to break out of
the low income trap which is often the root cause of hunger and
malnourishment. Often, too few people have access to the productive resources in the rural sector, including land ownership.
Institutional change in the context of redistribution of land
and tenancy reform can contribute significantly to increasing
the rural poor's access to the needed productive resources.

Moreover, we believe that rural and agricultural development policies must ensure effective participation of the rural
population in economic development and the political process.
Through economic and political participation people develop the
trust and confidence in the process which increases their contributions to it and allows them to make investments with longer-
term returns. Small farmers and rural worker organizations
should be involved in the implementation of programs of agrarian
reform, distribution of surplus land, credit, marketing assistance and other employment generation opportunities such as in
agro-industries. In addition, we suggest that national policies
emphasize the development of cooperatives, not only in the traditional areas of land, equipment and credit, but also in such
fields as transportation and distribution networks and marketing.

Rural employment and agricultural policies need to be closely coordinated as the supply of basic goods must increase in
parallel to the expansion of effective demand in rural areas.
Additionally, more attention to the supply of foods and services
in the rural sector must be paid to redress the adverse rural/
urban bias which exists in many countries.

SOCIO-ECONOMIC CHANGES AND AGRICULTURAL DEVELOPMENT
STATEMENT OF THE GERMAN DEMOCRATIC REPUBLIC
BY MR. S. ZACHMANN

Our own experience gathered in the development of agriculture
and food production confirm our view that highly effective and
long-lasting results can be achieved when fundamental socio-
economic changes lay the groundwork for the advance of agriculture, the development of those working in agriculture, and for
the distribution of foodstuffs. Whether progress will be made
in solving the food problem, largely depends on the willingness
to carry out fundamental progressive changes of a socio-economic
nature.

It was this realization which guided the World Food Conference in 1974 when it adopted the Declaration on the Eradication of Hunger and Malnutrition and Resolutions I and II by consensus. These decisions recommend that progressive agrarian price and tax reforms be carried out for the purpose of increasing food production in developing countries. They call for the development of cooperatives for progressive changes in the socio-economic structures of the rural areas, for promoting the active participation of smallholders and farm hands in the development process and for improving training and health care for the rural population. It is stated that the measures necessary for the development of food production are a responsibility of every State concerned.

We support this approach to solving the food problem of the developing countries.

13 Nutrition and the Eradication of Malnutrition

The Mexico Declaration forms the basis of the arguments for improving nutrition and eradicating malnutrition in the world. Several Member States and Specialized Agencies add important elements to the discussion.

IMPROVEMENT OF HUMAN NUTRITION AND REDUCTION OF HUNGER AND MALNUTRITION

The Mexico Declaration of the WFC

11. In pursuance of paragraph 1 of resolution V of the World Food Conference,* the developing countries, with bilateral and multilateral assistance, should make a practical assessment of the nature and extent of the problem of hunger and malnutrition, establish specific operational goals for nutritional improvement and develop and implement plans and policies and practical programmes and projects to achieve these goals.
12. Countries in their efforts to increase food production and improve nutrition should continue to consider practical ways and means to achieve a more equitable distribution of income and economic resources so as to ensure that food production increases result in a more equitable pattern of food consumption.
13. Governments should adopt the goal of eradicating vitamin-A deficiency and endemic goitre within a decade and establish measures to achieve this goal, the World Health Organization

---

* See Report of the World Food Conference, Rome, 5-16 November 1974 (United Nations publication, Sales No. 75.II.A.3), part one, chap. II.

should provide the Council at its fifth session with specific
proposals for an international effort in support of government
action, and Governments, the World Health Organization and other
relevant institutions should accelerate their efforts to improve
approaches to combating iron-deficiency anaemia.

14. Governments, international agencies and financing institutions should include, as far as possible, in the preparation of
major development projects, particularly in the agricultural
and rural sector, an assessment of their impact on hunger and
malnutrition giving priority to projects contributing to nutrition improvement; and full use should be made of the opportunities offered by many projects to incorporate specific nutrition
components into the design of development projects, such as
nutrition education and training, distribution of food supplements, development of production of nutritious indigenous foodstuffs and primary health care, with emphasis on the neediest
sectors of the rural and urban population, especially women and
children.

15. The United Nations system should make the eradication of
hunger and malnutrition a major objective and introduce specific nutrition-related goals into the system's operational programmes.

16. To make these goals effective, United Nations agencies,
with the support of the Administrative Committee on Co-ordination and its Sub-Committee on Nutrition, should accelerate
their efforts to implement the Manila Communique's recommendations on nutrition and present to the Council at its fifth session a programme of work identifying the resources and mechanisms for agency-government co-operation required:

(a) to encourage developing countries to institute a comprehensive programme to attack hunger and malnutrition;

(b) To speed up and improve assistance to developing countries in the formulation and implementation of food and nutrition policies and programmes, especially in the poorest countries;

(c) To help mobilize resources from all countries and the
institutions able to provide the assistance necessary to supplement such policies and programmes implemented by developing
countries;

(d) To intensify the exchange of information in the field
of nutrition and accelerate the Sub-Committee's present efforts
to establish a data and information bank on nutrition;

(e) To establish food and nutrition surveillance systems
as a basis for planning, monitoring and evaluating nutrition
policies and programmes, as well as for the early detection and
prevention of any nutrition deterioration.

17. All countries able to provide financial and technical assistance to eradicate malnutrition should increase substantially
or initiate at substantial levels such assistance through bilateral and multilateral channels and communicate to the Council

at its fifth session what concrete measures have been taken in
this respect.

18.   All interested countries and agencies of the United Nations
system should suggest improved means of co-operation in this
field between developed and developing countries, among developing countries themselves, and the agencies of the United Nations
system and the Council's secretariat should prepare a report on
these suggestions to the Council at its fifth session.

THE FUNDAMENTAL PROBLEM OF MALNUTRITION
STATEMENT OF THE GROUP OF 77 BY MR. MAHMOUD MESTIRI

Malnutrition – we are well aware – remains a serious problem, a
problem basically linked to inadequate production of essential
foodstuffs in the developing countries and to the inadequacy of
international co-operation in this sphere. The developing countries, for their part, are determined to continue, in the context of their integrated development plans, their efforts to
eradicate hunger and poverty. It is for this Committee to decide on the measures to be adopted by the donor countries and
international institutions to help the developing countries
attain their objectives in the field of nutrition.

SELF-RELIANT POVERTY-ORIENTED RURAL DEVELOPMENT
AND THE ERADICATION OF HUNGER

Statement by Mr. Nurul Islam of FAO

Coming now to the issue of the reduction of malnutrition and
rural poverty, it is essential that most of the faster increase
in production that I have so much exphasized should come from
the small producers and landless labourers who constitute the
vast majority of the rural poor. In order to increase their
income-earning and employment opportunities, they need improved
access to land and other productive resources. Suitable institutions are required for the effective delivery to them of technology and physical inputs and of the price incentives and credit needed to apply them, and for their full participation (including rural women) in development. Education and training,
particularly at the grass-roots level, are essential features
in such a concept of rural development, and represent a fruitful
field for increased international assistance.

     Technological progress, the mobilization of human and
material resources, and institutional changes, together with
appropriate international measures in support of them, should
all be geared to the objectives of both economic growth and the

alleviation of poverty. These are among the principal issues
with which the World Conference on Agrarian Reform and Rural
Development will be concerned in July this year.

I have just come from the meeting of the Preparatory Committee of the World Conference, which was held in Rome last
week. In addition to approving the provisional agenda for the
Conference, it gave preliminary consideration to the possible
structure of its conclusions, including a concrete Programme of
Action emphasizing the need for structural changes in rural
societies, for the reorientation of national policies and priorities towards a self-reliant poverty-oriented rural development
(with quantitative targets wherever feasible), and for international support for these measures in the context of the New
International Economic Order.

Mr. Chairman, I hope that your Committee will urge the
fullest support for the World Conference. Its conclusions
should be of the greatest importance for the preparation of the
new International Development Strategy. I was therefore glad
to note your intention to accept my Director-General's invitation to you to address the Conference.

While the eradication of hunger and malnutrition depends
ultimately on the eradication of poverty, much can be achieved
in the shorter run through special nutritional programmes, especially for vulnerable groups such as women and children,
through the better integration of nutritional goals in national
development plans, and the introduction of nutritional criteria
in the preparation and evaluation of development programmes and
projects. The newly-established ACC Sub-Committee on Nutrition,
with a secretariat located in Rome, is now providing a welcome
stimulus to increased and better coordinated efforts by the
United Nations Agencies in this important field.

THE IMPORTANCE OF THE WORLD CONFERENCE ON AGRARIAN REFORM
AND RURAL DEVELOPMENT IN ERADICATING MALNUTRITION

Statement of Finland by Mr. Jukka Valtasaari

In the opinion of the Finnish Government the World Conference
on Agrarian Reform and Rural Development has a great potential
in tackling many of the problems relating to improving the possibilities of nations to be self-reliant in terms of food production. It is, therefore, necessary that this meeting of the
Committee of the Whole tries to give its input to a successful
outcome of the WCARRD.

As to the issues related to nutrition, my delegation shares
the view expressed by Dr. Islam in his introductory statement
that the reduction of malnutrition is closely linked with the
conditions of the rural poor. It is indeed necessary that most

of the faster increase in production should come from the small
farmers and landless labourers. Thus the nutritional aspects
would be tackled within the general framework of solving the
equity problem in the context of increased production. There
is also another facet in this issue, namely the need for more
specialized nutritional measures. These measures require more
attention in the national development plans, preferably in the
form of specific and quantifiable programmes.

THE ROLE OF THE WORLD BANK IN THE
ERADICATION OF MALNUTRITION

Statement by Mr. Montague Yudelman of the World Bank

The Bank is attempting to reach malnourished people who live in
pockets of rural poverty and marginal productivity in middle
and upper income developing countries, as well as improve the
situation in the poorer countries where nutritional deprivation
is endemic. To this end the Bank is committed to assisting
small farmers many of whom have such low levels of productivity
that they are too poor to have adequate diets. Overall, the
last five years of lending were expected to help raise the productivity and incomes of as many as 60 million low income rural
inhabitants of the developing world. This impact should be
seen in the context of the estimate that a total of 500 million
live in absolute poverty and most of them live in rural areas.
    The alleviation of food problems has usually been sought,
by the World Bank and others, through the increased production
of food staples. However, we now know that increased production -
even when it benefits poor farm households which are themselves
malnourished - is a necessary but not sufficient way to meet
national security (preventing famine when harvests fail) and to
reduce the incidence of malnutrition (an objective which is not
necessarily met through food security, or production schemes).
It is personal income that is the major factor that determines
nutritional well being. Most of the malnourished are landless
laborers and small farmers who make up the bottom of the income
distribution ladder. Programs which provide more employment
for unskilled laborers in rural and urban areas are most important. So are special efforts to support food consumption by
the poor. Hitherto the World Bank has had little experience in
these kinds of programs. Clearly they will be more important
in the future.

THE EC AND THE ERADICATION OF MALNUTRITION

Statement of the EC by Mr. Jacques Leprette Representing

With regard to the improvement of human nutrition and the reduction of hunger and malnutrition, the Community has, on many
occasions, indicated that it supported the appeal made at the
Manila session of the World Food Council to the United Nations
system, to speed up its work in this sphere. In addition, the
Community's interventions through credits from the European
development fund, have increasingly been directed towards the
financing of activities designed primarily to promote the production of foodstuffs. This trend corresponds both to the
evolution of the objectives of the Community's partners and to
the Community's willingness to contribute to the improvement of
the formers' food situation by the local production of foodstuffs required for national consumption.

THE NEED FOR EXPLICIT MULTIDISCIPLINARY ACTIONS
TO ERADICATE MALNUTRITION

Statement by Mr. S. Mafatopoulos of WHO

It is well known that an attack on malnutrition requires a multi-
disciplinary approach: for example, increased food production
is essential but will of itself not meet the needs unless it is
associated with other measures leading to more equitable distribution of food and the alleviation of the disease load that
inhibits the effective use of food by the human organism. WHO,
within its own responsibilities, has recognized the multi-
dimensional nature of nutritional activities and has decided
that these should be a basic component of the delivery of primary health care as stated in the Declaration adopted at the
International Conference on Primary Health Care jointly sponsored by WHO and UNICEF at Alma Ata, USSR, in September of last
year. Particular attention will be given in this context to
the population at greatest risk; activities will include monitoring of nutritional status of children and pregnant women,
nutrition education and supplementary feeding. Other activities
not directly addressed to nutrition such as the control of diar-
rhoea and infectious diseases, and family planning which has
direct bearing on nutritional status, are to be combined in an
integrated approach. Any activities undertaken in this respect
will obviously require the full participation of the populations
concerned. Collaboration with concerned organizations within
and outside the UN system, is now greatly enhanced through the
ACC Subcommittee on Nutrition. Increased cooperation with

countries for the control of malnutrition is also within the
recently adopted policies of WHO which reflect a greater concern
for the social dimension of health development and for the role
of health for promoting economic and social development.

I should like to conclude by stressing that Governments
must give high priority to solve the problem of malnutrition,
bearing in mind its multisectoral nature and by developing and
implementing coordinated efforts for its solution. Indeed, Mr.
Chairman, explicit attention to nutrition as well as explicit
actions are required in the context of national development
policies and plans if the problem is to be reduced and ultimately eliminated. Endorsement and support from this Committee for
these actions would make a significant contribution to this
end.

Glossary

ACC	Administrative Committee on Co-ordination
AGRIS	International Information System for Agricultural Science and Technology
CARIS	Current Agricultural Research Information System
CFA	UN/FAO World Food Programme Committee on Food Aid Policies and Programmes
CFS	Committee on World Food Security
CGFPI	Consultative Group on Food Production and Investment
CGIAR	Consultative Group on International Agricultural Research
CIEC	Conference on International Economic Co-operation
CIRDAP	Centre for Integrated Rural Development for Asia and the Pacific
COPAL	Committee for the Promotion of Aid to Co-operatives
COW	Committee of the Whole
DAC	Development Assistance Council
DD2	Second United Nations Development Decade
EC	European Community
ECDC	Economic Co-operation Among Developing Countries
ECLA	Economic Committee for Latin America
ECOSOC	Economic and Social Council
EEC	European Economic Council
EEZ	exclusive economic zone
ESCAP	Economic and Social Commission for Asia and the Pacific
FAC	Food Aid Convention
FAO	Food and Agriculture Organization

FAOC	Food and Agriculture Conference
FAOCL	Food and Agriculture Council
FSAS	Food Security Assistance Scheme
GA	General Assembly
GSP	generalized system of preferences
GTZ	German Agency for Technical Co-operation
FAO/IDWG/WID	FAO Inter-Divisional Working Group on Women in Development
HYV	high-yielding varieties
IARC	International Agricultural Research Centre
IBPR	International Board for Plant Genetic Resources
IBRD	International Bank for Reconstruction and Development
ICARDA	International Center for Agricultural Research in Dry Areas
IDCAS	Industrial Development Centre for Arab States
IDA	International Development Association
IEFR	International Emergency Food Reserve
IER	International Emergency Reserve
IFAD	International Fund for African Development
ILCA	International Livestock Centre for Africa
ILO	International Labor Organization
ILRAD	International Laboratory for Research on Animal Diseases
IWC	International Wheat Council
MSA	most seriously affected countries
MTN	General Agreement on Tariffs and Trade (GATT) Multilateral Trade Negotiations
NIEO	New International Economic Order
ODA	official development assistance
OECD	Organization for Economic and Co-operative Development
OPEC	Organization of Petroleum-Exporting Countries
PAG	FAO Protein Advisory Group
OAU/STRC	Organization of African Unity/Scientific, Technical and Research Commission
SACRED	Scheme for Agricultural Credit Development
SELA	Latin American Economic System
SIDA	Swedish International Development Agency
SIDP	Seed Improvement and Development Programme
SOFA	State of Food and Agriculture
TCDC	UN Conference on Technical Co-operation among Developing Countries
TCP	FAO Technical Co-operation Programme
UN/ECA	United Nations Economic Council on Africa
UN/WFC	United Nations World Food Conference
UNCSTD	United Nations Conference on Science and Technology for Development

UNCTAD	United Nations Conference on Trade and Development
UNDP	United Nations Development Programme
UNEP	United Nations Environment Programme
UNFPA	United Nations Fund for Population Activities
UNICEF	United Nations International Children's Emergency Fund
UNIDO	United Nations International Development Organization
UNITAR	United Nations Institute for Training and Research
WARDA	West Africa Rice Development Association
WCARRD	World Conference on Agrarian Reform and Rural Development
WFC	World Food Council
WFP	UN/FAO World Food Programme
WHO	World Health Organization
WMO	World Meteorological Organization

Index

About the Editor

TOIVO MILJAN, Ph.D., is in the Political Science Department at Wilfred Laurier University, Waterloo, Ontario.